THE CHARLTON STANDARD CATALOGUE OF

ROYAL DOULTON BESWICK JUGS

THIRD EDITION

By
Jean Dale

Introduction By
Louise Irvine

W.K. Cross
Publisher

The Charlton Press

Birmingham, Michigan ✦ Toronto, Ontario

CANADIAN CATALOGUING IN PUBLICATION DATA

The National Library of Canada has catalogued
this publication as follows:
Main entry under title:

The Charlton standard catalogue of Royal Doulton jugs

1st ed. ([1991]) –
Biennial.
Title varies slightly.
ISSN 1183-711X
ISBN 0-88968-166-X (3rd ed.)

1. Royal Doulton character jugs – Catalogs.

NK4695.C518C442   738.8'0294   C92-030326-9

**Printed in Canada
in the Province of Quebec**

The Charlton Press

**Editorial Office
2010 Yonge Street
Toronto, Ontario M4S 1Z9
Telephone (416) 488-4653 Fax: (416) 488-4656
Telephone 1-800-442-6042 Fax: 1-800-442-1542**

EDITORIAL

Editor	Jean Dale
Assistant Editor	Sandra Tooze
Layout	Frank van Lieshout

SPECIAL THANKS

The publishers would like to thank Louise Irvine for writing the introduction to the third edition of *The Charlton Standard Catalogue of Royal Doulton Beswick Jugs*. Louise Irvine is an independent writer and lecturer on Royal Doulton's history and products and is not connected with the pricing of this catalogue.

Also, thanks to Stephen M. Mullins of the American Jug Museum, Chicago, Illinois, for allowing us to document and photograph parts of his toby jug collection.

CONTRIBUTORS

The following contributors graciously supplied photographs, price lists, data and other valuable information for the third edition, for which we offer a profound thank you:

Dealers

Arnie and Judi Berger, Yesterday's South, Miami, Florida; **Laura Campbell,** Site of the Green, Dundas, Ontario; **Anthony Cross,** Anthony Cross and The Englishman, Blackburn, England; **David Harcourt,** Thornton Antiques and Fine China Ltd., Wellington, New Zealand; **Mark Oliver,** Phillips, London, England; **Ed Pascoe,** Pascoe and Company, Miami, Florida; **Jamie and Mary Pole,** Seaway China Company, Marine City, Michigan; **Tom Power,** The Collector, London, England; **Stan Worrey,** Colonial House Antiques and Gifts, Berea, Ohio, and **Princess and Barry Weiss,** Yesterdays, New City, New York.

Collectors

R.J. Curtis, Newtown, Connecticut; **Terrence M. Durney,** El Paso, Texas; **Arlene and Barry Gillmain;** Oceanside New York; **Leonard Hamilton,** Kent, England; **Gil Harding,** Steubenville, Ohio; **Alan Matthew,** Bothwell, Washington; **K.K. Moser,** Omaha, Nebraska; **Henry E. Niemitz,** Maplewood, New Jersey, and **Scott M. Reichenberg,** North Smithfield, RI.

A SPECIAL NOTE TO COLLECTORS

We welcome and appreciate any comments or suggestions you may have regarding *The Charlton Standard Catalogue of Royal Doulton Beswick Jugs*. If you would like to participate in pricing or in supplying new data, such as information on unlisted jugs or varieties, please contact Jean Dale at (416) 488-4653.

CONTENTS

FOREWORD TO THE THIRD EDITION

This third edition has been expanded to include the jugs produced by Beswick between the years 1930 and 1980. Over 35 varieties of the jugs and their derivitives exist allowing the collector a new and exciting field to explore.

The Lambeth stoneware jugs have now been placed in a chapter on their own. This will allow for the correct positioning of these jugs historically and for expansion within a chapter in an orderly fashion when new varieties surface.

The first figure jugs were issued circa 1820 at Lambeth. Chronologically these pieces do not belong in either the toby or character jug sections of this book; however, in the interest of simplicity, they have been interspersed in this section. For example, if Nelson or Napoleon were listed chronologically, they would necessitate two different sections. As a result, we have taken the liberty of combining the Lambeth and early Burslem issues with the modern tobies and character jugs of the twentieth century. We apologize to those who would like to see a historical order preserved, but for those collectors who wish to easily trace the origins of their jugs, we believe our listing method is easier to use.

THE COLLECTOR AND THIS BOOK

The purpose of this book is twofold. One is to provide collectors with the comparative information and the illustrations necessary to help them build meaningful and rewarding collections. With this and subsequent editions, Charlton will present collectors with a comprehensive, technical guide on jugs.

The second purpose is to provide a timely price guide for Royal Doulton and Beswick jugs, in order that the collector can make intelligent decisions when purchasing jugs for his or her collection. This goal is more difficult to chieve. Pricing jugs is a difficult, ongoing task, and an explanation of our thoughts on pricing is needed.

A price guide is just that, a *guide* to the most current retail prices at the time of publication. It is not a fixed price list. It does not list prices at which dealers must sell their jugs. This publication is an indication of the current market price arrived at by submissions, price lists and auction results.

However, *The Charlton Standard Catalogue of Royal Doulton Beswick Jugs* goes one step further than any price guide has gone before. It lists the current market prices in three countries: the United Kingdom, the United States and Canada.

When using this guide, the collector must carefully assess the three market prices with the following points in mind:

1. The region of the prices listed.
2. The duties, taxes and shipping costs to move a jug from one region to another.
3. The foreign-exchange costs of moving funds between currencies.

Even with these points taken into account, there are major price differences between regional markets. The Royal Doulton and Beswick jug markets are not elastic; there is not a uniform demand across all markets. There is also not a uniform supply in all markets. The U.K. market, which is older and was supplied first by Doulton and Beswick, has more product available at any one moment. As a result, prices there should be lower.

Will dealers and collectors be able to use this guide to buy in the market that has the lowest prices? Maybe. But sellers will probably have the book also and will immediately adjust to the higher market, especially when it favours them. Nevertheless, a careful examination of prices is called for, as each market has its own peculiarities, and prices can and do vary.

THE ORIGINS OF THE TOBY JUG
Louise Irvine

Pottery jugs in the image of human beings have been made since the dawn of civilisation, and some impressive examples have survived from Greek and Roman times, as well as from the ancient cultures of South America. In Medieval England, potters poked fun at their contemporaries by creating figurative jugs, and these primitive vessels also provide interesting precedents for the toby jug, which first appeared in the Staffordshire Potteries in the late 18th century.

The toby jug traditionally represents a seated drinking character with a pot of foaming ale balanced on his knee. He is dressed in typical costume of the period, with a long coat and knee breeches, and his large tricorn hat forms the spout of the jug. There are several theories as to the origin of his name. Some suggest a connection with Shakespeare's convivial character Sir Toby Belch, others believe the notorious Yorkshire toper Henry Elwes was the model. He died in 1761 having consumed some 2,000 gallons of Stingo, a particularly strong ale, and was known as "Toby Fillpot." Potters might also have been inspired by an old English drinking song, *The Brown Jug*, written by the Reverend Francis Fawkes, which paid tribute to Toby Fillpot, "a thirsty old soul" who excelled in boozing. The popular verses were first published in 1761 and were soon distributed in print form, accompanied by a caricature of an enthusiastic drinker with a ruddy complexion and a huge beer belly.

Admiral Lord Nelson figure jug produced at the Doulton and Watts factory

By the early years of the 19th century, the Staffordshire potters were producing many variations on the original toby type, including standing figures flourishing pipes, sporting squires, jolly sailors and even female characters. Toby jugs were also made in other parts of England, notably London, where the Lambeth potteries used their favoured brown salt-glaze stoneware material to produce genial tobies astride barrels.

DOULTON LAMBETH JUGS

Brown stoneware tobies were amongst the earliest products of the Doulton and Watts factory, which was established on the banks of the river Thames in London in 1815. As well as complete figure jugs, the company also produced face jugs of famous personalities. The most impressive and best known is their portrait of the great naval hero Lord Nelson. Two different models are marked with the company's early trademark, Doulton and Watts. The complete bust stands 12 inches tall and the smaller head and shoulder design was made in three different sizes, the largest 7 1/2 inches tall. Replicas of both these models, clearly marked as such, were later made to celebrate the centenary of the Battle of Trafalgar in 1905, but even these are difficult to find today.

Stoneware portrait jug of Theodore Roosevelt modelled by Leslie Harradine

Nelson's great antagonist Napoleon has also been portrayed as a stoneware jug, and there are similar tributes to Wellington, the Iron Duke, but these are unmarked and could have been made by any of the London potters, as they frequently copied each other's. ideas. The Doulton pottery went on to honour many other military heroes, politicians and statesmen on flasks, jugs and vases, but the idea of the face jug was not revived until the early 1900s, when the celebrated modeller Leslie Harradine produced a stoneware portrait jug of Theodore Roosevelt, the 26th President of the United States. This was followed by a curious pair of Veteran Motorist jugs, an ugly Highwayman, a beaming Old King Cole and a humorous caricature of Mr. Pecksniff, from Dickens's *Martin Chuzzlewit*. The pattern books also refer to a Wee Mac jug in 1908, but to date this has not materialised and there may well be others still to come to light. Harradine left the Lambeth studio in 1912, but his colleague Mark Marshall occasionally dabbled in the toby tradition, producing a Soldier toby jug and a face jug, which bears a strong resemblance to John Barleycorn, the first character jug made at Royal Doulton's other factory in Burslem, Stoke-on-Trent.

Old King Cole modelled by Leslie Harradine

Charles Noke, the Burslem art director, was a regular visitor to Lambeth and was undoubtedly influenced by the achievements of the stoneware modellers. He was particularly impressed with the work of Harry Simeon, who contorted Toby Fillpot into a variety of useful shapes, including three styles of toby jugs, tobacco jars, ashpots, inkwells, candlesticks, decanters and even a teapot. A publicity leaflet of the mid 1920s indicates that the Simeon toby jugs were available in several sizes with modelling variations and alternative colourways. In addition the waistcoat could be coloured in a bright red enamel for a surcharge of 25 percent on the list price.

Simeon's toby wares all feature the full seated figure, with the exception of one model that depicts a happy smiling face on the marriage day, but when it is turned upside down, scowling features reveal what happens after marriage. The Marriage mug was made in three sizes and was included in the publicity leaflet for the rest of the stoneware toby collection. Although most of the Lambeth tobies were made of slip cast stoneware and produced in small editions, they are very hard to find today and count amongst the rarest of the Royal Doulton jugs.

BURSLEM CHARACTER AND TOBY JUGS

The Doulton family extended their business to Burslem, Stoke-on-Trent, in 1877, but initially they concentrated on the production of tablewares and other useful wares for the Victorian home. Gradually an art studio was developed, and in 1889 Charles Noke, who had trained at the Worcester factory, was appointed as a modeller of ornamental vases, mainly for exhibition purposes. Before long Noke was also producing figure models and had embarked on a mission to revive the Staffordshire figurative tradition. In 1913, following the launch of his famous HN collection of figures, he was promoted to art director, and he soon turned his attention to the revival of the toby jug.

His first models were quite different in style from the traditional smoking topers with brimful tankards of ale. In 1918, he introduced a portrait of the great silent movie star Charlie Chaplin in the form of a large toby jug, and this was followed a few years later by a similar portrait of George Robey, the popular music-hall comedian. In both models the characters' bowler hats come off to reveal the jugs underneath. George Robey, the "Prime Minister of Mirth," visited the Burslem factory in 1925, and the toby jug was probably made at that time.

Another early toby jug depicts a huntsman in scarlet, D4090, and this 1919 model was re-launched in more subdued colours as part of an extensive collection of tobies in 1950. The Huntsman was also issued in Kingsware, a distinctive treacle-brown ware which was developed by Noke in the early 1900s and used primarily for whisky flasks. A Kingsware Squire toby jug was also produced and a face jug of a Highlander was made around 1930 for D & J McCallum

The Kingsware Huntsman
modelled by Charles Noke, 1919

distillers in Edinburgh. It may have been this commission which gave Noke the idea for a collection of face jugs, for by 1933 he had modelled two designs, John Barleycorn, the personification of barley, and Old Charley, a typical night watchman, and they were launched the following year.

With the help of his chief modeller, Harry Fenton, Noke quickly introduced more personalities from literature, legend, folk-lore and song, and by 1935 the first models were also available in a small size (around 4 inches) as an alternative to the original large size (around 6 1/2 inches). A miniature size (around 2 1/2 inches) was added to the range by 1939, and the following year the first tinies (1 1/4 inches) were launched. These became the four standard sizes for the character jug range, although the dimensions have altered over the years, with some large-size jugs now measuring over 7 1/2 inches. There have also been occasional medium- or intermediate-size jugs (around 4 1/2 inches), as with the Dickens, Wild West and Beatles collections and an extra-large Tony Weller character jug, but these are exceptions to the usual sizes.

Although Charles Noke was in his mid seventies when he introduced character jugs, his fertile imagination was still working overtime, and by 1939 he had adapted the most popular personalities from the range to create a collection of useful gift items now known as the derivatives; for example, musical jugs, wall vases, tobacco jars, ashtrays, sugar bowls and teapots. He also developed a new range of toby jugs, several of which were closely based on early models by Harry Simeon at Doulton's Lambeth factory, in particular Double XX, Honest Measure and The Squire.

The bombing of the Burslem studio during the Second World War briefly interrupted Noke's creative output, but the conflict gave him an opportunity to pay tribute to the great war leader Winston Churchill, the first contemporary personality to be portrayed as a character or toby jug. Unfortunately Noke's character jug portrait, an unusual two-handled model in white, was not considered a good likeness and was quickly withdrawn from the range. It was the first character jug to be discontinued, and because of its brief production period, it is now very sought after. Early in 1941 Noke made a couple of attempts to remodel and colour the portrait, but only prototypes of these experiments are known to exist. Harry Fenton had considerably more success with his toby jug portrait of Churchill, which was launched in 1940 and remained in production for 50 years.

Charles Noke died in 1941, at the age of 83, and for several years Harry Fenton was the sole modeller. He continued to create excellent likenesses of contemporary characters, such as Monty and Smuts, but he was equally at home with historical or fictional characters, for example the Samuel Johnson and Robin Hood jugs which impart a vivid sense of reality. In 1949 Max Henk, who had been appointed as a tableware modeller, became interested in character jugs and his Uncle Tom Cobbleigh was introduced in 1952. When Fenton died in 1953, Henk was able to step into the breach and he soon set a new style for character jugs, which is most obvious in his approach to their handles. He fully exploited the handle's potential for elaborating on the story of the character portrayed; thus Scaramouche has his guitar and the handle of The Ugly Duchess is a flamingo, which she used as a croquet mallet in the story of Alice in Wonderland. Henk obviously loved delving into literature and legend for symbolic allusions such as these, and they add a new dimension to character jugs for the curious collector.

Apart from his own work, Henk had responsibility for training the next generation of artists. Geoff Blower was generally regarded as Henk's protégé and even before he had completed his five-year apprenticeship, he was contributing to the character jug range. His first jug in 1952 was Lord Nelson, and he followed this with several other popular models, such as Rip Van Winkle, which has been in production for nearly 40 years. Blower left the Burslem studio in 1956 to take up a career in teaching, but on his retirement he began modelling character jugs again and worked on the Collecting World series. His former colleague Garry Sharpe also started his career at Doulton but moved overseas in 1960, by which time he had modelled some of the best-selling character jugs in the range, including Old Salt and Merlin. Perhaps his success had something to do with Fenton's modelling tools, which Henk gave him in 1953 with the challenging remark, "If there is any of Harry's magic left in these modelling tools, you certainly need it!"

Henk's third apprentice was David Biggs, who joined the team in 1958 after an art school training. Working on his first jug, the Town Crier, he soon found out how difficult it is to create one face which typifies a profession or a hobby, but he then went on to specialise in this field, modelling the Golfer, the Yachtsman, the Punch and Judy Man and many other representative characters. When stuck for a particular expression, he would often reach for a mirror and manoeuvre his own face to achieve the desired effect.

To make way for all the exciting jugs from this new generation of modellers, around 30 early models were withdrawn from production in 1960. A few years later, Royal Doulton decided to discontinue the traditional earthenware body and make all the jugs in the newly developed English Translucent China. David Biggs was given the task of making all the new, more detailed models of existing jugs, which were required for the new process, and several more jugs were withdrawn at this stage to avoid all the costly remodelling. The changeover took place between 1968 and 1970, but the fine china jugs were only made for a few years before earthenware production was resumed in 1973 at the newly acquired John Beswick factory. The fine china jugs are therefore highly valued by collectors and can be recognised most easily by the slight difference in size. Biggs continued to model new character jugs until the early 1970s but for the last 20 years he has concentrated on tableware modelling, only occasionally reviving his character jug design skills, notably for W.C. Fields and Louis Armstrong in the Celebrity series. Hopefully some new work will join the range in the future.

In 1972 a special studio was established for the development of figures and character jugs, and Eric Griffiths was appointed the new head of sculpture, ultimately becoming art director. Griffiths was a portrait painter by training and he particularly enjoyed modelling famous people for the jug range, notably Henry VIII, Mark Twain and Ronald Reagan. He also portrayed John Doulton, the founder of the company, as the first character jug especially for members of the Royal Doulton International Collectors Club, which was founded in 1980. There have been many more exclusive commissions for members in the intervening years, including a revival of the tiny size for the Beefeater and Old King Cole jugs.

The 1980s was an exciting time for character jug fans. The club provided a lot of useful information on the subject, stimulating many new collections, and the first major reference book by Desmond Eyles had just been published in 1979. Another informative book was produced by Jocelyn Lukins to celebrate the 50th anniversary of character jugs in 1984, and there were a number of price guides reflecting the buoyant market. New record prices were continuously being set in the sale rooms and amongst the most exceptional was the Toby Gillette jug, which was modelled by Eric Griffiths in a limited edition of three for a popular British TV show, "Jim'll Fix It." The jug sold for over £15,000 at Christie's auction rooms in 1984 to raise money for charity.

Several limited edition collections of character jugs were launched during the 1980s, beginning with the novel two-faced portraits for the Antagonists series by Michael Abberley, a young Royal Doulton figure painter who taught himself to model jugs in his spare time. The Antagonists were extremely popular, and the edition of 9,500 was soon over-subscribed. Abberley followed his first success with another two-faced collection, the Star-Crossed Lovers, and he also worked on some unlimited series, including the Wives of Henry VIII and characters from Shakespeare.

Such was the popularity of character jugs by the mid 1980s that many independent companies requested special designs for advertising purposes. This was not a new idea, as famous firms such as Charringtons had commissioned specially branded tobies in the 1930s and in 1956 the American industrialist Cliff Cornell even had a toby jug made in his own image to impress his customers. Thirty years later another American firm, Quaker Oats, ordered a character jug of Mr. Quaker and Pick Kwik Wines and Spirits of Derby purchased a large range of character jug containers for their liquor during the 1980s. Mail order companies, fair organisers and leading retailers all wanted exclusive jugs for promotional events and colourways of existing jugs were sold in special editions. At first the very small editions were snapped up , as with the colourway of the Mad Hatter made to commemorate the opening of the Royal Doulton Shop at Higbees of Cleveland in 1985, but collectors eventually became jaded with the number of colourways, and the company concentrated resources on new subjects instead.

Since the 1980s most new character jug subjects have been conceived as part of sets, thus creating interesting themes for collectors. In response to the demand for American subjects, Royal Doulton introduced the Wild West and the Celebrity series. The 50th anniversary of the Second World War led to several commemorative series, the Heroic Leaders, the Armed Forces and Heroes of the Blitz, and other important historical events have inspired individual jugs, notably

Columbus, which was produced to mark the 500th anniversary of his famous voyage to the New World. Established themes have also been developed to create new series; for example, the Beefeater was joined by lots of other London characters, and Henk's early characters from *Alice's Adventures in Wonderland* were joined by The Red Queen and The March Hare. To date this is the only animal character in the range, but the designer Bill Harper has also considered a grinning Cheshire Cat and White Rabbit, so it will be interesting to see if any others appear in the future. Harper is perhaps best known as a figure modeller, but he has produced a number of character jugs, as well as the amusing Doultonville collection of 25 small-size tobies, which were produced between 1983 and 1991.

Since 1992 there have also been limited-edition toby jugs of traditional characters, such as the Jester and the Clown. These were designed by Stan Taylor, a retired art teacher from Bristol, and he has been responsible for the majority of character jugs introduced since 1982. His subjects are extremely diverse, ranging from portraits of circus performers to typical characters encountered on a journey through Britain, such as a postman and a policeman. He also allowed his imagination to run riot for his Witch and Genie jugs. These are now in demand, having only been in production for six months because of the extensive withdrawal of character jugs at the end of 1991. The range was reduced from 157 models to 59 — all the early toby jugs were withdrawn and the miniature-size jug was discontinued altogether.

The rationalisation of the character jug range coincided with the appointment of a new art director, Amanda Dixon, who is in charge of all the Royal Doulton design studios. She continues to commission character jugs from Stan Taylor and Bill Harper but other younger modellers from the John Beswick studio, notably Martyn Alcock and Warren Platt, have also been encouraged to try their hands at modelling jugs. They work under the guidance of studio manager Graham Tongue, who has several advertising jugs to his credit, including the superb portrait of William Grant.

As well as all this new talent, recent marketing initiatives have also been well received by collectors. The Character Jug of the Year concept has proved very successful, with huge sales for Winston Churchill, the 1992 exclusive. The prestige limited-edition jugs with two or more handles have also been popular, notably the Henry VIII and William Shakespeare designs. After a brief period of concern about wide-ranging withdrawals and colourways, the future now looks very bright for character jug collectors.

BUILDING A COLLECTION

Collections start in many different ways. Often a surprise gift will be responsible for starting a life-long enthusiasm or it could be a legacy that starts an instant collection. Perhaps a chance discovery in an antique market might also spark off a new collector's curiosity and hunting for more will become an absorbing hobby. One thing is certain, the first acquisition is rarely alone for long.

A few dedicated collectors have acquired all the Royal Doulton character and toby jugs in the standard range and then gone on to add rare prototypes, colourways, modelling variations and unusual backstamps. However, this goal requires considerable time and energy as well as substantial financial resources. Most collectors are content to concentrate on specific themes, sizes or types of jugs and can build some fascinating collections in this way.

Collecting By Type

Lambeth Stoneware Jugs

The scarcity of the early jugs from the Lambeth factory has meant that they are not as widely publicised as the Burslem models. However, there is a committed group of collectors who specialise in English stonewares and seek out the Doulton tobies and face jugs along with other brown salt-glaze stoneware products, such as reform flasks, hunting jugs, bottles, mugs and jars. Competition is stiff, therefore, to include representative examples in Doulton jug collections. A little more accessible are the Lambeth toby wares, modelled by Harry Simeon, which were made in small editions during the 1920s. A number of collectors have specialised in this field, delighting in all the ingenious uses devised for Toby Fillpots, be it a candlestick, tobacco jar, ink pot or traditional jug. One of the largest collections, built up over ten years, included more than 75 examples in various sizes and colour schemes. Collectors' discoveries have added greatly to the archive information over the years, but it is still impossible to produce a definitive list, which is part of the fun of collecting these Simeon tobies.

Toby Jugs

The term "toby" is frequently used to describe all Royal Doulton jugs, but strictly speaking it should only be applied to jugs in the form of a full seated or standing figure. Although Royal Doulton began by producing toby jugs at their Burslem factory, they are better known for their character jugs, which feature only the head and shoulders. Nevertheless, there is a lot of scope for collectors in the toby jug range alone.

Two of the earliest Burslem tobies are also the rarest, the large portraits of Charlie Chaplin and George Robey, which stand around 11 inches tall. Most of the traditional tobies, with their tankards of foaming ale, were introduced in 1939, and the majority remained in production for over 50 years, so they are relatively easy to find. The best-selling toby portrait of Winston Churchill is also readily available in three different sizes and should not be confused, as has often happened, with the rare Churchill character jug. Also confusing is the similarity between the Winston Churchill toby and the toby of Cliff Cornell. This American industrialist was a great admirer of Churchill, and in 1956 he commissioned a portrait toby of himself in the image of the great statesman – even smoking a cigar. Three different colourways were produced in two sizes, with Cornell wearing either a brown, blue or tan suit and various matching ties. The base was suitably inscribed to promote his Cleveland Flux company, and he

sent them to his friends and associates as Thanksgiving gifts. Today they are becoming hard to find, particularly the tan suit variation, which was made in smaller quantities than the others. Advertising toby jugs were also commissioned by Charrington's to promote their Toby Ale, and three versions with different inscriptions have been recorded from the 1930s.

Completely different in style from the rest of the range are the little Dickens tobies (4 1/2 inches high), which verge on caricature. There are six characters to find in this desirable collection, which was produced between 1948 and 1960, and there is a lot of competition from Dickens fans. This whimsical style of toby jug was revived by Bill Harper for his Doultonville collection in 1983. He created 25 larger-than-life characters from the imaginary town of Doultonville for this appealing set and all have appropriate comical names. One of the rarest is Albert Sagger, the Potter, which was only made for a six-month period especially for Collectors Club members.

George Robey (c1925) and Charlie Chaplin (1918)
designed by Charles Noke, Art Director

In 1992 Royal Doulton launched their first limited-edition toby jugs in a new style and size (5 1/2 inches). The collection has grown rapidly and their instant popularity has inspired a revival of interest in Royal Doulton tobies. The subjects have varied from traditional characters, like the Jester and the Clown, to unusual double-sided designs like The Judge and Thief.

In 1994, Royal Doulton launched a new tiny size for their toby jugs, reinterpreting some of the first toby designs, such as Old Charley and Happy John, in this miniature scale. The set of six tiny tobies has been well received and it will be interesting to see if more follow.

Character Jugs

The standard character jug range has included around 300 different subjects, not to mention all the different sizes which have been available, so there is a lot of scope for collectors. It is the ambition of many keen collectors to find all of them, but as the range expands, so the task becomes more daunting and choices have to be made.

The most accessible jugs are the ones in current production, which can be purchased in local china shops or by mail order through specialist dealers. The Doulton catalogues currently list around 40 different subjects, some of which are available in large size, some in small size and some in both. There are also limited editions, subject to availability, and a few special commissions from Lawleys By Post and other companies. This number changes every year as new designs are added and models are withdrawn from production.

Once a piece has been discontinued in the Doulton catalogues, it is only available on the secondary market. Prices will depend on the demand for the retired model, which is often influenced by how long it was in production. Obviously there will be lots of Bacchus jugs around, as it was made for over 30 years before being discontinued in 1991, whereas the Genie and the Witch jugs were in production for less than a year before being caught up in the sweeping withdrawals of 1991.

There are different styles of discontinued character jugs, and it may be that a specific era or the work of a particular artist appeals. Harry Fenton, who was active in the 1930s and 40s, modelled rugged, wrinkly faces (with warts and all!), whereas in the 1950s and 60s his successor, Max Henk, favoured smoother complexions with exaggerated features. It was Henk and his assistants who saw the potential of the character jug's handle which had been mostly plain and functional in the early years, and many collectors delight in the creativity and ingenuity of the designs, which have included animals, birds, boats, various weapons, sporting equipment, musical instruments and even parts of buildings. Miniature faces or figures have often been incorporated in the handle and the latest representation of Henry VIII features all six of his wives on two handles – seven portraits in one jug! There has even been a prestigious three-handled jug recently, King Charles I. Occasionally new handles have been modelled for promotional purposes or just to ring the changes, and in the case of the Santa Claus and Father Christmas jugs, several different handles have been issued over the years.

Themes and Series

Part of the fun of collecting character jugs is researching the symbolism of the handles and finding out more about the characters behind the jugs. For bookworms there have been lots of characters from literature, beginning with the novels of Charles Dickens, a particular favourite of the art director, Charles Noke. Just looking for all the different Dickens character jugs, tobies, derivatives and limited-edition jugs could keep a collector very busy for several years. Those interested in England's past will find an abundance of kings and queens, colourful London characters and military heroes to create a historical pageant of jugs. As an island nation, the sea has been particularly important in British history, and not surprisingly there are many seafaring characters which could form part of a nautical collection. Patriotic Americans can look out for all the presidents, Civil War generals, Williamsburg pioneers, Hollywood film stars and Wild West cowboys represented in the collection. In many cases these have been presented in themed sub-collections, some in limited editions, and issued on an annual basis by Royal Doulton. A list of all the different self-contained series is listed below in alphabetical order for easy reference:

Alice in Wonderland
> The Cook and the Cheshire Cat; Mad Hatter; The March Hare; The Red Queen; Ugly Duchess; The Walrus and the Carpenter

Antagonists (limited)
> Chief Sitting Bull and George Armstrong Custer; Davy Crockett and Santa Anna; George III and George Washington; Ulysses S. Grant and Robert E. Lee

Armed Forces (limited)
> The Airman (style one); The Sailor (style one); The Soldier (style one)

Beatles
> George Harrison; John Lennon; Paul McCartney; Ringo Starr

Canadians (limited)
> The Airman (style two); The Sailor (style two); The Soldier (style two)

Canadian Centennial Series 1867-1967
> The Lumberjack; North American Indian; The Trapper

Celebrity Series
> Clark Gable; Groucho Marx; Jimmy Durante; Louis Armstrong; Mae West; W.C. Fields

Characters from Life
> The Angler; The Baseball Player (style two); The Bowls Player; The Gardener (style two); The Golfer (style two); The Jockey (style two); The Snooker Player

Characters from Literature
> Aramis; Athos; D'Artagnan; Don Quixote; Falstaff; Long John Silver; Merlin; Porthos; Rip Van Winkle; Robin Hood (style two); Scaramouche (style two)

Charles Dickens Characters
> Bill Sykes; Buz Fuz; Cap'n Cuttle; Charles Dickens (styles one, two and three); Fat Boy; Sairey Gamp; Mr. Micawber; Mr. Pickwick (styles one and two); Sam Weller; Tony Weller

Charles Dickens Commemorative Tinies
> Artful Dodger; Betsy Trotwood; Bill Sykes; Charles Dickens; David Copperfield; Fagin; Little Nell; Mr Bumble; Mrs Bardell; Oliver Twist; Scrooge; Uriah Heep

Christmas Miniatures
Caroler; Elf; Mrs. Claus; Santa Claus (style five);
Snowman

Circus Performers
The Clown (style two); The Elephant Trainer;
The Juggler; The Ringmaster

Collecting World (limited)
The Antique Dealer; The Auctioneer; The Collector

Diamond Collection
Dick Turpin; Granny; Jester; John Barleycorn;
Parson Brown; Simon the Cellarer

Dickens Tobies
Cap'n Cuttle; Fat Boy; Mr. Micawber; Mr.
Pickwick; Sairey Gamp; Sam Weller

Doultonville Tobies
Albert Sagger the Potter; Alderman Mace the
Mayor; Betty Bitters the Barmaid; Captain Prop
the Pilot; Capt. Salt the Sea Captain; Charlie
Cheer the Clown; Dr. Pulse the Physician; Flora
Fuchsia the Florist; Fred Fearless the Fireman;
Fred Fly the Fisherman; Len Lifebelt the
Lifeboatman; Madam Crystal the Clairvoyant;
Major Green the Golfer; Mike Mineral the Miner;
Miss Nostrum the Nurse; Miss Studious the
Schoolmistress; Monsieur Chasseur the Chef; Mr.
Brisket the Butcher;
Mr. Furrow the Farmer; Mr. Litigate the Lawyer;
Mr. Tonsil the Town Crier; Mrs. Loan the
Librarian; Pat Parcel the Postman; Rev. Cassock
the Clergyman; Sgt. Peeler the Policeman

English Civil War (limited)
Charles I; Oliver Cromwell

Flambé (limited)
Aladdin's Genie; Confucius

Football Supporters
Arsenal; Aston Villa; Celtic; Everton; Leeds
United; Liverpool; Manchester United; Rangers;
Sheffield Wednesday

Great Generals (limited)
Duke of Wellington; General Eisenhower;
General Gordon

Henry VIII and his Wives
Anne Boleyn; Anne of Cleves; Catherine of Aragon;
Catherine Howard; Catherine Parr; Henry VIII;
Jane Seymour; (Sir Thomas More)

Heroes of the Blitz (limited)
ARP Warden; Auxiliary Fireman; Home Guard

Heroic Leaders (limited)
Earl Mountbatten of Burma; Sir Winston Churchill;
Viscount Montgomery of Alamein

Journey through Britain (limited)
The Engine Driver; The Fireman (style two);
The Policeman; The Postman

Kings and Queens of the Realm (limited)
Charles I; Elizabeth I; Edward VII; Henry V;
Henry; VIII; Victoria

Laurel and Hardy
Hardy; Laurel

London
Beefeater; The Busker; Chelsea Pensioner;
City Gent; The Guardsman; The London 'Bobby';
Lord Mayor of London; Pearly King; Pearly
Queen;
Yeoman of the Guard

Mystical Characters
Genie; Witch; The Wizard

National Service
The Airman (style three); The Sailor (style three);
The Soldier (style three)

Presidential (limited)
Abraham Lincoln; George Washington; Thomas
Jefferson

**Royal Doulton International Collectors Club
Commissions**
Albert Sagger the Potter (toby); Beefeater (tiny);
Charles Dickens (style two); Christopher
Columbus (style two); Earl Mountbatten (large
size); John Doulton (style one and two); Nelson
(small size); Old King Cole (tiny); Punch and
Judy (large size); Sir Henry Doulton (small size)

Shakespearean
Hamlet; Henry V; Macbeth; Othello; Romeo;
William Shakespeare

Star-Crossed Lovers (limited)
Antony and Cleopatra; King Arthur and
Guinevere;
Napoleon and Josephine; Samson and Delilah

Status Quo (limited)
Francis Rossi; Rick Parfitt

Suites From Playing Cards
King and Queen of Clubs; King and Queen of
Diamonds

Three Musketeers
Aramis, Athos, D'Artagnan; Porthos

Tinies
'Arry; 'Arriet; Auld Mac; Beefeater; Charles I;
Dick Turpin; Edward VII; Elizabeth I; Fat Boy;
Granny; Henry V; Henry VIII; Jester; John
Barleycorn; John Peel; Mr. Micawber; Mr.
Pickwick; Old Charley; Old King Cole; Paddy;
Parson Brown; Sairey Gamp; Sam Weller; Santa
Claus (styles four, six and seven); Simon the
Cellarer; Victoria

Waterloo
Napoleon (style two); Wellington

Wild West
Annie Oakley; Buffalo Bill (style two); Doc
Holliday;
Geronimo; Wild Bill Hickock; Wyatt Earp

Characters from Williamsburg
Apothecary; Blacksmith; Bootmaker;
Cabinetmaker; Gaoler; Guardsman; Gunsmith;
Night Watchman

Collecting by Size

Potential display space is one of the factors to consider when embarking on a collection of character jugs as many subjects have been available in four different sizes – large, small, miniature and tiny. Some keen collectors purchase their favourite jugs in all the sizes along with the toby version and the various derivatives, and in the case of Sairey Gamp, that makes 12 different portraits of her to collect!

The majority of collectors look out for one specific size of character jug and the large has tended to be the most popular. In the past Royal Doulton always launched the large size first and, if it was well received, smaller versions would follow within a few years. Sometimes the subject never appeared in the small or miniature sizes, much to the chagrin of those who were collecting these. In recent years, the Royal Doulton International Collectors Club has commissioned a number of small-size jugs exclusively for their members, and Lawleys By Post, the mail-order division of the company, also prefers the small size for their special series, and these are not produced in any other size.

The smaller the jug, the less detail it is possible to achieve, and the costs do not decrease in proportion to the scale, which has tended to make the miniature-size character jug the least popular choice. In 1992 Royal Doulton discontinued this size jug altogether, so there are now set limits to a miniature character jug collection. However, some models will be hard to find, notably Trapper and Lumberjack, which were not officially launched, yet some examples have appeared on the market. On several occasions miniature prototypes were developed many years before they were put into production, as with The Golfer, where the miniature followed 15 years after the large size, or Old Salt, where there was an interval of 23 years.

To date Royal Doulton have only produced 40 tiny-size character jugs, making this a diminutive collection in more ways than one. Their obvious appeal is reflected in the high prices commanded by the original set of 12, which are out of all proportion to their Lilliputian scale. The tinies require expert decorating skills, and the artists have to balance the minute jugs on the end of their little fingers, which is very time consuming and consequently expensive. Such tiny jugs are also difficult to display in china shops, which has meant that the recent models have tended to be special commissions; for example, a set of Kings and Queens of the Realm characters for Lawleys By Post customers and the tiny Beefeater and Old King Cole jugs for members of the RDICC.

LIMITED AND SPECIAL-EDITION CHARACTER AND TOBY JUGS

Limited-edition jugs are comparatively recent developments, as the first character jug was not commissioned until 1978 and the first toby in 1992. It was Michael Doulton's first American tour that inspired the reproduction of the company's very first jug, John Barleycorn, and it was issued in a limited edition of 7,500, appropriately numbered and marked on the base. A few years later, in 1983, the first limited-edition collection was launched with Grant

and Lee as the initial pair of Antagonists. The novel two-faced design proved to be very popular, and the edition of 9,500 was quickly sold out. The other three jugs in the series were also very successful, and so they were quickly followed in 1985 by the Star-Crossed Lovers, another two-faced collection.

In 1984 Royal Doulton had the honour of designing a character jug portrait of President Ronald Reagan as a fund-raiser for the Republican National Committee, and number one of the edition of 2,000 was presented to the President at the White House. This prestigious commission was followed by many other requests for special character jugs to promote various companies, products and events. A character jug of Mr. Quaker was produced in a limited edition of 3,500 to mark the 85th year of Quaker Oats Limited in 1985, and the restricted distribution amongst this company's customers and employees has made this a very desirable jug today. Pick-Kwik Wines and Spirits of Derby commissioned a range of small-size character jugs, some adapted as liquor containers, to promote their various whiskies. As well as the traditional pre-announced limited editions, they also issued collectors editions and special editions – new terms coined to describe commissions by independent companies that are not individually numbered limited editions in the strictest sense. Special editions have included colourways (discussed in the section on colour variations) and entirely new jugs, such as the Collecting World Series for Kevin Francis and the Great Generals series for UK International Ceramics.

There have also been occasional special commissions, which are limited by time and distribution rather than by numbers. For example, in 1984 only members of the Royal Doulton International Collectors Club could purchase a small-size Henry Doulton character jug, and in 1986 the offer was a small Doultonville toby of Albert Sagger, the Potter. Similarly, only customers attending Michael Doulton's special appearances in 1988 and 1989 could buy the character jug portrait of him. In 1991 Royal Doulton launched their new Character Jug of the Year concept, which limits the model to one year's production, and this has proved very popular.

In the last few years there has been a new approach to limited character jugs with the launch of several exceptionally complex and detailed models in low editions at premium prices. Some of these prestige jugs had two handles, or even three, and gold or silver embellishments. The first of this type was Henry VIII, issued in 1991 in a limited edition of 1,991 to mark the 500th anniversary of his birth. The edition was quickly oversubscribed, endorsing collectors' very positive reactions to these ambitious designs. Another recent development which has generated a lot of interest is the collection of limited-edition toby jugs, which began in 1992 with the Jester.

PROTOTYPES AND VARIATIONS

Once all the standard range jugs have been acquired, the ultimate challenge for many serious collectors is to find as many prototypes and variations as possible. This usually requires a very healthy bank balance, as huge sums of money can change hands for these rare pieces.

Prototypes

Prototype jugs are the samples taken from the master mould, and they are often described as pilots or trials. Usually two or three jugs are cast at this early stage, any more would wear down the detail in the master mould, and they are given different decorative treatments. If one of the prototypes is approved, then lots of production moulds will be made, but if it is rejected, the model will only exist in prototype form. There have been lots of character jugs and at least a few toby jugs that did not get past the prototype stage for various reasons.

In the 1920s Charles Noke modelled a toby jug of John Wesley, the founder of Methodism, but when the prototypes came from the kiln, he had misgivings about the propriety of portraying a strict abstainer as a toby. He therefore abandoned the project, giving one of the prototype jugs to the decorator Ted Eley, another was later presented to the Museum of the Wesley Church in Tasmania.

Prototype of The Maori
modelled by Harry Fenton in 1939

During the 1930s most of the jugs that were modelled seem to have gone into production, but the war interrupted several plans. In the Royal Doulton archives there are references to an Old Scrooge jug and one called Red Wing, but no illustrations have survived. Harry Fenton modelled two portraits of a New Zealand Maori, one of which was approved in July 1939, but it did not subsequently go into the general range. A few examples survive in private collections around the world, and the last one to come on the market in 1986 sold for £12,000. No records survive for the Buffalo Bill jug, which presumably also dates from the war years and was modelled by Fenton.

The 1950s seem to have passed with only two casualties. The Scarlet Pimpernell, which was submitted by Geoff Blower, surfaced in 1987 and changed hands for over £15,000. Blower's colleague Garry Sharpe remembered his portrait of Alice in Wonderland being turned down in 1959 because of copyright restrictions, but no examples have come to light, so perhaps it did not get beyond the clay stage.

During the 1960s a rejected Village Blacksmith was rescued from a Doulton rubbish skip by a factory labourer, and his family recently sold it at Phillips Auction rooms in London for over £7,000. It is probably the work of design manager Max Henk, and it was given a pattern number D6549 in 1961, so it is strange that it was never launched.

David Biggs was responsible for many of the successful character jugs produced during the 1960s, but several of his prototypes were rejected at the end of the decade, possibly because of the re-appraisal of the collection and the change-over to bone china production, which took place at that time. He remembers submitting a Racing Driver, but this has not come to light. However, his models of of a Fisherman (1968), John Gilpin (1968) and two colourways of The Baseball Player (1971) are in private collections, and his ambitious Pilgrim Father was discovered at Royal Doulton in 1988.

Several new modellers joined the design department in the 1970s, and inevitably some of their early work was not accepted for production. Robert Tabbenor's character jug of Uncle Tom Cobbleigh was rejected in 1975 and Peter Gee's Jester toby in 1977. Although both artists later produced popular jugs, they made figure modelling their speciality. Michael Abberley's Cabinet Maker of Williamsburg, which he modelled in 1979, caused a lot of confusion, as it was publicised in the 1981 catalogue but was not launched then, as it was decided to discontinue the Williamsburg range. In August 1995 it will finally join the collection at the RDICC convention in Williamsburg to mark the 15th anniversary of the club. Bill Harper's first character jug of a pirate was rejected in 1976, but he has gone on to contribute a wide range of subjects to the range. Unfortunately his admirable portrait of Pierre Trudeau (1986) missed the boat as the Canadian Prime Minister had left office before the jug was ready to be launched. In 1987 Bill was keen to produce a *Canterbury Tales* series of jugs but it was felt that the Miller and The Wife of Bath were not sufficiently well known internationally, and so they remain in prototype form in Royal Doulton's own collection. Bill also submitted a portrait of Elvis Presley for the Celebrity collection, but it was not approved by the singer's estate. Several stars in this hapless series did not get beyond the prototype stage, but they have found their way on to the market. In 1992 one of the Marilyn Monroe prototypes was auctioned in Canada for $17,500 and a Humphrey Bogart prototype has also changed hands recently for a significant sum. A portrait of Clark Gable had got beyond the prototype stage and several hundred had been made in 1984 before it was recalled for copyright reasons, so although not unique, it is still a rare model.

A few more jugs "got away" in the late 1980s, including a portrayal of Robin Hood by Eric Griffiths, Uncle Sam by Harry Sales and a Prison Warder by Stan Taylor, and no doubt there will be more in the future, although the art director's ideal is not to reach the expensive prototype stage until all the production problems have been ironed out. For this reason original clay models are smashed or left to dry out and crumble to dust if they do not come up to scratch.

Often the design of the character jug is basically acceptable, but there are reservations about the handle. Usually this is resolved at the clay stage, as with the Collectors Club jug of Henry Doulton, which originally incorporated a drainpipe in the handle to symbolise the firm's original achievements. It was felt that this was too mundane a reminder and the vase motif was emphasised instead. Occasionally alternative handles have been moulded, and for the Catharine of Aragon character jug two different designs featuring a cornet and a scroll were considered before the version with the tower was agreed upon.

It is not only aesthetic considerations which lead to modifications, cost is also an important factor and handles occasionally need to be simplified. For example, the prototype of Groucho Marx included the other Marx brothers peeping out from behind his cigar, and they were subsequently removed for the production model. Eagle-eyed collectors have often noticed other minor modifications. The original version of the Fireman character jug, which was used for publicity purposes, featured the badge of the London Fire Brigade, but this was changed when permission to use it was not granted. Discrepancies such as these have always had a particular fascination for jug collectors, and premium prices are paid when original-version prototypes come up for sale.

Modelling Variations

If a character jug is altered once it has gone into production, it can no longer be described as a prototype, but there is still a lot of interest in such modelling variations, and there are more of them around for collectors to find. The Anne of Cleves character jug is a celebrated example. When it was launched in 1980, the ears on the horse handle were erect, but as these were easily chipped they were soon remodelled to lie flat. A premium is now paid for the first "ears up" version. Similarly with the original handle of the Macbeth jug, the large protruding noses on the witches were prone to damage and consequently the heads were turned inwards. It would appear that only a few of the original jugs had been made before modification, so the "noses out" version is extremely rare.

Some of the early character jugs have also been modified, although the reasons for the changes are not so apparent. Harry Fenton's Granny, which was introduced in 1935, was revamped within a few years. The proportions of her face were altered and a white frill was added to the front of her bonnet, but the most significant addition was a prominent front tooth. This resulted in the original version being dubbed the "Toothless Granny," and she commands considerably more in the marketplace than the second version, which continued in production until 1983. Fenton's Cavalier also exists in two versions; the original from 1940 features a goatee beard, which is missing from the later version, but it now makes a big difference in price if he is bearded.

Style One: Hatless Drake

The war years seem to have been a period of change and reappraisal generally. Apart from the modifications already mentioned, Drake acquired a plumed hat, making the original, hatless version something of a rarity, and Pearly Boy lost his relief-modelled buttons to become plain 'Arry. His companion, Pearly Girl, was not remodelled, but was decorated differently to become 'Arriet. The original Pearly Boy and Girl character jugs are now amongst the rarest production models to find.

Colour Variations

Changes of colour can make a significant difference to the desirability of jugs, as has been seen with the Pearly Girl. The presence of a lime green and pink hat, as opposed to the drab green worn by 'Arriet, will attract a substantial premium. Pearly Boy has also worn different coloured outfits, and the blue version is considered to be much rarer than the brown. Another expensive variation is Fenton's Old King Cole. The original, which dates from 1939, has a yellow crown, and the second common version an orange one. There are also slight modelling variations in the ruff, but the colour differences are the most pronounced.

The Clown character jug features the most radical of the early colour changes. In the first version, introduced in 1937, he has a white painted face with bright red hair, whilst the post-war version has natural flesh tones with white hair. There is also a brown-hair variation, which is contemporary with the red-haired model. All the clowns are desirable additions to a collection, but the red- and brown-haired versions are priced higher.

In the early years alternative colour schemes for character jugs were unusual, but from the mid 1980s it became standard practice to offer the most popular models in different outfits. A few of these went into the general range, but most were special commissions in limited editions. The first, in 1985, was a colourway of the large-size Mad Hatter, which was produced in an edition of 250 to celebrate the opening of the Royal Doulton room at Higbees department store in the US, and it sold out on the day of issue. Many more special colourway editions followed this early success, but their appeal gradually diminished until ultimately the practice ceased at the end of the decade.

During long production runs, colours have frequently been altered for technical reasons, and the results of the new recipes are often noticed by serious collectors. The most obvious in recent years was the Beefeater, who received an on-glaze red jacket in 1987 instead of the early underglaze maroon shade. There have also been other modifications to this long-lived jug. In the first year or so of production, the Royal Cypher GR was picked out in gold, and this is now very rare. When Queen Elizabeth was crowned in 1953, the handle was altered again to feature her cypher ER.

Character and toby jugs are all painted individually by different artists, and so inevitably there will be slight variations in colour between one and another, even though everybody is following the same standard. Occasionally mistakes are made, colours might be reversed or omitted, and they can cause a lot of interest amongst collectors when they slip through the system. An interesting error was spotted in 1984, when the first Custer and Sitting Bull character jugs left the factory. The Indian chief was depicted with grey eyes and, when it was pointed out that this was genetically unlikely, the eyes were altered to brown. There are no prizes for guessing which variation is the most sought after! Around the same time a small quantity of Henry V jugs left the factory without the on-glaze red and gold decoration, and initially they caused some excitement in the marketplace before it was realised they were seconds. Colour variations do not always command premium prices, but it is still fun looking out for them.

DERIVATIVES

Novelty coupled with practicality became Charles Noke's maxim during the 1930s, as his fertile imagination contorted many of his favourite character jug personalities into all sorts of useful items, including teapots, tobacco jars, ashtrays and wall vases. Collecting these derivatives, as they are known, can add another dimension to Doulton displays. It is possible to find Old Charley in 15 different guises, including character jugs, tobies and derivatives, and Sairey Gamp comes a close second in the variety of her appearances, so putting together displays of these characters alone could be fun.

It may be that Noke was given the idea for the derivatives from the novel toby wares made by Harry Simeon at the Lambeth studio, and it is probably not a coincidence that the Burslem factory was also commissioned to model character decanters for Aspreys and Co. The resulting Scotsman and Irishman whisky containers were issued in 1934 and can be considered forerunners of the derivatives. Bookends, busts and napkin rings of Dickens personalities followed, and although they have more in common with Noke's figures from the HN series, they are still sought after by jug enthusiasts.

The first true character jug derivatives were the ashtrays of 1936, which are essentially miniature-size jugs with trays added. These must have been successful, for larger ashbowls and tobacco jars were soon added to the range. Generally only minor modifications were required to suit the character jugs for their new purposes. The musical jugs, for instance, had an extended hollow base to accommodate the Thorens Swiss movement which played the appropriate tune. In contrast, Harry Fenton's creative powers were fully stretched to incorporate Sairey Gamp, Tony Weller and Old Charley into teapots! Although it is highly unlikely that these figurative teapots were used, they soon had matching sugar bowls. Perhaps milk jugs would have followed if it had not been for the outbreak of war, which abruptly curtailed production of all these whimsical gift items. Consequently all the early derivatives are considered rare.

Complete set of Sairey Gamp character jugs together with a sugar bowl and bust

It was not until the late 1950s that designers were once again able to turn their attention to the novelty gift market. A range of table lighters in the form of jug personalities was launched in 1958, and some of these now prove elusive. As well as the 14 lighters recorded in the catalogues, a prototype Granny lighter has also made an appearance in the market. Most of the post-war derivatives have been liquor containers made to order for various distillers and bottlers, including W. Walklate, Pick-Kwik and William Grant, and perhaps there will be more in the future. The Royal Doulton International Collectors Club has also played its part in keeping the derivatives in focus by reviving the potty teapot tradition. In 1988 they commissioned the Old Salt Teapot especially for members, and this led to the introduction of several new character teapots of The Old Balloon Seller, Long John Silver and Falstaff. As they were only in the range for a brief period, they will eventually become as hard to find as some of the early derivatives.

LIMITED-EDITION LOVING CUPS AND JUGS

A few years before the successful launch of character jugs, Charles Noke and Harry Fenton had already collaborated on a spectacular range of limited-edition loving cups and jugs. These large, colourful pieces are vigorously modelled in low relief, and they feature many of the characters who were later portrayed as jugs. Thus in terms of subject and style, they are closely related to character and toby jugs, and consequently many keen collectors seek them out as display centrepieces. Unfortunately they are not easy to find, as most were only made for a short period during the 1930s, and they were produced in very small editions of 300 to 1,000, some of which were never completed. Also it is inevitable that some have been broken in the intervening years, so not surprisingly, they are expensive when they do appear on the market.

Wandering Minstrel Loving Cup

These loving cups and jugs were Royal Doulton's very first limited-edition pieces and, as such, represent the zenith of Noke's achievements as art director. The accompanying certificates of authenticity are almost as splendid as the items they describe, with elaborate illustrations, ribboned seals and Noke's signature written in ink. Understandably many collectors have these documents framed as works of art in their own right. Further authentification and the unique number of the loving cup or jug appears on the base, which is usually equally decorative, with appropriate motifs or symbols. Perhaps the most novel is the treasure chart on the base of The Treasure Island jug.

The majority of the loving cups and jugs stand around 10 inches high, and the scene unfolds in relief, painted in glowing underglaze colours. The handles are often ingeniously linked to the subject; for instance, the John Peel loving cup has a riding crop and fox head, whilst the Guy Fawkes jug has a flaming torch. It is interesting that symbolic handles such as these later became a major feature of the character jug range.

Many of the subjects reflect Noke's literary interests, which he regularly explored in the series ware, figures and character jug collections, in particular the writings of Dickens and Shakespeare and popular adventure stories such as *The Three Musketeers* and *Treasure Island*. The exploits of real-life seafaring heroes, such as Drake, Nelson and Cook, were also celebrated in the range.

Noke realised at an early stage that these prestige pieces were ideal for commemorating important historical and royal events, and so the bicentenary of the birth of George Washington in 1932 was marked with a patriotic American jug, bedecked in stars and stripes, whilst the anniversary of the founding of New South Wales was recalled by the launch of the Captain Phillip jug. There was no shortage of royal events to celebrate during the 1930s, and loving cups with portraits of the monarchs, emblazoned with flags and regalia, were issued for the Silver Jubilee of George V and the coronation of George VI. There are even three different coronation loving cups for Edward VIII, who, of course, was never crowned, but some of the editions had been sold before his abdication. Years later these ceremonial loving cups were revived for the Coronation and Silver Jubilee of Queen Elizabeth II in 1953 and 1977 respectively, and perhaps they will be used again for important royal occasions in the future.

In 1982 the Royal Doulton International Collectors Club commissioned a loving cup in traditional style depicting Pottery in the Past, and as it was only made in small numbers for members, it is becoming increasingly difficult to find.

Collecting all the limited-edition loving cups and jugs will prove to be something of a challenge, and as with all Royal Doulton wares, there are also some tantalising prototypes and variations. To date nobody has found the trials of Roger Solemel, Cobbler and I.T. Wigg, Broom-man, but one lucky collector has a prototype George Washington presentation jug with a different stars and stripes handle. This variation was not recorded in the Royal Doulton archives, and there may well be others to be found, so happy hunting.

MAKING CHARACTER AND TOBY JUGS

Each Royal Doulton character and toby jug goes through the hands of many skilled and experienced individuals. From the designer to the painter to the kiln manager, each person is responsible for ensuring the quality of the finished article.

Today the diverse ideas for new jugs usually originate in the company's marketing department, and following discussions with the design managers, the modeller is briefed about the required subject. A great deal of research goes into the initial concept. If a historical personality is to be depicted, contemporary paintings, photographs and other records are studied to ensure accuracy in features and costume. For a fictional character, the designer needs to read the relevant book and consider any illustrations before embarking on sketches. Some Royal Doulton artists submit drawings of their proposed subject, others prefer to work directly with the modelling clay to visualise their ideas.

A careful balance must be achieved between portraiture and caricature, good humour and dignity, to create a jug suitable for the Royal Doulton range. The symbolism of the handle, which is now such an important element of the design, also requires a lot of thought and ingenuity. When the modeller is completely satisfied with his work, it goes for approval to the art and marketing directors, who occasionally suggest modifications to improve the design or avert potting problems. It is vital that everybody is happy with the jug at this stage, because the lines and details of this master model will determine the exact appearance of the finished piece.

The mould-maker then takes over and carefully disects the original to create plaster of Paris moulds of each part. Usually a four-part mould is required, for the head and the handle are moulded separately. A few sample jugs, known as prototypes, will be cast from the master mould for further discussion and colour trials. Ideally only two or three prototypes are produced, as with each casting the intricate detail of the mould is gradually worn away. If the prototype is approved at one of the design conferences, a rubber working "case" is made from the master mould, and it is from this case that all the subsequent plaster of Paris production moulds are made.

In the casting department a liquid clay mixture known as slip is poured into the production moulds through a hole in the top. The porous plaster absorbs the water in the slip and a layer of solid clay is formed in the interior of the mould. When this has reached the required thickness, the excess slip is drained away and the mould is taken apart for the various cast sections to be extracted. The separate parts of the jug are assembled using slip as an adhesive and the rough edges and seams smoothed away in a process known as fettling.

After drying at a controlled temperature, the jugs are ready to receive their first firing in the electric tunnel kiln. This is known as the "biscuit" firing because of the texture of the jug when it emerges from the kiln. On completion the fragile clay body has shrunk by about an eighth of its original size, becoming hard and durable.

The white biscuit jug is then taken to the decorating studio, where special pigments suitable for underglaze painting are used. Painting directly onto the porous biscuit body gives the rugged character lines and wrinkles required in many jug subjects. Considerable care and expertise is required at this stage, as some colours can change during the fixing process in the hardening — on kiln.

After this second, low-temperature firing, the jug is ready to be glazed, and this is done by either spraying it with a liquid glass mixture or dipping it into a vat of the same mixture. The glossy, protective finish is achieved by firing the jug again, this time in a glost kiln. In many cases, this completes the process, but some brightly coloured jugs have a further coat of paint applied on top of the glaze, and they need to be fired a fourth time to seal the colours permanently. Before leaving the factory, the finished jugs are inspected by the quality control staff to ensure there are no flaws, and they are then packed for despatch all over the world.

Collectors are invited to see the jug-making process at the John Beswick factory. For opening times and tour bookings, contact the Tour Organiser, John Beswick, Gold Street, Longton, Stoke-on-Trent ST3 2JP.

BODIES AND GLAZES

Stoneware

The first Doulton jugs were produced at the Lambeth factory in London, and these were made of salt-glaze stoneware, a high-fired ceramic body which is literally glazed with salt thrown into the kiln at peak temperatures. Bodies range from a plain buff to a rich brown, which is sometimes dipped in a darker coloured slip to create a two-tone effect. Muted colours can be achieved in this high-temperature process, but only the Simeon toby wares were additionally coloured with a bright red on-glaze enamel colour.

Earthenware, Kingsware and China

The first character and toby jugs produced at Royal Doulton's factory in Nile Street, Burslem, were mostly made of white earthenware, although the treacle-coloured Kingsware body was used for some early commissions. For a brief period, between 1968 and 1973, character jugs were made in English Translucent China, a porcelain body pioneered by Doulton chemists in 1959. All the jugs had to be remodelled for this process, and so collectors will notice differences in detail between earthenware and ETC jugs. However, the most obvious variation is the size, as the china body fires about a half- inch smaller than the earthenware.

Following Royal Doulton's acquisition of the John Beswick factory, it was decided to concentrate the production of jugs at this location in Longton, and the earthenware body was revived. Consequently, since 1973 new models have been produced in earthenware and painted under the glaze, although some recent designs also have on-glaze decoration, particularly to achieve bright reds, blues or metallic effects.

In the early 1980s there was some research at the Nile Street factory to revive the china body for character jugs, in order to cope with the demand for the Antagonists and Beatles collections, and although the experiment was short-lived, occasional china examples come on to the market.

White Jugs

From time to time, white-glazed versions of standard character jugs appear on the market, and these are highly valued by collectors. Most were made from the late 1930s to the early 1950s when wartime restrictions prohibited the production of decorated china for the UK market. It is believed that white biscuit jugs with slight flaws, which could not be decorated for the export market, were glazed for sale to company employees.

These white substandard jugs should not be confused with the white character jug portrait of Winston Churchill, which was originally conceived undecorated, no doubt because of the UK embargo. Examples are rare because it did not remain in production for long.

During the 1930s D&J McCallum, the whisky distillers, commissioned a white version of their Highlander jug, as well as the better-known Kingsware variety. Numbers were limited to around 1,000 and they are hard to find today. Fifty years later Pick-Kwik Wines and Spirits of Derby commissioned two undecorated variations in their extensive range of promotional jugs. Only 100 of each were made of the Micawber character jug and spirit container for internal promotional use.

Occasionally modern white character jugs have turned up at local auctions and markets, but it would appear that these have "escaped" from the factory in an undecorated state and been glazed to cater for the strong market demand for white jugs.

CARE AND REPAIR

Character and toby jugs are relatively robust and easy to look after. The glaze seals and protects the colours permanently, and occasional dusting will maintain the shiny finish. If the jugs are displayed on open shelves, it is a good idea to fill the interior with crumpled tissue paper, as this catches the dust and can be replaced easily at cleaning times. When necessary, jugs can be washed in luke-warm water using a mild detergent, then rinsed thoroughly and dried naturally or buffed with a soft cloth. Care should be taken not to knock jugs against the tap or each other – the rims and handles are the most vulnerable parts. If an accident does happen, there are professional restorers who can make "invisible" repairs to chips and cracks, even hairlines.

Obviously when buying on the secondary market, it is advisable to check very carefully for restorations such as these, as they are not immediately obvious to the naked eye. Expert dealers have many different ways of spotting repairs. Rarely do they carry an ultraviolet lamp that will highlight problem areas, instead they become sensitive to the different vibrations given by the softer restored areas when tapped with a metallic object or even bitten with the teeth! Reputable dealers will stand by any guarantees they give regarding restorations. Prices should reflect the level of damage sustained and the quality of the restoration.

Occasionally old jugs have been used as containers, and these can appear at flea markets quite dirty and stained. If washing fails, petroleum jelly will usually remove stubborn rust marks. It is worth persevering — apparently the rare, coloured Churchill character jug, which made over £16,000 at auction in 1989, had originally been used as a storage jar under the kitchen sink.

A GUIDE TO BACKSTAMPS AND DATING

The marks on the base of a character jug can be a useful guide for dating the piece, particularly if it has been in production for a while. However, it is impossible to be precise, as stocks of old-style backstamps continued to be used up after changes had been implemented. Nevertheless, jugs can usually be placed in a specific time period and, very occasionally, if there is a date code, an exact year of manufacture can be determined.

The Royal Doulton Trademark

Most prominent on the base is the Royal Doulton factory mark, which has featured a lion standing on a crown ever since the company was awarded the Royal Warrant in 1901. It is unusual for a jug not to have a Royal Doulton trademark, but occasionally prototypes have been found with a blank base, and these have been authenticated by the company in Stoke-on-Trent.

Lion and Crown
Backstamp 1901 to 1930s

Made in England
was added in the 1930s

The early Royal Doulton trademark is found on some of the first Burslem toby jugs, such as Charlie Chaplin, and on the McCallum character jugs. By the early 1930s, the words "Made in England" had been incorporated in the lion and crown trademark, and this style of backstamp has been recorded, with no other information, on some of the first character jugs. Most of the toby jugs issued between 1939 and 1950 are marked with this backstamp and the title of the character portrayed. Copyright information was either nonexistent or kept to a minimum, unlike the character jugs.

The 1930s

In order to protect their designs from being copied, Royal Doulton registered them at the UK patent office, and the resulting registration number (e.g. RdNo782778 for John Barleycorn) is often printed underneath the backstamp. The year the jug was registered can be worked out from the table of numbers published by the patent office. Usually registration was a year before the jug went into production, but on occasion the number was not issued in time and the words "Reg. applied for" were added to the backstamp (this has also been found misspelt "Registeration"). It should be noted that the registration number does not give the date of manufacture for a specific piece, only when the design was first protected.

R^dN°782778

Registered Mark below backstamp
Printed numeral '14' stands for 1941

"Micawber."

R^dN°822825.
REG^d IN AUSTRALIA

Regd in Australia
Name in inverted commas

Around 1938 Royal Doulton also began to register their designs in Australia, and the information "Regd in Australia" was added to the backstamp.

By the late 1930s, the name of the jug in inverted commas was usually included above the registration number (e.g. "The Cavalier"). Jugs produced during the 1930s might also have a hand-painted D pattern number, which was added by the decorator when the jug was completed. This practice continued until the Second World War.

All the above details will help date a piece to the 1930s, but the only way to determine the exact year of manufacture is with the date code, if it has one. This numbering system began in 1928 with the number one. The date-code number is immediately to the right of the lion and crown symbol, and the year of manufacture can be calculated by adding it to 1927. Thus the code number 11 will give a date of 1938, and 15 indicates 1942. This code system can be found on character jugs from the 1930s and 40s.

The 1940s and 1950s

A capital *A* on the left of the lion and crown symbol is known as the A mark and it is a kiln control mark denoting a specific type of earthenware body known as Georgian. Sometimes an A mark appears on a character jug without any other information. It was used on a variety of Royal Doulton products between 1939 and 1955, so its presence on character jugs will date the piece to within that time period.

After the war Royal Doulton found it necessary to register their designs in more of their main export markets, and a new style backstamp was devised in 1947. This gives a copyright date for Doulton and Co Limited and four different registration numbers for the UK, Australia, South Africa and

New Zealand. A few jugs introduced in 1950 only have three registration numbers.

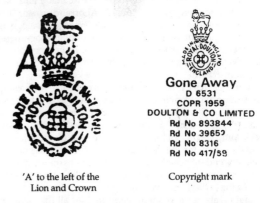

Gone Away
D 6531
COPR 1959
DOULTON & CO LIMITED
Rd No 893844
Rd No 39652
Rd No 8316
Rd No 417/59

'A' to the left of the
Lion and Crown

Copyright mark

From circa 1952 a printed D pattern number appears above the copyright date, and a few years later the inverted commas around the character's name were dropped. Several different typefaces appear to have been used.

The 1960s and 1970s

New UK copyright laws in 1966 gave protection in each country without separate design registrations. Protection was extended to articles previously registered, and as the period of registration ran out, the relevant numbers were withdrawn from the backstamp. By circa 1973 the lists had disappeared altogether and a new copyright symbol was adopted, "C" in place of "Copr." From 1975 the company's new name, Royal Doulton Tableware Ltd, began to appear in the copyright notice, and many collectors were puzzled by this reference to tableware on gift items.

The 1980s and 1990s

A large elegant script was adopted for the character names in the early 1980s, and by 1983 the first reference to hand made and hand decorated had been included underneath. The new Doultonville tobies also adopted this improved style. An entirely new design of backstamp was introduced in 1984,

Doultonville
Tobies backstamp

The Fireman
Backstamp

featuring the new styling for the company name, Royal Doulton, the subject of the jug in bold capitals, the modeller's facsimile signature and the words "Hand made and hand decorated" forming an arch around the lion and crown. These changes were implemented in order to acknowledge the talents of individual artists and to seek public recognition of the specialist production skills involved. Initials or dots and dashes on the base are decorator's marks, but no records exist to identify these.

In the last ten years backstamps have become increasingly interesting and attractive, as evocative images and typefaces are chosen to capture the spirit of the subject matter; for example, the Journey through Britain series has lots of novel backstamp motifs, including a hose for the Fireman jug and postage stamp for the Postman. The Celebrity collection has a Hollywood-billboard typeface and relevant quotes from the characters portrayed. This is not a completely new idea, as one of the earliest jugs, Mephistopheles, was inscribed with a quotation about the devil by Rabelais. Not all the jugs carry this inscription, however, and keen collectors are prepared to pay a slight premium for this feature.

Promotional and Commemorative Backstamps

There are many other interesting backstamp variations which ardent collectors will seek out. During the 1930s several independent companies commissioned standard character jugs with their name printed on the base for promotional purposes, and this can now add to the value of the jug. Amongst the names to look for are Coleman's, Bentall's, Darley and Sons and the Salt River Cement Works. In 1967, to celebrate the Canadian Centenary, the North American Indian and Trapper jugs were launched with a special backstamp in North America only, and this was deleted for worldwide sales the following year. The presence of this commemorative backstamp will double the price of these jugs.

This practice of pre-releasing has continued in recent years for Royal Doulton's important customers. For example, the first two jugs in the Celebrity series, W.C. Fields and Mae West, were produced in a premier edition for American Express, and a small premium is payable for this backstamp.

Generally speaking the backstamps on toby jugs do not excite collectors, the exception being the portrait of Winston Churchill, which originally had a backstamp commemorating "Winston Churchill Prime Minister of Great Britain 1940." This was deleted after 1940, and so jugs with this mark are very rare and consequently expensive.

Other Guides to Dating

Much can obviously be gleaned from the backstamp as to the age of a character jug, but occasionally there are some other clues. It used to be the practice with large-size jugs to continue painting inside the rim, and this is referred to by collectors as bleeding. As this method was discontinued by 1973, it is possible to date jugs with this trait before then. Having checked the rim, look into the character's eyes! It is not as strange as it sounds, for early-style modelling was to indent the iris, and this continued until the early 1960s. For a few years between 1968 and 1973, character jugs were produced in a type of porcelain known as ETC, so pieces in this body must have been made during this short period.

Other clues are specific to certain models; for example, early versions of Auld Mac have "Owd Mac" on the backstamp and also impressed in the tammy. Toby Philpots was spelt with a double *t* until circa 1952, so those spelt Toby Philpotts date from the 1930s or 40s. The Beefeater has a couple of unique clues. Until circa 1953 it was called "Beefeaters" on the backstamp, and following the coronation of Queen Elizabeth in 1953, the handle was remodelled with a new Royal cypher (see Modelling Variations).

SECONDS

Seconds character jugs are no longer sold through retailers, but examples do tend to appear in the marketplace, following sales to Royal Doulton employees. Jugs which have not been approved by the company's quality control department have their backstamps defaced. Nowadays a hole is drilled into the interlacing D device of the trademark, but in the past a cross was scratched through.

"Coleman's Compliments"
Backstamp

"Winston Churchill
Prime Minister of
Great Britain 1940"

WHERE TO BUY

Discontinued Royal Doulton toby and character jugs can be found in antique shops, markets and fairs, as well as in auction houses. Specialist dealers in Royal Doulton jugs attend many of the venues and events below.

UNITED KINGDOM

Auction Houses

Phillips
101 New Bond Street
London W1

Christie's South Kensington
85 Old Brompton Road
London SW5

Bonhams
Montpelier Street
London SW7

Sotheby's
Summer's Place
Billingshurst, West Sussex

Louis Taylor
Percy Street
Hanley, Stoke-on-Trent

Peter Wilson
Victoria Gallery
Market Street
Nantwich, Cheshire

Antique Fairs

UK Doulton Collectors Fair
The Queensway Hall
Civic Centre
Dunstable, Bedfordshire

Stafford International Doulton Fair
Stafford County Showground
Stafford

Doulton and Beswick Collectors Fair
National Motor Cycle Museum
Meriden, Birmingham

Antique Markets

Portobello Road Market
London W11
Saturday only

New Caledonian Market
Bermondsey Square
London SE1
Friday morning

Alfie's Antique Market
13-25 Church Street
London NW8
Tuesday - Saturday

Camden Passage Market
(off Upper Street)
London N1
Wednesday and Saturday

USA

Auction Houses

Phillips New York
406 East 79th Street
New York, NY 10021

Antique Fairs

Florida Doulton Convention
Guest Quarters Suite Hotel
Cypress Creek
555 NW 62nd Street
Fort Lauderdale, Florida 33309

Doulton Show
Sheraton Poste House
Cherry Hill, New Jersey

Doulton Show
Holiday Inn
Independence, Ohio

CANADA

Auction Houses

D & J Ritchies
429 Richmond Street
Toronto, Ontario M5A 1R1

Antique Shows

The International Doulton Collectors
Weekend
Holiday Inn
Airport Road
Mississauga, Ontario

Antique Markets

Harbourfront Antique Market
390 Queens Quay West
Toronto, Ontario
(Tuesday - Sunday)

PLACES TO VISIT

John Beswick Studio
Gold Street
Longton
Stoke-on-Trent ST3 2JP

CLUBS AND SOCIETIES

The Royal Doulton Collectors Club was founded in 1980 to provide an information service on all aspects of the company's products, past and present. The club's magazine, *Gallery*, is published four times a year, and local branches also publish newsletters. There are also several regional groups in the USA, which meet for lectures and other events, and some publish newsletters. Contact the USA branch for further information.

Headquarters and UK Branch

Royal Doulton
Minton House
London Road
Stoke-on-Trent ST4 7QD

Canadian Branch

Royal Doulton Canada Inc.
850 Progress Avenue
Scarborough, Ontario
M1H 3C4

USA Branch

Royal Doulton USA Inc.
P.O. Box 1815
Somerset, New Jersey
08873

Australia Branch

Royal Doulton Australia Pty Ltd.
17 - 23 Merriwa Street
Gordon, NSW 2072

New Zealand Branch

Royal Doulton
P.O. Box 2059
Auckland

FURTHER READING

Figures and Character Jugs

Royal Doulton Figures, by Desmond Eyles, Richard Dennis and Louise Irvine
The Charlton Standard Catalogue of Royal Doulton Figurines, by Jean Dale
Collecting Character and Toby Jugs, by Jocelyn Lukins
The Original Price Guide to Royal Doulton Discontinued Character Jugs,by Princess and Barry Weiss
The Character Jug Collectors Handbook, by Kevin Pearson
The Doulton Figure Collectors Handbook, by Kevin Pearson

General

The Doulton Story, by Paul Atterbury and Louise Irvine
Royal Doulton Series Wares, (vols. 1 – 4), by Louise Irvine
Royal Doulton Bunnykins Figures, by Louise Irvine
Bunnykins Collectors Book, by Louise Irvine
Limited Edition Loving Cups and Jugs, by Louise Irvine and Richard Dennis
Doulton for the Collector, by Jocelyn Lukins
Doulton Kingsware Flasks, by Jocelyn Lukins
Collecting Doulton Animals, by Jocelyn Lukins
Doulton Burslem Advertising Wares, by Jocelyn Lukins
Doulton Lambeth Advertising Wares, by Jocelyn Lukins
The Doulton Lambeth Wares, by Desmond Eyles
The Doulton Burslem Wares, by Desmond Eyles
Hannah Barlow, by Peter Rose
George Tinworth, by Peter Rose
Sir Henry Doulton Biography, by Edmund Gosse
Phillips Collectors Guide, by Catherine Braithwaite
Discovering Royal Doulton, by Michael Doulton
Royal Doulton, by Jennifer Queree
Doulton Divvy Magazine, by Betty Weir and David Gilman
Collecting Doulton Magazine, published by Francis Jodeph, edited by Doug Pinchin
Thorndon Antiques and Fine China Ltd., by David Harcourt

DOULTON
LAMBETH
JUGS

ADMIRAL LORD NELSON

STYLE ONE: NELSON MODELLED TO THE CHEST

The Admiral Lord Nelson jug was produced in the 1820s by Doulton and Watts in Lambeth. Although originally called a figure mug, this jug must be considered one of the first character jugs. This jug was reissued in 1905 to commemorate the 100th anniversary of the Battle of Trafalgar in which Nelson defeated the French fleet.

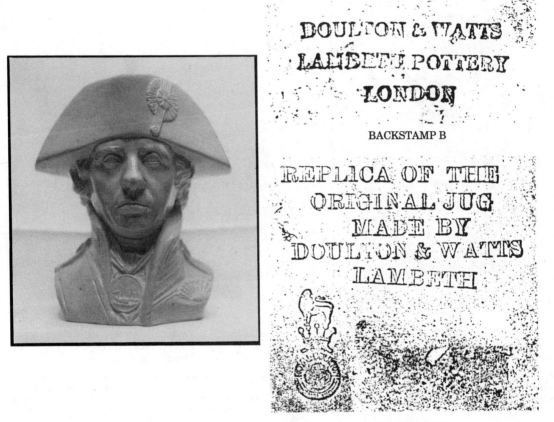

DOULTON & WATTS
LAMBETH POTTERY
LONDON

BACKSTAMP B

REPLICA OF THE
ORIGINAL JUG
MADE BY
DOULTON & WATTS
LAMBETH

BACKSTAMP C

Designer: Unknown	**Backstamps:** A. Doulton & Watts
Handle: Rope	B. Doulton & Watts,
Colourway: Saltglaze; light tan	Lambeth Pottery London
	C. Doulton

Model Number	Size	Backstamp	Height	Intro.	Discon.	U.K. £	U.S. $	Can. $
—	Large	A and B	6 - 7 1/2"	1821	1830	600.00	1,000.00	1,250.00
—	Large	C	6"	1905	Unknown	400.00	650.00	750.00
—	Small	A and B	5"	1821	1830	500.00	800.00	1,000.00
—	Miniature	A and B	2 1/2"	1821	1830	350.00	600.00	700.00

Current Market Value

ADMIRAL LORD NELSON

STYLE TWO: NELSON MODELLED TO THE WAIST

The inscription around the base of this jug is Nelson's famous words spoken before the Battle of Trafalgar, "England Expects Every Man to do his Duty." As in style one, this jug was reproduced to commemorate the 100th anniversary of Trafalgar.

BACKSTAMP A

Designer: Unknown
Handle: Hair tied with a bow
Colourway: Saltglaze; light brown

Backstamp: A. Doulton & Watts
Lambeth Pottery, London
B. Doulton Burselm

Model Number	Size	Backstamp	Height	Intro.	Discon.	Current Market Value U.K. £	U.S. $	Can. $
—	Large	A	11 3/4"	1845	Unknown	1,200.00	2,500.00	2,500.00
—	Large	B	11 3/4"	1905	Unknown	1,000.00	2,000.00	2,000.00

ARTHUR WELLESLEY
FIRST DUKE OF WELLINGTON

Arthur Wellesley (1769-1852) had a distinguished military career and was endowed with numerous honours, including the title of first Duke of Wellington after the Battle of Toulouse, France, in 1814. He became a Member of Parliament in 1806 and Prime Minister in 1827.

Produced in the 1820s by Doulton and Watts in Lambeth, this jug is also considered a figure mug.

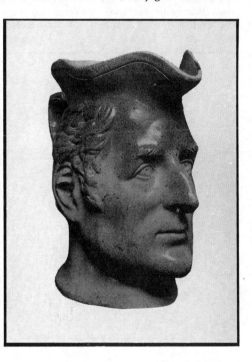

Designer: Unknown   **Backstamp:** Unknown
Handle: Plain
Colourway: Saltglaze; light tan

Model Number	Size	Backstamp	Height	Intro.	Discon.	Current Market Value U.K. £	U.S. $	Can. $
—	Large	Unknown	7 1/2"	1821	1830	800.00	1,500.00	1,600.00

THE BEST IS NOT TOO GOOD

STYLE ONE: SMILING FACE; EYES OPEN; LEFT HAND HOLDING A PIPE
15 BUTTONS

Issued circa 1925, this jug by Harry Simeon was the forerunner of The Best is not too Good by Harry Fenton. It is wider and darker than the later version. The character has white hair, a closed mouth, a dark waistcoat with 15 light-coloured buttons, a smooth face and his whole hand encloses the pipe. The Harry Fenton jug is lighter, and the character has dark hair, white teeth on a smiling face, no tie, a dark waistcoat with 11 buttons, his face is detailed and his index finger holds the pipe.

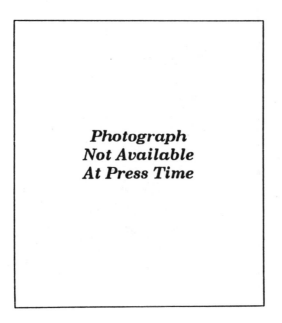

Photograph Not Available At Press Time

Designer: Harry Simeon
Handle: Plain
Colourway: Unknown

Backstamp: Doulton Lambeth

Model Number	Size	Backstamp	Height	Intro.	Discon.	Current Market Value U.K. £	U.S. $	Can. $
—	Small	Doulton	4 1/2"	c.1925	Unknown	400.00	700.00	800.00

THE BEST IS NOT TOO GOOD

STYLE TWO: SMILING FACE; LEFT EYE WINKING; LEFT HAND HOLDING A PIPE; 15 BUTTONS

Designer: Harry Simeon
Handle: Plain
Colourway: Slate blue jacket; white waistcoat; brown breeches

Backstamp: Doulton Lambeth

Model Number	Size	Backstamp	Height	Intro.	Discon.	Current Market Value U.K. £	U.S. $	Can. $
8588	Small	Doulton	3"	c.1925	Unknown	300.00	500.00	600.00

The Best is not too Good Derivative

The neck of this flask is hallmarked sterling silver. The outer edge of the flask is blue.

Designer: Harry Simeon
Colourway: Slate blue jacket; orange waistcoat; olive-green breeches
Inscription: No inscription around base

Backstamp: Doulton Lambeth

Model Number	Item	Height	Intro.	Discon.	Current Market Value U.K. £	U.S. $	Can. $
—	Liquor flask	8 1/2"	c.1925	Unknown	650.00	1,800.00	2,000.00

Note: See page 35 for the continuation of this jug in china.

THE BEST IS NOT TOO GOOD

STYLE THREE: SMILING FACE; EYES OPEN; LEFT HAND HOLDING LAPEL;
13 BUTTONS

Designer: Harry Simeon   **Backstamp:** Doulton Lambeth
Handle: Plain
Colourway: Variation No. 1 — Slate blue jacket; orange waistcoat; brown breeches
Variation No. 2 — Slate blue jacket olive green waistcoat; brown breeches

Model Number	Variation	Backstamp	Height	Intro.	Discon.	Current Market Value U.K. £	U.S. $	Can. $
8588	Var. 1	Doulton Lambeth	4 1/2"	c.1925	Unknown	350.00	700.00	800.00
8588	Var. 2	Doulton Lambeth	4 1/2"	c.1925	Unknown	350.00	700.00	800.00

THE BEST IS NOT TOO GOOD

STYLE FOUR: SOMBRE FACE; EYES OPEN; LEFT HAND HOLDING LAPEL; 13 BUTTONS

Designer: Harry Simeon		**Backstamp:** Doulton Lambeth
Handle: Plain		
Colourway: Slate blue jacket; white waistcoat; olive-green breeches		

Model Number	Size	Backstamp	Height	Intro.	Discon.	Current Market Value U.K. £	U.S. $	Can. $
554	Small	Doulton Lambeth	3 3/4"	c.1925	Unknown	300.00	600.00	700.00

The Best is not too Good Derivative

Designer: Harry Simeon		**Backstamp:** Doulton Lambeth
Colourway: Slate blue jacket; white waistcoat; olive green breeches		

Model Number	Item	Height	Intro.	Discon.	Current Market Value U.K. £	U.S. $	Can. $
8593	Tobacco jar	4 1/2"	c.1925	Unknown	700.00	1,200.00	1,400.00

HIGHWAYMAN

This design by Leslie Harradine could very well be interpreted as the forerunner of the Doulton line of character jugs.

Designer: Leslie Harradine
Handle: Strands of hair
Colourway: Saltglaze

Backstamp: Doulton Lambeth

Model Number	Backstamp	Height	Intro.	Discon.	Current Market Value		
					U.K. £	**U.S. $**	**Can. $**
—	Doulton Lambeth	Unknown	c. 1912	Unknown		Extremely rare	

HONEST MEASURE

Ink Pot
(Removable Head)

Designer: Harry Simeon
Colourway: Variation No. 1 — Olive-green jacket; orange waistcoat; slate blue breeches
Variation No. 2 — Brown jacket; white waistcoat; black breeches
Backstamp: Doulton Lambeth

Model Number	Variation	Backstamp	Height	Intro.	Discon.	Current Market Value U.K. £	U.S. $	Can. $
8583	Var. 1	Doulton Lambeth	2 3/4"	c.1925	Unknown	400.00	800.00	900.00
8583	Var. 2	Doulton Lambeth	2 3/4"	c.1925	Unknown	400.00	800.00	900.00

Ash Pot
(Removable Hat)

Designer: Harry Simeon
Colourway: Variation No. 1 — Olive-green jacket; dark green waistcoat; black breeches
Variation No. 2 — Olive-green jacket; orange waistcoat; slate blue breeches
Backstamp: Doulton Lambeth

Model Number	Variation	Backstamp	Height	Intro.	Discon.	Current Market Value U.K. £	U.S. $	Can. $
8584	Var. 1	Doulton Lambeth	4 "	c.1925	Unknown	400.00	800.00	900.00
8584	Var. 2	Doulton Lambeth	4 "	c.1925	Unknown	400.00	800.00	900.00

MARRIAGE DAY

This saltglaze jug was issued with the words "Marriage Day" and "After Marriage" inscribed atop either the smiling or frowning faces.

  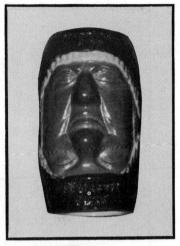

MARRIAGE DAY	MARRIAGE DAY	AFTER MARRIAGE
JUG UPRIGHT	JUG UPSET	JUG UPRIGHT

Designer: Harry Simeon **Backstamp:** Doulton Lambeth
Handle: Plain
Colourway: Blue, brown and white

Doulton Number	Size	Description	Height	Intro.	Discon.	Current Market Value U.K. £	U.S. $	Can. $
8595	1/2 pint	Frown upright	4 3/4"	c.1925	Unknown	300.00	800.00	800.00
8595	1/2 pint	Smile upright	4 3/4"	c.1925	Unknown	300.00	800.00	800.00
8596	1/4 pint	Frown upright	3 1/2"	c.1925	Unknown	250.00	700.00	700.00
8596	1/4 pint	Smile upright	3 1/2"	c.1925	Unknown	250.00	700.00	700.00
8595	Miniature	Frown upright	2"	c.1925	Unknown	200.00	600.00	600.00
8595	Miniature	Smile upright	2"	c.1925	Unknown	200.00	600.00	600.00

Note: A plain white stoneware jug exists (model number X7590).

MR PECKSNIFF

VARIATION No. 1:   Colourway — Ivory

VARIATION NO. 1

VARIATION NO. 2

Designer: Leslie Harradine
Handle: Plain
Colourway: Variation No. 1 — Ivory
Variation No. 2 — Treacle glaze

Backstamp: Doulton Lambeth

Model Number	Variation	Backstamp	Height	Intro.	Discon.	Current Market Value U.K. £	U.S. $	Can. $
15354	Var. 1	Doulton Lambeth	7 1/2"	c.1912	Unknown	500.00	2,500.00	2,500.00
15354	Var. 2	Doulton Lambeth	7 1/2"	c.1912	Unknown	500.00	2,500.00	2,500.00

OLD KING COLE

Designer: Leslie Harradine   **Backstamp:** Doulton Lambeth
   Handle: Plain
Colourway: Saltglaze stoneware

Model Number	Size	Backstamp	Height	Intro.	Discon.	Current Market Value		
						U.K. £	**U.S. $**	**Can. $**
—	Large	Doulton Lambeth	Unknown	c.1910	Unknown		Extremely rare	

SEATED TOBY

STYLE ONE: KNEES TOGETHER

Designer: Harry Simeon
Handle: Plain
Colourway: Variation No. 1 — Slate blue jacket; orange waistcoat; olive green breeches
Variation No. 2 — Slate blue jacket; olive green waistcoat; white breeches
Backstamp: Doulton Lambeth

Model Number	Variation	Backstamp	Height	Intro.	Discon.	Current Market Value U.K. £	U.S. $	Can. $
8599	Var. 1	Doulton Lambeth	3 1/8"	c.1925	Unknown	200.00	600.00	600.00
8599	Var. 2	Doulton Lambeth	3 1/8"	c.1925	Unknown	200.00	600.00	600.00

Seated Toby Derivative

Designer: Harry Simeon   **Backstamp:** Doulton Lambeth
Colourway: Slate blue jacket; orange breeches

Model Number	Item	Height	Intro.	Discon.	Current Market Value U.K. £	U.S. $	Can. $
559	Candlestick	3 3/4"	c.1925	Unknown	300.00	650.00	650.00

SEATED TOBY

STYLE TWO: KNEES APART

Designer: Harry Simeon
Colourway: Slate blue jacket; olive green waistcoat; brown breeches
Backstamp: Doulton Lambeth

Model Number	Size	Backstamp	Height	Intro.	Discon.	Current Market Value U.K. £	U.S. $	Can. $
8594	Tiny	Doulton Lambeth	2 1/2"	c.1925	Unknown	200.00	600.00	600.00

Seated Toby Derivative

Designer: Harry Simeon
Colourway: Variation No. 1 — Slate blue jacket; white waistcoat
Variation No. 2 — Cream jacket; tan waistcoat
Variation No. 3 — Slate blue jacket; brown waistcoat
Variation No. 4 — Slate blue jacket; olive green waistcoat; olive green breeches
Backstamp: Doulton Lambeth

Model Number	Variation	Item	Height	Intro.	Discon.	Current Market Value U.K. £	U.S. $	Can. $
8594	Candlestick	Var. 1	2 1/2"	c.1925	Unknown	200.00	600.00	600.00
8594	Candlestick	Var. 2	2 1/2"	c.1925	Unknown	200.00	600.00	600.00
8594	Candlestick	Var. 3	2 1/2"	c.1925	Unknown	200.00	600.00	600.00
8594	Candlestick	Var. 4	2"	c.1925	Unknown	200.00	600.00	600.00

SEATED TOBY

STYLE THREE: ARMCHAIR VARIETY

VARIATION NO. 1   VARIATION NO. 5

Designer: Harry Simeon
Colour: Variation No. 1 — Blue jacket; cream waistcoat; dark brown breeches
Variation No. 2 — Brown jacket; orange waistcoat; dark brown breeches
Variation No. 3 — Royal blue jacket; burgundy waistcoat; green breeches
Variation No. 4 — Slate blue jacket; orange waistcoat; brown breeches
Variation No. 5 — Green jacket; rust waistcoat; black breeches
Advertisement for "Ye Olde Cock Tavern 22 Fleet Street Founded 1549"
Backstamp: Doulton Lambeth

Model Number	Variation / Description	Height	Intro.	Discon.	Current Market Value U.K. £	U.S. $	Can. $
8586	Var. 1 / Blue, white, brown	4"	c.1925	Unknown	250.00	650.00	700.00
543	Var. 2 / Brown, orange, blue	4"	c.1925	Unknown	250.00	650.00	700.00
543	Var. 3 / Royal blue, burgundy	4"	c.1925	Unknown	250.00	650.00	700.00
543	Var. 4 / Slate blue, orange	6"	c.1925	Unknown	350.00	800.00	900.00
551	Var. 5 / Green, rust, black	6"	c.1925	Unknown	350.00	800.00	900.00

Note:: There is a liquor flask of the 6" Seated Toby.

SOLDIER BOY

Designer: Mark Mitchell
Handle: Plain
Colourway: Saltglaze stoneware

Backstamp: Doulton Lambeth

Model Number	Size	Backstamp	Height	Intro.	Discon.	Current Market Value		
						U.K. £	U.S. $	Can. $
—	Large	Doulton Lambeth	Unknown	c.1910	Unknown		Extremely rare	

THE STANDING MAN

STYLE ONE: SMILING FACE

Designer: Harry Simeon
Handle: Plain
Colourway: Variation No. 1 — Slate blue jacket; orange waistcoat; brown breeches;
                  waistcoat buttons are either white or gold
           Variation No. 2 — Slate blue jacket; olive green waistcoat; olive green breeches
Issued: c.1925 — Unknown
Backstamp: Doulton Lambeth

Model Number	Size	Variation — Description	Height	Current Market Value U.K. £	U.S. $	Can. $
8572	Large	Var. 1 — White waistcoat buttons	8 3/4"	350.00	750.00	800.00
8572	Large	Var. 1 — Silver rim, white waistcoat buttons	8 3/4"	450.00	900.00	1,000.00
8572	Medium	Var. 1 — White waistcoat buttons	8 3/4"	300.00	650.00	700.00
8572	Medium	Var. 1 — Gold waistcoat buttons	7"	325.00	700.00	800.00
8572	Medium	Var. 1 — Silver rim, white waistcoat buttons	7"	375.00	850.00	950.00
8572	Medium	Var. 1 — Silver rim, gold waistcoat buttons	7"	375.00	850.00	950.00
8572	Medium	Var. 1 — White waistcoat buttons	7"	325.00	700.00	800.00
8572	Medium	Var. 1 — Silver rim, white waistcoat buttons	7"	375.00	850.00	950.00
8572	Medium	Var. 1 — White waistcoat buttons	6 1/4"	250.00	650.00	750.00
8572	Medium	Var. 2 — Slate blue; olive green	6"	250.00	650.00	750.00
8572	Small	Var. 1 — White waistcoat buttons	4 1/2"	200.00	600.00	750.00

Note: Large and medium size jugs are found with sterling silver rims hallmarked Birmingham, 1928 or 1929.

THE STANDING MAN

STYLE TWO: SOMBRE FACE

The sombre-face, standing-man variety has two buttons on the left lapel of his jacket.

Designer: Harry Simeon   **Backstamp:** Doulton Lambeth
Handle: Plain
Colourway: Slate blue jacket; brown waistcoat;
brown breeches; white or gold waistcoat buttons
Issued: c.1925 - Unknown

Model Number	Size	Variation \ Description	Height	Current Market Value U.K. £	U.S. $	Can. $
8572	Large	White waistcoat buttons	8 3/4"	300.00	750.00	800.00
8572	Large	Gold waistcoat buttons	8 3/4"	300.00	800.00	900.00
8572	Medium	White waistcoat buttons	6 1/4"	250.00	600.00	700.00
8572	Small	White waistcoat buttons	4 1/2"	175.00	500.00	600.00
8572	Tiny	White waistcoat buttons	2 3/4"	125.00	450.00	500.00

THEODORE ROOSEVELT

Designer: Leslie Harradine
Handle: Plain
Colourway: Saltglaze stoneware

Backstamp: Doulton Lambeth

Model Number	Size	Backstamp	Height	Intro.	Discon.	Current Market Value		
						U.K. £	U.S. $	Can. $
—	Large	Doulton Lambeth	Unknown	c.1910	Unknown		Extremely rare	

TOBY XX

HAND HOLDS JUG OF ALE, WITH HANDLE

STYLE ONE: SALTGLAZE STONEWARE

VARIATION No. 2

Designer: Unknown
Handle: Hair tied with a bow
Colourway: Variation No. 1 — Light brown overall glaze; no dark brown overglaze
　　　　　Variation No. 2 — Light brown overall glaze, different sections with dark brown overglaze
　　　　　Variation No. 3 — Light brown overall glaze; "XX" is replaced with "W. Dow & Co. India Pale Ale" on barrel
Backstamp: Doulton Lambeth

Model Number	Variation	Backstamp	Height	Intro.	Discon.	Current Market Value U.K. £	U.S. $	Can. $
6365	Var. 1	Doulton Lambeth	14 1/2"	1863	Unknown	450.00	1,500.00	1,500.00
6365	Var. 1	Doulton Lambeth	8 1/2"	1863	Unknown	250.00	750.00	750.00
6365	Var. 2	Doulton Lambeth	12 1/2"	1863	Unknown	350.00	1,250.00	1,250.00
6365	Var. 2	Doulton Lambeth	10 1/2"	1863	Unknown	300.00	900.00	900.00
6365	Var. 2	Doulton Lambeth	8 1/2"	1863	Unknown	250.00	750.00	750.00
6365	Var. 3	Doulton Lambeth	14 1/2"	1891	Unknown	Rare		

Note: Some examples carry a registration number 169753, which is a design registration by Doulton, circa 1891.

TOBY XX

HAND HOLDS JUG OF ALE, WITH HANDLE

STYLE TWO: SALTGLAZE COLOURED STONEWARE

Designer: Harry Simeon
Handle: Strands of hair
Colourway: Variation No. 1 — Slate blue jacket; brown waistcoat; green breeches
Variation No. 2 — Slate blue jacket; orange waistcoat; green breeches
Variation No. 3 — Slate blue jacket; brown waistcoat; brown breeches
Variation No. 4 — Slate blue jacket; orange waistcoat; olive-green breeches
Variation No. 5 — Slate blue jacket; green waistcoat; olive-green breeches
Variation No. 6 — Black jacket; olive-green waistcoat; slate blue breeches
Backstamp: Doulton Lambeth

Model Number	Variation	Backstamp	Height	Intro.	Discon.	Current Market Value U.K. £	U.S. $	Can. $
8590	Var. 1	Doulton Lambeth	8"	c.1925	Unknown	300.00	800.00	900.00
8590	Var. 2	Doulton Lambeth	8"	c.1925	Unknown	300.00	800.00	900.00
8592	Var. 3	Doulton Lambeth	8"	c.1925	Unknown	275.00	750.00	850.00
8589	Var. 4	Doulton Lambeth	6 3/4"	c.1925	Unknown	250.00	700.00	850.00
8589	Var. 5	Doulton Lambeth	6 3/4"	c.1925	Unknown	250.00	700.00	850.00
8589	Var. 6	Doulton Lambeth	6 3/4"	c.1925	Unknown	250.00	700.00	850.00

Toby XX Derivative

This liquor container is supported by a silver-plated stand, produced by Finnigans Limited, Manchester.

Designer: Harry Simeon   **Backstamp:** Doulton Lambeth
Handle: None
Colourway: Slate blue jacket; orange waistcoat;
              brown breeches

Model Number	Item	Height	Intro.	Discon.	U.K. £	Current Market Value U.S. $	Can. $
8589	Liquor container	10 1/4"	c.1925	Unknown	500.00	950.00	1,000.00

TOBY XX

HANDS REST ON KNEES, WITHOUT HANDLE

STYLE ONE: SALTGLAZE STONEWARE

VARIATION No. 1   VARIATION No. 2

Designer:	Unknown
Handle:	None
Colourway:	Variation No. 1 — Light brown overall glaze; no dark brown overglaze
	Variation No. 2 — Light brown overall; different sections with dark brown overglaze
Backstamp:	Doulton Lambeth
	Doulton Lambeth, Phillips Oxford St. London

Model Number	Variation	Backstamp	Height	Intro.	Discon.	Current Market Value U.K. £	U.S. $	Can. $
8547	Var. 1	Doulton Lambeth	5 3/4"	c.1925	Unknown	300.00	600.00	600.00
8547	Var. 2	Lambeth/Phillips	5 3/4	c.1925	Unknown	300.00	600.00	600.00

TOBY XX

HANDS REST ON KNEES, WITHOUT HANDLE

STYLE TWO: SALTGLAZE COLOURED STONEWARE

Designer: Unknown
Handle: None
Colourway: Variation No. 1 — Olive-green jacket; white waistcoat; olive-green breeches
Variation No. 2 — Slate blue jacket; orange waistcoat; brown breeches
Variation No. 3 — Slate blue jacket; green waistcoat; green breeches
Backstamp: Doulton Lambeth

Model Number	Variation	Backstamp	Height	Intro.	Discon.	Current Market Value U.K. £	U.S. $	Can. $
8591	Var. 1	Doulton Lambeth	5 3/4"	c.1925	Unknown	300.00	600.00	600.00
8591	Var. 2	Doulton Lambeth	5 1/2"	c.1925	Unknown	300.00	600.00	600.00
547	Var. 3	Doulton Lambeth	5 1/2"	c.1925	Unknown	300.00	600.00	600.00

VETERAN MOTORISTS

| STYLE ONE | STYLE TWO |

Designer: Leslie Harradine   **Backstamp:** Doulton Lambeth
Handle: Plain
Colourway: Saltglaze stoneware

Model Number	Size	Style	Height	Intro.	Discon.	Current Market Value U.K. £	U.S. $	Can. $
—	Large	Style one	Unknown	c.1905	Unknown		Extremely rare	
—	Large	Style two	Unknown	c.1905	Unknown		Extremely rare	

Note: Both style one and style two have sterling silver hallmarked rims dated 1906.

WEE MAC

**Photograph
Not Available
At Press Time**

Designer: Unknown
Handle: Unknown
Colourway: Saltglaze stoneware

Backstamp: Doulton Lambeth

Model Number	Backstamp	Height	Intro.	Discon.	Current Market Value		
					U.K. £	U.S. $	Can. $
—	Doulton Lambeth	Unknown	c.1908	Unknown		Extremely rare	

TOBY JUGS

ALBERT SAGGER THE POTTER

THE DOULTONVILLE COLLECTION,
ONE OF 25

This jug was issued for the Royal Doulton International Collectors Club in 1986.

ALBERT SAGGER THE POTTER
FROM THE DOULTONVILLE COLLECTION
EXCLUSIVELY FOR
COLLECTORS CLUB
© 1986 ROYAL DOULTON (U.K.)
MODELLED BY

Designer: William K. Harper
Handle: Plain
Colourway: Brown apron; white shirt; dark green cap; light green vase

Backstamp: Doulton/RDICC

Doulton Number	Size	Backstamp	Height	Intro.	Discon.	Current Market Value U.K. £	Current Market Value U.S. $	Current Market Value Can. $
D6745	Small	Doulton/RDICC	4"	1986	1986	90.00	180.00	225.00

ALDERMAN MACE THE MAYOR

THE DOULTONVILLE COLLECTION,
ONE OF 25

Designer: William K. Harper
Handle: Plain
Colourway: Red coat trimmed with gold; white collar and scarf;
black hat trimmed with gold and white feathers

Backstamp: Doulton

Doulton Number	Size	Backstamp	Height	Intro.	Discon.	Current Market Value		
						U.K. £	U.S. $	Can. $
D6766	Small	Doulton	4"	1987	1991	50.00	95.00	125.00

THE BEST IS NOT TOO GOOD

STYLE TWO: BURSLEM, 11 BUTTONS

This jug was modelled on an earlier Harry Simeon Lambeth design of about 1920. There are, however, several obvious differences on this later piece. See page 6 for an outline of these differences.

The Best is not too Good was one of six toby jugs remodelled by William K. Harper and reissued as tinies in 1994 in a limited edition of 2,500. The others were Happy John, Honest Measure, Jolly Toby, Old Charlie and Toby XX. The issue price was U.K. £225.00 for the complete set and a display stand.

The Best is not too good.

Designer: Harry Fenton	**Backstamp:** Doulton
Model No.: 8338	
Handle: Plain	
Colourway: Green jacket; burgundy trousers; mustard waistcoat with double row of black buttons; brown hat with gold trim	
Inscription: "The Best is not too Good"	

Doulton Number	Size	Backstamp	Height	Intro.	Discon.	Current Market Value U.K. £	U.S. $	Can. $
D6107	Small	Doulton	4 1/2"	1939	1960	225.00	550.00	550.00
D6977	Tiny	Doulton	1 1/2"	1994	Ltd. ed.	45.00	—	—

BETTY BITTERS THE BARMAID

THE DOULTONVILLE COLLECTION,
ONE OF 25

Designer: William K. Harper
Handle: Plain
Colourway: Green blouse; burgundy skirt; yellow hair

Backstamp: Doulton

Doulton Number	Size	Backstamp	Height	Intro.	Discon.	Current Market Value		
						U.K. £	U.S. $	Can. $
D6716	Small	Doulton	4"	1984	1990	50.00	95.00	125.00

CAP'N CUTTLE

DICKENS TOBIES,
ONE OF SIX

Designer: Harry Fenton
Handle: Plain
Colourway: Light brown suit; blue highlights on
jacket lapels and waistcoat

Backstamp: Doulton

Doulton Number	Size	Backstamp	Height	Intro.	Discon.	Current Market Value		
						U.K. £	U.S. $	Can. $
D6266	Small	Doulton	4 1/2"	1948	1960	125.00	250.00	300.00

CAPTAIN PROP THE PILOT

THE DOULTONVILLE COLLECTION,
ONE OF 25

Designer: William K. Harper
Handle: Plain
Colourway: Brown coat and gloves; grey cap; cream scarf

Backstamp: Doulton

Doulton Number	Size	Backstamp	Height	Intro.	Discon.	Current Market Value		
						U.K. £	U.S. $	Can. $
D6812	Small	Doulton	4"	1989	1991	60.00	90.00	125.00

CAPT. SALT THE SEA CAPTAIN

THE DOULTONVILLE COLLECTION,
ONE OF 25

Designer: William K. Harper   **Backstamp:** Doulton
Handle: Plain
Colourway: Blue-black coat; blue-black cap trimmed with yellow

Doulton Number	Size	Backstamp	Height	Intro.	Discon.	Current Market Value U.K. £	U.S. $	Can. $
D6721	Small	Doulton	4"	1985	1991	50.00	90.00	125.00

CHARLES DICKENS

The 125th anniversary of the death of Charles Dickens is being commemorated in 1995 with this toby jug of Dickens. The jug was issued in a limited edition of 2,500 and is available through Lawleys By Post.

Designer: Stanley J. Taylor
Handle: Plain
Colourway: Black

Backstamp: Doulton

Doulton Number	Size	Backstamp	Height	Intro.	Discon.	Current Market Value U.K. £	U.S. $	Can. $
D6997	Small	Doulton	5"	1995	Ltd. ed.	75.00	—	—

CHARLIE

This figure of Charlie Chaplin has a removable bowler hat. He stands on a green base and the name "Charlie" is incised around the base.

Designer: Unknown	**Backstamp:** Doulton
Handle: Plain	
Colourway: Black suit and bowler hat; green and red plaid waistcoat; red-brown tie; green base	

Doulton Number	Size	Backstamp	Height	Intro.	Discon.	Current Market Value U.K. £	U.S. $	Can. $
D —	Large	Doulton	11 1/4 "	1918	Unknown	2,000.00	6,000.00	6,000.00

CHARLIE CHEER THE CLOWN

THE DOULTONVILLE COLLECTION,
ONE OF 25

Designer: William K. Harper
Handle: Plain
Colourway: Orange jacket; blue tie; green cap;
yellow hair; pink sausages

Backstamp: Doulton

Doulton Number	Size	Backstamp	Height	Intro.	Discon.	Current Market Value U.K. £	U.S. $	Can. $
D6768	Small	Doulton	4"	1987	1991	60.00	120.00	150.00

CHARRINGTON & CO. LTD.

According to the Bass Museum, Burton-on-Trent, Staffordshire, these jugs originated from Hoare & Co., a London brewery which had been purchased by Charrington, another London brewery. The original Charrington toby jugs were made by Doulton, but there are no records of the numbers manufactured. The three variations below were made as promotional pieces for Charrington & Co., Mile End, London. They differ only in the wording on their bases and were in production from the 1930s. Charrington closed Hoare & Co. in 1933.

VARIATION No. 1:   Inscription around base — "Toby Ale"

Designer: Unknown

Handle: Plain

Colourway: Black hat; green coat; maroon trousers

Backstamp: Doulton

Doulton Number	Variation	Inscription	Height	Intro.	Discon.	Current Market Value		
						U.K. £	U.S. $	Can. $
D8074	Var. 1	Toby Ale	9"	1934	1938	200.00	550.00	600.00

VARIATION No. 2:   Inscription around base — "One Toby Leads to Another"

Doulton Number	Variation	Inscription	Height	Intro.	Discon.	Current Market Value		
						U.K. £	U.S. $	Can. $
D8074	Var. 2	One Toby	9"	1937	1938	250.00	1,000.00	1,000.00

VARIATION No. 3:   Inscription around base — "Charrington's Toby"

Doulton Number	Variation	Inscription	Height	Intro.	Discon.	Current Market Value		
						U.K. £	U.S. $	Can. $
D8074	Var. 3	Charrington's	9 1/4"	1938	1939	400.00	1,000.00	1,000.00

CLIFF CORNELL

In 1956 an American industrialist commissioned these toby jugs as gifts to friends and associates. The inscription on the base reads, "Greetings Cliff Cornell 'Famous Cornell Fluxes' Cleveland Flux Company."

Approximately 500 pieces were issued for the large size blue and dark brown jugs and 375 pieces for the small sizes. The number of light brown jugs produced is unknown.

VARIATION No. 1: Colourway — Tan suit

GREETINGS
CLIFF CORNELL

"FAMOUS CORNELL FLUXES"
CLEVELAND FLUX COMPANY

Designer: Unknown
Handle: Plain
Colourway: Light brown suit; brown and cream striped tie

Backstamp: Doulton

Doulton Number	Size	Variation	Height	Intro.	Discon.	Current Market Value U.K. £	U.S. $	Can. $
D —	Large	Var. 1	9"	1956	1956	350.00	1,000.00	1,000.00
D —	Small	Var. 1	5 1/2"	1956	1956	350.00	1,500.00	1,500.00

VARIATION No. 2   VARIATION No. 3

VARIATION No. 2: Colourway — Dark blue suit; red tie with cream polka dots

Doulton Number	Size	Variation	Height	Intro.	Discon.	Current Market Value		
						U.K. £	U.S. $	Can. $
D —	Large	Var. 2	9"	1956	1956	250.00	450.00	500.00
D —	Small	Var. 2	5 1/2"	1956	1956	250.00	450.00	500.00

VARIATION No. 3: Colourway — Dark brown suit; green, black and blue design on tie

Doulton Number	Size	Variation	Height	Intro.	Discon.	Current Market Value		
						U.K. £	U.S. $	Can. $
D —	Large	Var. 3	9"	1956	1956	250.00	450.00	500.00
D —	Small	Var. 3	5 1/2"	1956	1956	250.00	450.00	500.00

THE CLOWN

This jug was issued in a limited edition of 3,000.

Royal Doulton®
THE CLOWN
D 8935
Modelled by

Stanley James Taylor

© 1992 ROYAL DOULTON
ISSUED IN A LIMITED
EDITION OF 3,000.
THIS IS N° 129

Designer: Stanley J. Taylor
Handle: Plain, black
Colourway: Green shirt; blue trousers; yellow bow tie
with blue polka dots; yellow and red drum

Backstamp: Doulton

Doulton Number	Size	Backstamp	Height	Intro.	Discon.	Current Market Value U.K. £	U.S. $	Can. $
D6935	Medium	Doulton	5 1/2"	1993	Ltd. ed.	69.95	175.00	235.00

DR. PULSE THE PHYSICIAN

THE DOULTONVILLE COLLECTION,
ONE OF 25

Designer: William K. Harper
Handle: Plain
Colourway: Light brown jacket; grey hair

Backstamp: Doulton

Doulton Number	Size	Backstamp	Height	Intro.	Discon.	Current Market Value U.K. £	U.S. $	Can. $
D6723	Small	Doulton	4"	1985	1991	50.00	90.00	100.00

FALSTAFF

FALSTAFF

BACKSTAMP B

Designer: Charles Noke
Model No.: 8328
Handle: Plain
Colourway: Burgundy clothes; black hat with burgundy feathers

Backstamps: **A.** Sir John Falstaff
B. Falstaff

Doulton Number	Size	Backstamp	Height	Intro.	Discon.	Current Market Value		
						U.K. £	U.S. $	Can. $
D6062	Large	Doulton	8 1/2"	1939	1991	75.00	175.00	200.00
D6063	Small	Doulton	5 1/4"	1939	1991	45.00	100.00	125.00

FAT BOY

DICKENS TOBIES,
ONE OF SIX

Designer: Harry Fenton
Handle: Plain
Colourway: Brown

Backstamp: Doulton

Doulton Number	Size	Backstamp	Height	Intro.	Discon.	Current Market Value		
						U.K. £	U.S. $	Can. $
D6264	Small	Doulton	4 1/2"	1948	1960	125.00	300.00	300.00

FATHER CHRISTMAS

A holly wreath is incorporated into the backstamp of the Father Christmas toby jug. Produced in a limited edition of 3,500, each jug is issued with a certificate of authenticity.

Designer: William K. Harper
Handle: Plain
Colourway: Red and white

Backstamp: Doulton

Doulton Number	Size	Backstamp	Height	Intro.	Discon.	Current Market Value		
						U.K. £	U.S. $	Can. $
D6940	Small	Doulton	5 1/2"	1993	Ltd. ed.	49.95	125.00	250.00

FLORA FUCHSIA THE FLORIST

THE DOULTONVILLE COLLECTION,
ONE OF 25

Designer: William K. Harper
Handle: Plain
Colourway: Light blue uniform; brown hair;
red, yellow and white flowers

Backstamp: Doulton

Doulton Number	Size	Backstamp	Height	Intro.	Discon.	Current Market Value		
						U.K. £	U.S. $	Can. $
D6767	Small	Doulton	4"	1987	1990	50.00	120.00	135.00

FRED FEARLESS THE FIREMAN

THE DOULTONVILLE COLLECTION,
ONE OF 25

Designer: William K. Harper
Handle: Plain
Colourway: Dark blue uniform with green buttons;
yellow helmet

Backstamp: Doulton

Doulton Number	Size	Backstamp	Height	Intro.	Discon.	Current Market Value		
						U.K. £	**U.S. $**	**Can. $**
D6809	Small	Doulton	4"	1989	1991	50.00	95.00	120.00

FRED FLY THE FISHERMAN

THE DOULTONVILLE COLLECTION,
ONE OF 25

Designer: William K. Harper
Handle: Plain
Colourway: Light brown coat; tan hat; grey fish and net

Backstamp: Doulton

Doulton Number	Size	Backstamp	Height	Intro.	Discon.	Current Market Value U.K. £	U.S. $	Can. $
D6742	Small	Doulton	4"	1986	1991	50.00	110.00	125.00

GEORGE ROBEY

George Robey, a star of the British Music Hall, entertained thousands during his long career. The hat on this jug is detachable, and his name is incised on the base.

Designer: Charles Noke
Handle: Plain
Colourway: Black suit and hat; grey shirt; green base

Backstamp: Doulton

| Doulton Number | Size | Backstamp | Height | Intro. | Discon. | Current Market Value | | |
						U.K. £	U.S. $	Can. $
—	Large	Doulton	9 3/4"	c.1925	Unknown	2,000.00	7,000.00	7,000.00

HAPPY JOHN

Happy John was one of six toby jugs remodelled by William K. Harper and reissued as tinies in 1994 in a limited edition of 2,500. The others were Honest Measure, Jolly Toby, Old Charlie, The Best is not too Good and Toby XX. The issue price was U.K. £225.00 for the complete set and a display stand.

HAPPY JOHN

Designer: Harry Fenton
Handle: Plain
Colourway: Black hat; light green coat; yellow scarf with blue polka dots; orange breeches

Backstamp: Doulton

Doulton Number	Size	Backstamp	Height	Intro.	Discon.	Current Market Value U.K. £	U.S. $	Can. $
D6031	Large	Doulton	8 1/2"	1939	1991	85.00	175.00	200.00
D6070	Small	Doulton	5 1/4"	1939	1991	50.00	90.00	100.00
D6979	Tiny	Doulton	2 1/2"	1994	Ltd. ed.	50.00	90.00	100.00

HONEST MEASURE

Honest Measure was one of six toby jugs remodelled by William K. Harper and reissued as tinies in 1994 in a limited edition of 2,500. The others were Happy John, Jolly Toby, Old Charlie, The Best is not too Good and Toby XX. The issue price was U.K. £225.00 for the complete set and a display stand.

Honest Measure

Designer: Harry Fenton	**Backstamp:** Doulton
Handle: Plain	

Colourway: Green coat; orange waistcoat with black buttons; burgundy trousers; brown hat with gold trim

Inscription: "Honest Measure: Drink at Leisure"

Doulton Number	Size	Backstamp	Height	Intro.	Discon.	Current Market Value U.K. £	U.S. $	Can. $
D6108	Small	Doulton	4 1/4"	1939	1991	50.00	120.00	135.00
D6974	Tiny	Doulton	2"	1994	Ltd. ed.	45.00	90.00	100.00

THE HUNTSMAN

VARIATION No. 1: Burslem
Colourway — Bright orange coat

Designer: Charles Noke
Handle: Plain
Colourway: Bright orange coat; yellow waistcoat;
silver rim around top of hat

Backstamp: Doulton Burslem

Model Number	Size	Variation	Height	Intro.	Discon.	Current Market Value U.K. £	U.S. $	Can. $
4090	Large	Var. 1	8"	c.1919	Unknown		Extremely rare	

VARIATION No. 2:   Burslem
Colourway — Red coat

This variation may be found with or without the sterling silver rim around the hat. The variety recorded has a silver rim.

Designer: Charles Noke
Handle: Plain
Colourway: Red coat with yellow buttons; yellow waistcoat; white shirt

Backstamp: Doulton Burslem

Model Number	Size	Variation	Height	Intro.	Discon.	Current Market Value U.K. £	U.S. $	Can. $
4090	Large	Var. 2	7 3/4"	c. 1919	1930	600.00	1,200.00	1,200.00

VARIATION No. 3:   Doulton Kingsware
Colourway — Browns

Designer: Charles Noke	**Backstamp:** Doulton
Handle: Plain	
Colourway: Browns	

Doulton Number	Size	Variation	Height	Intro.	Discon.	Current Market Value U.K. £	U.S. $	Can. $
—	Large	Var. 3	7 1/4"	1910	c.1927	600.00	1,200.00	1,200.00

VARIATION No. 4: Doulton
Colourway — Black hat; maroon coat

This is the Harry Fenton adaption of Noke's original design.

THE HUNTSMAN

Designer:	Harry Fenton	**Backstamp:** Doulton
Handle:	Plain	
Colourway:	Black hat; maroon coat; white shirt; gold waistcoat; grey trousers	

Doulton Number	Size	Variation	Height	Intro.	Discon.	U.K. £	Current Market Value U.S. $	Can. $
D6320	Large	Var. 4	7"	1950	1991	80.00	165.00	175.00

JESTER

The Jester jug was issued in a limited edition of 2,500.

Designer: Stanley J. Taylor
Handle: Plain, black
Colourway: Mauve and brown costume with yellow bobbles

Backstamp: Doulton

Doulton Number	Size	Backstamp	Height	Intro.	Discon.	Current Market Value		
						U.K. £	U.S. $	Can. $
D6910	Medium	Doulton	5"	1992	Ltd. ed. (1993)	120.00	225.00	250.00

JOHN WESLEY

PROTOTYPE

Designer: Charles Noke
Handle: Plain
Colourway: Black

Backstamp: Doulton

Doulton Number	Size	Backstamp	Height	Intro.	Discon.	Current Market Value		
						U.K. £	U.S. $	Can. $
—	Large	Doulton	Unknown	c.1925	Unknown	Only two recorded		

JOLLY TOBY

Jolly Toby was one of six toby jugs remodelled by William K. Harper and reissued as tinies in 1994 in a limited edition of 2,500. The others were Happy John, Honest Measure, Old Charlie, The Best is not too Good and Toby XX. The issue price was U.K. £225.00 for the complete set and a display stand.

Designer: Harry Fenton
Handle: Riding crop
Colourway: Black hat; burgundy coat; yellow vest

Backstamp: Doulton

Doulton Number	Size	Backstamp	Height	Intro.	Discon.	Current Market Value		
						U.K. £	U.S. $	Can. $
D6109	Medium	Doulton	6"	1939	1991	60.00	140.00	150.00
D6976	Tiny	Doulton	2"	1994	Ltd. ed.	45.00	90.00	100.00

THE JUDGE AND THIEF

This is a double-sided toby jug with the caricatures of a stern judge and a smirking robber.

Royal Doulton®
THE JUDGE AND THIEF
D 6988
Modelled by
Stanley James Taylor
© 1994 ROYAL DOULTON

Designer: Stanley J. Taylor
Handle: Plain
Colourways: Red, white, black and brown

Backstamp: Doulton

Doulton Number	Size	Backstamp	Height	Intro.	Discon.	Current Market Value U.K. £	U.S. $	Can. $
D6988	Medium	Doulton	5 1/4"	1995	Current	69.95	185.00	295.00

KING AND QUEEN OF CLUBS

SUITES FROM PLAYING CARDS,
ONE OF FOUR

This is the second jug issued in this series. It was produced in a limited edition of 2,500.

Designer: Stanley J. Taylor
Handle: Plain
Colourway: King in red; Queen in blue;
both wear yellow crowns

Backstamp: Doulton

Doulton Number	Size	Backstamp	Height	Intro.	Discon.	Current Market Value U.K. £	U.S. $	Can. $
D6999	Small	Doulton	5"	1995	Ltd. ed. (1994)	99.95	275.00	415.00

KING AND QUEEN OF DIAMONDS

SUITES FROM PLAYING CARDS,
ONE OF FOUR

This is one of a series of four tobies illustrating the four suites of playing cards. This is the first double-sided toby jug in this series, and it was issued in a limited edition of 2,500.

Designer: Stanley J. Taylor	**Backstamp:** Doulton
Handle: Plain	
Colourway: Yellow, blue, red and cream	

Doulton Number	Size	Backstamp	Height	Intro.	Discon.	Current Market Value U.K. £	U.S. $	Can. $
D6969	Small	Doulton	5"	1994	Ltd. ed. (1994)	99.95	275.00	415.00

LEN LIFEBELT THE LIFEBOATMAN

THE DOULTONVILLE COLLECTION,
ONE OF 25

Designer: William K. Harper
Handle: Plain
Colourway: Yellow life jacket and sou'wester;
blue sweater; white life preserver

Backstamp: Doulton

Doulton Number	Size	Backstamp	Height	Intro.	Discon.	Current Market Value U.K. £	U.S. $	Can. $
D6811	Small	Doulton	4"	1989	1991	50.00	100.00	110.00

LEPRECHAUN

This jug was issued in a worldwide limited edition of 2,500. It was sold out in 1994.

1115

Royal Doulton®
LEPRECHAUN
D 6948
Modelled by
Stanley James Taylor.
© 1993 ROYAL DOULTON
LIMITED EDITION OF 2,500
THIS IS Nº 370

Designer: Stanley J. Taylor
Handle: Plain
Colourways: Light and dark green and brown

Backstamp: Doulton

Doulton Number	Size	Backstamp	Height	Intro.	Discon.	Current Market Value		
						U.K. £	U.S. $	Can. $
D6948	Medium	Doulton	5"	1994	Ltd. ed. (1994)	60.00	125.00	150.00

MADAME CRYSTAL THE CLAIRVOYANT

THE DOULTONVILLE COLLECTION,
ONE OF 25

Designer:	William K. Harper	**Backstamp:** Doulton
Handle:	Plain	
Colourway:	Green headscarf; burgundy skirt; mauve shawl with blue fringe	

Doulton Number	Size	Backstamp	Height	Intro.	Discon.	Current Market Value		
						U.K. £	U.S. $	Can. $
D6714	Small	Doulton	4"	1984	1989	60.00	100.00	110.00

MAJOR GREEN THE GOLFER

THE DOULTONVILLE COLLECTION,
ONE OF 25

Designer:	William K. Harper		**Backstamp:** Doulton
Handle:	Plain		
Colourway:	Light brown waistcoat; yellow shirt; green cap		

Doulton Number	Size	Backstamp	Height	Intro.	Discon.	Current Market Value U.K. £	U.S. $	Can. $
D6740	Small	Doulton	4"	1986	1991	60.00	110.00	120.00

MIKE MINERAL THE MINER

THE DOULTONVILLE COLLECTION,
ONE OF 25

Designer:	William K. Harper
Handle:	Plain
Colourway:	Light green shirt; grey helmet;
	blue scarf; light brown belt

Backstamp: Doulton

Doulton Number	Size	Backstamp	Height	Intro.	Discon.	Current Market Value		
						U.K. £	U.S. $	Can. $
D6741	Small	Doulton	4"	1986	1989	100.00	225.00	250.00

MISS NOSTRUM THE NURSE

THE DOULTONVILLE COLLECTION,
ONE OF 25

Designer: William K. Harper
Handle: Plain
Colourway: Blue uniform; white apron;
blue and white cap

Backstamp: Doulton

Doulton Number	Size	Backstamp	Height	Intro.	Discon.	Current Market Value U.K. £	U.S. $	Can. $
D6700	Small	Doulton	4"	1983	1991	50.00	95.00	100.00

MISS STUDIOUS THE SCHOOLMISTRESS

THE DOULTONVILLE COLLECTION,
ONE OF 25

Designer: William K. Harper
Handle: Plain
Colourway: Yellow blouse; green waistcoat;
dark burgundy skirt

Backstamp: Doulton

Doulton Number	Size	Backstamp	Height	Intro.	Discon.	Current Market Value		
						U.K. £	U.S. $	Can. $
D6722	Small	Doulton	4"	1985	1989	60.00	100.00	120.00

MONSIEUR CHASSEUR THE CHEF

THE DOULTONVILLE COLLECTION,
ONE OF 25

Designer: William K. Harper
Handle: Plain
Colourway: White chef's coat and hat; blue scarf

Backstamp: Doulton

Doulton Number	Size	Backstamp	Height	Intro.	Discon.	Current Market Value U.K. £	U.S. $	Can. $
D6769	Small	Doulton	4"	1987	1991	60.00	100.00	120.00

MR. BRISKET THE BUTCHER

THE DOULTONVILLE COLLECTION,
ONE OF 25

Designer: William K. Harper
Handle: Plain
Colourway: Pale blue shirt; white apron;
yellow hat with brown band

Backstamp: Doulton

Doulton Number	Size	Backstamp	Height	Intro.	Discon.	Current Market Value		
						U.K. £	U.S. $	Can. $
D6743	Small	Doulton	4"	1986	1991	60.00	100.00	120.00

MR. FURROW THE FARMER

THE DOULTONVILLE COLLECTION,
ONE OF 25

Designer: William K. Harper

Handle: Plain

Colourway: Dark brown coat; cream trousers; light brown hat

Backstamp: Doulton

Doulton Number	Size	Backstamp	Height	Intro.	Discon.	Current Market Value U.K. £	U.S. $	Can. $
D6701	Small	Doulton	4"	1983	1989	60.00	120.00	130.00

MR. LITIGATE THE LAWYER

THE DOULTONVILLE COLLECTION,
ONE OF 25

Designer: William K. Harper
Handle: Plain
Colourway: Black robes; yellow waistcoat;
grey wig and trousers

Backstamp: Doulton

Doulton Number	Size	Backstamp	Height	Intro.	Discon.	Current Market Value		
						U.K. £	U.S. $	Can. $
D6699	Small	Doulton	4"	1983	1991	60.00	100.00	110.00

MR. MICAWBER

DICKENS TOBIES,
ONE OF SIX

Designer: Harry Fenton
Handle: Plain
Colourway: Browns

Backstamp: Doulton

Doulton Number	Size	Backstamp	Height	Intro.	Discon.	Current Market Value		
						U.K. £	U.S. $	Can. $
D6262	Small	Doulton	4 1/2"	1948	1960	130.00	275.00	300.00

MR. PICKWICK

DICKENS TOBIES,
ONE OF SIX

Designer: Harry Fenton
Handle: Plain
Colourway: Browns

Backstamp: Doulton

Doulton Number	Size	Backstamp	Height	Intro.	Discon.	Current Market Value U.K. £	U.S. $	Can. $
D6261	Small	Doulton	4 1/2"	1948	1960	130.00	275.00	300.00

MR. TONSIL THE TOWN CRIER

THE DOULTONVILLE COLLECTION,
ONE OF 25

Designer: William K. Harper
Handle: Plain
Colourway: Burgundy coat trimmed with gold; brown
hat trimmed with gold; white scarf

Backstamp: Doulton

Doulton Number	Size	Backstamp	Height	Intro.	Discon.	Current Market Value U.K. £	U.S. $	Can. $
D6713	Small	Doulton	4"	1984	1991	50.00	95.00	100.00

MRS. LOAN THE LIBRARIAN

THE DOULTONVILLE COLLECTION,
ONE OF 25

Designer: William K. Harper
Handle: Plain
Colourway: Dark green blouse trimmed with white;
light green skirt; yellow book

Backstamp: Doulton

Doulton Number	Size	Backstamp	Height	Intro.	Discon.	Current Market Value		
						U.K. £	U.S. $	Can. $
D6715	Small	Doulton	4"	1984	1989	50.00	90.00	100.00

OLD CHARLIE

Old Charlie was one of six toby jugs remodelled by William K. Harper and reissued as tinies in 1994 in a limited edition of 2,500. The others were Happy John, Honest Measure, Jolly Toby, The Best is not too Good and Toby XX. The issue price was U.K. £225.00 for the complete set and a display stand.

Old Charlie.

Designer: Harry Fenton
Handle: Plain
Colourway: Brown hat; green coat; burgundy trousers

Backstamp: Doulton

Doulton Number	Size	Backstamp	Height	Intro.	Discon.	Current Market Value		
						U.K. £	**U.S. $**	**Can. $**
D6030	Large	Doulton	8 1/2"	1939	1960	200.00	450.00	475.00
D6069	Small	Doulton	5"	1939	1960	150.00	350.00	375.00
D6978	Tiny	Doulton	2 1/2"	1994	Ltd. ed.	45.00	—	—

PAT PARCEL THE POSTMAN

THE DOULTONVILLE COLLECTION,
ONE OF 25

Designer:	William K. Harper	
Handle:	Plain	
Colourway:	Dark blue uniform trimmed with red; grey postbag	

Backstamp: Doulton

Doulton Number	Size	Backstamp	Height	Intro.	Discon.	Current Market Value U.K. £	U.S. $	Can. $
D6813	Small	Doulton	4"	1989	1991	55.00	95.00	100.00

REV. CASSOCK THE CLERGYMAN

THE DOULTONVILLE COLLECTION,
ONE OF 25

Designer: William K. Harper
Handle: Plain
Colourway: Black coat; grey shirt; brown cap

Backstamp: Doulton

Doulton Number	Size	Backstamp	Height	Intro.	Discon.	Current Market Value		
						U.K. £	U.S. $	Can. $
D6702	Small	Doulton	4"	1983	1990	55.00	95.00	100.00

SAIREY GAMP

DICKENS TOBIES,
ONE OF SIX

Designer: Harry Fenton
Handle: Plain
Colourway: Browns

Backstamp: Doulton

Doulton Number	Size	Backstamp	Height	Intro.	Discon.	Current Market Value		
						U.K. £	**U.S. $**	**Can. $**
D6263	Small	Doulton	4 1/2"	1948	1960	150.00	325.00	350.00

SAM WELLER

DICKENS TOBIES,
ONE OF SIX

Designer: Harry Fenton
Handle: Plain
Colourway: Browns

Backstamp: Doulton

Doulton Number	Size	Backstamp	Height	Intro.	Discon.	Current Market Value		
						U.K. £	**U.S. $**	**Can. $**
D6265	Small	Doulton	4 1/2"	1948	1960	125.00	275.00	300.00

SGT. PEELER THE POLICEMAN

THE DOULTONVILLE COLLECTION,
ONE OF 25

Designer: William K. Harper
Handle: Plain
Colourway: Blue-black uniform

Backstamp: Doulton

Doulton Number	Size	Backstamp	Height	Intro.	Discon.	Current Market Value		
						U.K. £	U.S. $	Can. $
D6720	Small	Doulton	4"	1985	1991	60.00	100.00	110.00

SHERLOCK HOLMES

The inscription on the base of this jug reads "Issued to Commemorate the 50th Anniversary of the Death of Sir Arthur Conan Doyle (1859 - 1930)."

© ROYAL DOULTON
TABLEWARE LTD. 1980

Sherlock Holmes

D.6661
ISSUED TO COMMEMORATE
THE 50th ANNIVERSARY
OF THE DEATH OF
SIR ARTHUR CONAN DOYLE
(1859 - 1930)

Designer: Robert Tabbenor
Handle: Plain, black
Colourway: Green hat and cloak; green-brown coat

Backstamp: Doulton

Doulton Number	Size	Backstamp	Height	Intro.	Discon.	Current Market Value U.K. £	U.S. $	Can. $
D6661	Large	Doulton	9"	1981	1991	95.00	200.00	225.00

SIR FRANCIS DRAKE

The inscription on the base of this jug reads "Issued to commemorate the 400th Anniversary of the circumnavigation of the world."

© ROYAL DOULTON
TABLEWARE LTD. 1980

Sir Francis Drake

D.6660
ISSUED TO COMMEMORATE
THE 400th ANNIVERSARY
OF THE CIRCUMNAVIGATION
OF THE WORLD

Designer: Michael Abberley
Handle: Plain
Colourway: Black hat with white feather;
yellow with brown tunic; tan boots

Backstamp: Doulton

Doulton Number	Size	Backstamp	Height	Intro.	Discon.	Current Market Value		
						U.K. £	U.S. $	Can. $
D6660	Large	Doulton	9"	1981	1991	95.00	200.00	225.00

THE SQUIRE

VARIATION No. 1: Kingsware
Colourway — Browns; sterling silver rim around neck of jug

Designer: Unknown	**Backstamp:** Doulton
Handle: Plain	
Colourway: Browns	

Model Number	Variation	Backstamp	Height	Intro.	Discon.	Current Market Value U.K. £	U.S. $	Can. $
—	Var. 1	Doulton	6"	c.1910	Unknown	450.00	1,100.00	1,100.00

Note: We believe there is a possibility that an early Squire jug, issued circa 1910, exists in earthenware. If anyone has any information regarding this jug, please contact us.

VARIATION No. 2:   Earthenware
                             Colourway — Green coat; brown hat

The Squire
D6319
COPR 1950
DOULTON & CO LIMITED

Designer: Harry Fenton
Handle: Plain
Colourway: Brown hat; green coat; mustard waistcoat
with black buttons

Backstamp: Doulton

Doulton Number	Size	Variation	Height	Intro.	Discon.	Current Market Value		
						U.K. £	U.S. $	Can. $
D6319	Medium	Var. 2	6"	1950	1969	300.00	650.00	650.00

TOBY XX

STYLE FOUR: BURSLEM, EARTHENWARE, BURGUNDY COAT, WITH HANDLE

Style four is a modification of the 1925 design by Harry Simeon. Toby XX is also known as The Man on the Barrel and Double XX.

This jug was one of six remodelled by William K. Harper and reissued as tinies in 1994 in a limited edition of 2,500. The others were Happy John, Honest Measure, Jolly Toby, Old Charlie and The Best is not too Good. The issue price was U.K. £225.00 for the complete set and a display stand.

"Toby XX."

Rᵈ Nº 837178.
Regᵈ in Australia

Designer:	Harry Fenton	**Backstamp:**	Doulton
Model No.:	8337		
Handle:	Plain		
Colourway:	Burgundy coat; orange shirt; blue bow tie; black trousers; dark brown hat; green-grey hair and handle; cream barrel		

Doulton Number	Size	Backstamp	Height	Intro.	Discon.	Current Market Value U.K. £	U.S. $	Can. $
D6088	Medium	Doulton	7"	1939	1969	200.00	550.00	550.00
D6975	Tiny	Doulton	2"	1994	Ltd. ed.	45.00	—	—

TOWN CRIER

The Town Crier jug was issued in a limited edition of 2,500.

Royal Doulton®
TOWN CRIER
D 6920
Modelled by
Stanley James Taylor
Ⓒ 1992 ROYAL DOULTON
ISSUED IN A LIMITED
EDITION OF 2,500.
THIS IS Nº 770

Designer: Stanley J. Taylor
Handle: Plain, black
Colourway: Scarlet great coat trimmed with yellow; black tricorn hat trimmed with yellow; white feather

Backstamp: Doulton

Doulton Number	Size	Backstamp	Height	Intro.	Discon.	Current Market Value		
						U.K. £	U.S. $	Can. $
D6920	Medium	Doulton	5"	1992	Ltd. ed.	100.00	250.00	275.00

WINSTON CHURCHILL

WINSTON CHURCHILL
PRIME MINISTER
OF GREAT BRITAIN
— 1940 —

BACKSTAMP A

WINSTON CHURCHILL

BACKSTAMP B

Designer:	Harry Fenton
Handle:	Plain
Colourway:	Black hat; brown overcoat; black-green suit

Backstamps: A. "Winston Churchill Prime Minister of Great Britain 1940" Model No. 8360 B
B. "Winston Churchill" only

Doulton Number	Size	Backstamp	Height	Intro.	Discon.	Current Market Value U.K. £	U.S. $	Can. $
D6171	Large	A. Doulton	9"	1940	1940	250.00	500.00	525.00
D6171	Large	B. Doulton	9"	1941	1991	90.00	150.00	175.00
D6172	Medium	A. Doulton	5 1/2"	1940	1940	175.00	400.00	425.00
D6172	Medium	B. Doulton	5 1/2"	1941	1991	55.00	100.00	110.00
D6175	Small	A. Doulton	4"	1940	1940	150.00	275.00	300.00
D6175	Small	B. Doulton	4"	1941	1991	50.00	85.00	100.00

ROYAL DOULTON
CHARACTER JUGS

ABRAHAM LINCOLN

PRESIDENTIAL SERIES,
ONE OF THREE
PRESIDENTS OF THE UNITED STATES

First in a series of Presidents of the United States of America, issued in a limited edition of 2,500. The American flag and Lincoln's famous speech that begins "Four score and seven years ago..." form the handle.

Royal Doulton®
PRESIDENTIAL SERIES
ABRAHAM LINCOLN
D 6936
Modelled by

Stanley James Taylor.

© 1992 ROYAL DOULTON
A SPECIALLY COMMISSIONED
LIMITED EDITION OF 2,500
THIS IS Nº 767

Designer: Stanley J. Taylor
Handle: U.S. flag and Gettysburg Address
Colourway: Black and white

Backstamp: Doulton

Doulton Number	Size	Backstamp	Height	Intro.	Discon.	Current Market Value U.K. £	U.S. $	Can. $
D6936	Large	Doulton	6 3/4"	1992	Ltd. ed.	150.00	190.00	250.00

THE AIRMAN
(Royal Air Force)

ARMED FORCES SERIES,
ONE OF THREE

This series pays tribute to those servicemen of the Royal Air Force, the Royal Army and the Royal Navy who fought in World War II. An airman belongs to the Royal Air Force, as either a pilot or another member of the crew.

STYLE ONE: HANDLE — GERMAN PLANE

VARIATION No. 1: White scarf without cypher

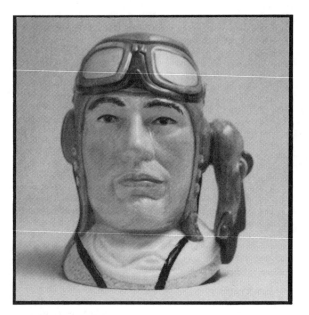

Royal Doulton®
THE AIRMAN
D 6870
Modelled by

William K. Harper

© 1990 ROYAL DOULTON

Designer: William K. Harper
Handle: German fighter plane shot down in flames
Colourway: Light brown cap; dark brown flight jacket with cream collar; white scarf

Backstamp: Doulton

Doulton Number	Size	Backstamp	Height	Intro.	Discon.	Current Market Value U.K. £	U.S. $	Can. $
D6870	Small	Doulton	4 1/2"	1991	Current	35.00	69.50	110.00

THE AIRMAN
(Royal Canadian Air Force)

THE CANADIANS SERIES,
ONE OF THREE

The Airman jug was commissioned by The British Toby of Ontario, Canada, in a limited edition of 250 pieces. It sold originally as part of a set of three at Can. $465.00.

STYLE ONE: HANDLE — GERMAN PLANE

VARIATION No. 2: Red scarf with cypher "RCAF"

Designer:	William K. Harper
Handle:	German fighter plane shot down in flames
Colourway:	Dark brown cap; flight jacket with biege collar; red scarf with cypher

Backstamp: Doulton/British Toby

Doulton Number	Size	Backstamp	Height	Intro.	Discon.	Current Market Value U.K. £	U.S. $	Can. $
D6903	Small	Doulton/British	4 1/2"	1991	Ltd. ed. (1991)	150.00	275.00	300.00

THE AIRMAN

NATIONAL SERVICE SERIES,
ONE OF THREE

Commissioned by Lawleys By Post, one could have a National Service Number incorporated within the accompanying certificate.

STYLE TWO: HANDLE — OXYGEN MASK

Designer: William K. Harper
Handle: A oxygen mask
Colourway: Cream, brown and grey

Backstamp: Doulton

Doulton Number	Size	Backstamp	Height	Intro.	Discon.	Current Market Value U.K. £	U.S. $	Can. $
D6982	Small	Doulton	4 1/2"	1994	Sp. ed.	49.50	—	—

ALADDIN'S GENIE

FLAMBÉ SERIES,
ONE OF TWO

Issued in a limited edition of 1,500, this was the first jug to be decorated in flambé.

Designer: David Biggs
Handle: Lamp, ghost form and tassle
Colourway: Flambé

Backstamp: Doulton

Doulton Number	Size	Backstamp	Height	Intro.	Discon.	Current Market Value		
						U.K. £	U.S. $	Can. $
D6971	Large	Doulton	7 1/2"	1994	Ltd ed.	125.00	335.00	485.00

ALFRED HITCHCOCK

This jug commemorates the achievements of Alfred Hitchcock (1899-1990) in producing superb movie thrillers. The handle features the shower curtain from *Psycho* and a bird from *The Birds*.

The original design of this jug had the shower curtain painted pink and the backstamp was the usual Royal Doulton design. This was later changed to a white shower curtain with blue shading and a backstamp that incorporated the MCA Universal Copyright.

VARIATION No. 1: Colourway — Pink shower curtain

Royal Doulton®
ALFRED HITCHCOCK
D 6987
Modelled by
David B Biggs
© 1994 ROYAL DOULTON

Designer: David Biggs
Handle: Shower curtain, bird and film
Colourway: White, black and pink

Backstamp: Doulton

Doulton Number	Size	Backstamp	Height	Intro.	Discon.	Current Market Value U.K. £	U.S. $	Can. $
D6987	Large	Doulton	7 1/2"	1995	1995		Rare	

VARIATION No. 2: Colourway — White shower curtain with blue shading

Backstamp: Doulton/MCA Universal Copyright

Doulton Number	Size	Backstamp	Height	Intro.	Discon.	Current Market Value U.K. £	U.S. $	Can. $
D6987	Large	Doulton/Universal	7 1/2"	1995	Current	79.95	200.00	265.00

THE ANGLER

CHARACTERS FROM LIFE SERIES,
ONE OF SEVEN

Royal Doulton®

THE ANGLER
D 6866
Modelled by
Stanley James Taylor
© 1990 ROYAL DOULTON

Designer: Stanley J. Taylor
Handle: A fish and lure
Colourway: Green jacket; brown hat;
cream pullover

Backstamp: Doulton

Doulton Number	Size	Backstamp	Height	Intro.	Discon.	Current Market Value		
						U.K. £	**U.S. $**	**Can. $**
D6866	Small	Doulton	4"	1990	Current	29.95	69.50	110.00

ANNE BOLEYN

HENRY VIII AND HIS SIX WIVES SERIES,
ONE OF EIGHT

Anne Boleyn (1502-1536) became the second wife of Henry VIII in a secret ceremony performed in January 1533. Their marriage was officially sanctioned in May by the Archbishop of Canterbury, Thomas Cranmer, and she was crowned Queen on June 1, 1533, in Westminster Hall. Unable to produce the son Henry VIII desired, Anne was imprisoned in the Tower of London on false grounds of adultery. She was beheaded with a sword on May 19, 1536, in a courtyard of the Tower of London (the modeller's use of an axe to form the handle was incorrect). Anne Boleyn was the mother of Queen Elizabeth I, born on September 7, 1533.

Designer: Douglas V. Tootle
Handle: An axe and chopping block
Colourway: Black and grey

Backstamp: Doulton

Doulton Number	Size	Backstamp	Height	Intro.	Discon.	Current Market Value U.K. £	U.S. $	Can. $
D6644	Large	Doulton	7 1/4"	1975	1990	95.00	160.00	175.00
D6650	Small	Doulton	3 1/2"	1980	1990	60.00	115.00	125.00
D6651	Miniature	Doulton	2 1/2"	1980	1990	75.00	140.00	150.00

ANNE OF CLEVES

HENRY VIII AND HIS SIX WIVES SERIES, ONE OF EIGHT

In a political arrangement by Thomas Cromwell, Anne of Cleves (1515-1557) was chosen to marry Henry VIII. Upon seeing his dull and unattractive betrothed, whom he later referred to as his "Flanders Mare," Henry attempted unsuccessfully to break the contract. Anne became his fourth wife on January 6, 1540, for only a brief time. Henry had the marriage annulled on July 8th of that year and gave Anne a pension for life.

VARIATION No. 1:   Handle — Horse's ears pointing up

VARIATION NO. 2, EARS FLAT   VARIATION NO. 1, EARS POINTING UP

Designer: Michael Abberley
Handle: Head of a horse; ears pointing up
Colourway: Black and red

Backstamp: Doulton

Doulton Number	Size	Variation	Height	Intro.	Discon.	Current Market Value U.K. £	U.S. $	Can. $
D6653	Large	Var. 1	7 1/4"	1980	1981	175.00	400.00	425.00

VARIATION No. 2: Handle — Horse's ears flat against head. Because the upright ears tended to break off during packaging and shipping, the design was changed so the ears lay flat against the head.

Royal Doulton
ANNE OF CLEVES
D 6653
Modelled by

Michael Abberley

© ROYAL DOULTON TABLEWARE
LIMITED 1979

LARGE JUG BACKSTAMP

Royal Doulton ©
ANNE OF CLEVES
D 6753
Designed by M. Abberley
Modelled by

Peter A Gee

© 1979 ROYAL DOULTON (UK)

SMALL JUG BACKSTAMP

Backstamp: Doulton

Designer: Large size: Michael Abberley
Small and miniature size: Peter Gee
Handle: Head of a horse; ears flat
Colourway: Black and red

Doulton Number	Size	Variation	Height	Intro.	Discon.	Current Market Value		
						U.K. £	U.S. $	Can. $
D6653	Large	Var. 2	7 1/4"	1980	1990	100.00	200.00	225.00
D6753	Small	Var. 2	4 1/4"	1987	1990	65.00	145.00	160.00
D6754	Miniature	Var. 2	2 1/2"	1987	1990	75.00	140.00	150.00

ANNIE OAKLEY

THE WILD WEST COLLECTION,
ONE OF SIX

Phoebe Anne Moses (1860-1926) learned to shoot at the age of eight and helped support her family by killing game for a hotel in Cincinnati, Ohio. At 15, she defeated professional marksman Frank Butler in a shooting contest. She married him in 1876 and became a regular performer in shooting exhibitions, using the stage name Annie Oakley. She was a star of Buffalo Bill's Wild West Show from 1885 until 1901, when she was injured in a train accident and forced to retire. During World War I she trained American soldiers in marksmanship.

Royal Doulton
THE WILD WEST
Collection
ANNIE OAKLEY
D6732
Modelled by
Stanley James Taylor.
© ROYAL DOULTON TABLEWARE
LIMITED 1984

Designer: Stanley J. Taylor	**Backstamp:** Doulton
Handle: Rifle and belt	
Colourway: Yellow hair; cream hat; brown tunic	

Doulton Number	Size	Backstamp	Height	Intro.	Discon.	Current Market Value U.K. £	U.S. $	Can. $
D6732	Mid	Doulton	5 1/4"	1985	1989	60.00	140.00	150.00

THE ANTIQUE DEALER

THE COLLECTING WORLD,
ONE OF THREE

This jug was commissioned by Kevin Francis Ceramics Ltd. (KFC) in 1988 in a special edition of 5,000 pieces. It is interesting to note that Kevin Francis jugs have the handle on the left side.

Designer: Geoff Blower
Handle: Flintlock handgun and candlestick
Colourway: Black hat; blue coat

Backstamp: Doulton/Kevin Francis

Doulton Number	Size	Backstamp	Height	Intro.	Discon.	Current Market Value U.K. £	U.S. $	Can. $
D6807	Large	Doulton/KFC	7 1/4"	1988	Sp. ed.	75.00	250.00	265.00

ANTONY AND CLEOPATRA

PROTOTYPE

A prototype of this character jug exists where Antony has a pudgy face, wide eyes and brown hair, and Cleopatra has lighter eye make-up, lighter beads around her neck and a dark red headdress. Only one is known to exist.

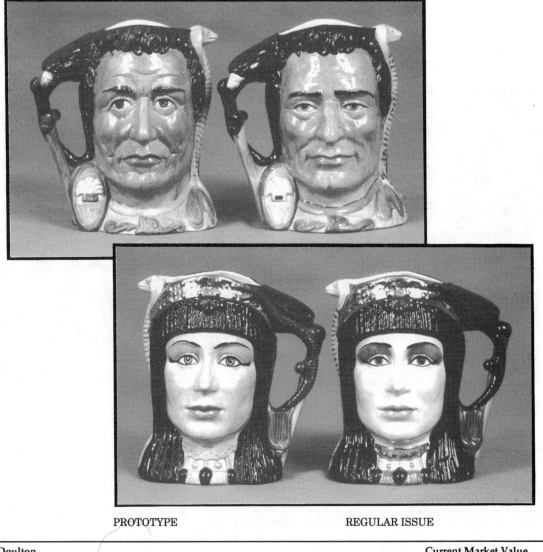

PROTOTYPE   REGULAR ISSUE

Doulton Number	Size	Variation	Height	Intro.	Discon.	Current Market Value U.K. £	Current Market Value U.S. $	Current Market Value Can. $
D6728	Large	Prototype	7 1/4"	1984	1984		Unique	

ANTONY AND CLEOPATRA

THE STAR-CROSSED LOVERS COLLECTION (TWO-FACED JUG), ONE OF FOUR

Marcus Antonius (83-30 B.C.) was a skilled soldier and co-ruler of Rome with Caesar's nephew Octavian from 43 to 32 B.C.

Cleopatra (68-30 B.C.), well known for her charm and beauty, was queen of Egypt and an ally and lover of Julius Caesar. In 41 B.C. Antony and Cleopatra met and fell in love, marrying in 37 B.C. Antony gave Cleopatra and their children a share of his Roman provinces in 34 B.C., a move which enraged Octavian, who waged war on the couple, pursuing them in their defeat to Alexandria.

Antony, hearing a false rumour of Cleopatra's death, stabbed himself in grief. He was carried to her and died in her arms. In turn, Cleopatra committed suicide by placing an asp on her chest, apparently from fear of Octavian,

The jugs were issued in 1985 in a limited edition of 9,500 pieces.

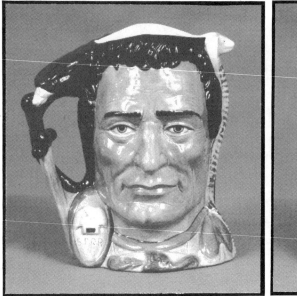 

Designer: Michael Abberley
Handle: Eagle's head, dagger and shield; asp and harp
Colourway: Black, grey, brown
Backstamp: Doulton

Doulton Number	Size	Backstamp	Height	Intro.	Discon.	Current Market Value U.K. £	U.S. $	Can. $
D6728	Large	Doulton	7 1/4"	1985	Ltd. ed. (1990)	100.00	225.00	250.00

APOTHECARY

CHARACTERS FROM WILLIAMSBURG,
ONE OF EIGHT

Along with the other characters in the Williamsburg Series, the apothecary was central to colonial life in 18th century America.

Character Jugs from Williamsburg

Apothecary

D 6567
COPR 1962
DOULTON & CO LIMITED
Rd No 906337
Rd No 43444
Rd No 9223
Rd No 287/62

Designer: Max Henk
Handle: Mortar and pestle
Colourway: Green coat with white cravat; white wig

Backstamp: Doulton

Doulton Number	Size	Backstamp	Height	Intro.	Discon.	Current Market Value U.K. £	U.S. $	Can. $
D6567	Large	Doulton	7"	1963	1983	95.00	175.00	190.00
D6574	Small	Doulton	4"	1963	1983	50.00	120.00	130.00
D6581	Miniature	Doulton	2 1/2"	1963	1983	60.00	100.00	115.00

ARAMIS

THE THREE MUSKETEERS, ONE OF FOUR,
NOW PART OF THE CHARACTERS FROM LITERATURE, ONE OF 11

One of the three musketeers, Aramis joined Athos, Porthos and D'Artagnan in a life of adventure in Alexandre Dumas's 19th century novel, following their code "All for one, and one for all."

The wording "One of the Three Musketeers" was included in the earlier backstamp to indicate that Aramis was one of the famous Musketeers.

VARIATION No. 1: Colourway — Black hat; white feather; brown tunic

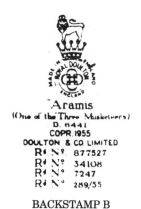

Aramis
((One of the Three Musketeers)
D. 6441
COPR. 1955
DOULTON & CO. LIMITED
R¢ N°. 877527
R¢ N° 34108
R¢ N° 7247
R¢ N° 289/55

BACKSTAMP B

Designer: Max Henk
Handle: Handle of a sword
Colourway: Black hat; white feather; brown tunic

Backstamps: A. Doulton
B. Doulton/One of the Three Musketeers

Doulton Number	Size	Backstamp	Height	Intro.	Discon.	Current Market Value U.K. £	U.S. $	Can. $
D6441	Large	A. Doulton	7 1/4"	1956	1991	75.00	150.00	165.00
D6441	Large	B. Doulton	7 1/4"	1956	1970	75.00	150.00	165.00
D6454	Small	B. Doulton	3 1/2"	1956	1991	40.00	90.00	100.00
D6508	Miniature	A. Doulton	2 1/2"	1960	1991	45.00	90.00	100.00

VARIATION No. 2:   Colourway — Yellow hat; maroon tunic

This jug was commissioned by Peter Jones China Ltd., England, and issued in 1988 in a limited edition of 1,000.

Royal Doulton®
ARAMIS
D 6829
Modelled by

© 1955 ROYAL DOULTON
NEW COLOURWAY 1988
SPECIAL COMMISSION 1000
PETER JONES CHINA
LEEDS AND WAKEFIELD

Backstamp: Doulton / Peter Jones China Ltd.

Doulton Number	Size	Backstamp	Height	Intro.	Discon.	Current Market Value		
						U.K. £	U.S. $	Can. $
D6829	Large	Doulton/Jones	7 1/4"	1988	Ltd. ed.	95.00	225.00	250.00

'ARD OF 'EARING

With hand held to cup his ear, this cockney gentleman is a comic representation of a deaf man. After being discontinued in 1967, this jug has increased in value and is difficult to find.

'ard of 'earing
D 6 5 8 6
COPR 1963
DOULTON & CO LIMITED
Rd No 913137
Rd No 45356
Rd No 9681
Rd No 81 1/63

Designer: David Biggs
Handle: A hand held to the ear
Colourway: Dark purple tricorn; green, white and yellow clothing

Backstamp: Doulton

Doulton Number	Size	Backstamp	Height	Intro.	Discon.	Current Market Value U.K. £	U.S. $	Can. $
D6588	Large	Doulton	7 1/2"	1964	1967	900.00	1,750.00	1,750.00
D6591	Small	Doulton	3 1/2"	1964	1967	600.00	1,100.00	1,100.00
D6594	Miniature	Doulton	2 1/2"	1964	1967	600.00	1,550.00	1,500.00

ARP WARDEN

HEROES OF THE BLITZ,
ONE OF THREE

The ARP (Air Raids Precautions) Wardens were charged with the responsibility of insuring that people were as secure as possible during an air raid. Armed only with his whistle, he would patrol the streets enforcing the "lights out please" signal and see that all citizens took cover as quickly as possible. The Heroes of the Blitz jugs were commissioned by Lawleys By Post in a limited edition of 9,500 sets.

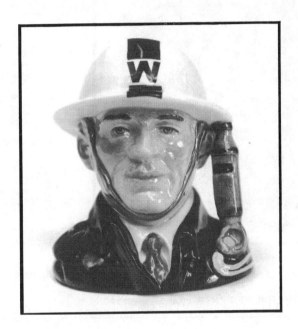

Designer: Stanley J. Taylor
Handle: Grey whistle
Colourway: Dark blue jacket; white helmet with black stripe and the initial W (Warden)

Backstamp: Doulton

Doulton Number	Size	Backstamp	Height	Intro.	Discon.	Current Market Value U.K. £	U.S. $	Can. $
D6872	Small	Doulton	4"	1991	Ltd. ed.	90.00	190.00	210.00

'ARRIET

'Arriet is a coster or costermonger, a cockney woman who sold fruits and vegetables from a barrow in the streets of London. She is a variation of the Pearly Girl character jug (see page 365).

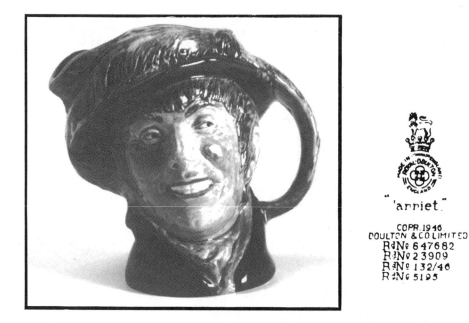

Designer: Harry Fenton
Handle: Hat feather
Colourway: Green hat; brown coat; yellow scarf

Backstamp: Doulton

Doulton Number	Size	Backstamp	Height	Intro.	Discon.	U.K. £	U.S. $	Can. $
						Current Market Value		
D6208	Large	Doulton	6 1/2"	1947	1960	150.00	350.00	375.00
D6236	Small	Doulton	3 1/4"	1947	1960	75.00	175.00	200.00
D6250	Miniature	Doulton	2 1/4"	1947	1960	55.00	120.00	135.00
D6256	Tiny	Doulton	1 1/4"	1947	1960	100.00	275.00	300.00

'ARRY

'Arriet's husband 'Arry is also a costermonger, plying his trade in London. He is a variation of the Pearly Boy (see page 362) character jug. The original design featured the word "Blimey" across the back, but it was never produced.

Designer: Harry Fenton
Handle: Plain
Colourway: Brown hat and coat; red and yellow scarf

Backstamp: Doulton

Doulton Number	Size	Backstamp	Height	Intro.	Discon.	Current Market Value U.K. £	U.S. $	Can. $
D6207	Large	Doulton	6 1/2"	1947	1960	150.00	350.00	375.00
D6235	Small	Doulton	3 1/2"	1947	1960	75.00	175.00	200.00
D6249	Miniature	Doulton	2 1/2"	1947	1960	55.00	120.00	135.00
D6255	Tiny	Doulton	1 1/2"	1947	1960	100.00	275.00	300.00

ARSENAL (FOOTBALL CLUB)

THE FOOTBALL SUPPORTERS,
ONE OF NINE

Designer: Stanley J. Taylor
Handle: Team coloured scarf
Colourway: Red and white uniform

Backstamp: Doulton

Doulton Number	Size	Backstamp	Height	Intro.	Discon.	Current Market Value U.K. £	U.S. $	Can. $
D6927	Mid	Doulton	5"	1992	Current	32.50	—	—

ARTFUL DODGER

CHARLES DICKENS COMMEMORATIVE SET,
DICKENS TINIES, ONE OF 12

The Artful Dodger was a member of a gang of thieves who enlisted Oliver Twist in Dickens's novel of Victorian London. It was issued to commemorate the 170th anniversary of the birth of Charles Dickens. There are 12 jugs in this set, each issued with a certificate of authenticity. A mahogany display shelf completes the set. The set was first sold by Lawleys By Post in the U.K. from 1982 to 1988, and from 1985 in North America and Australia.

Artful
Dodger
D 6678

Backstamp: Doulton

Designer: Peter Gee
Handle: Plain
Colourway: Yellow and black

Doulton Number	Size	Backstamp		Height	Intro.	Discon.	Current Market Value		
							U.K. £	U.S. $	Can. $
D6678	Tiny	Doulton		1 1/2"	1982	1989	35.00	55.00	65.00
		Display stand for 12 tinies					65.00	45.00	50.00

ASTON VILLA (FOOTBALL CLUB)

THE FOOTBALL SUPPORTERS,
ONE OF NINE

Designer: Stanley J. Taylor
Handle: Team coloured scarf
Colourway: Maroon and blue uniform

Backstamp: Doulton

Doulton Number	Size	Backstamp	Height	Intro.	Discon.	Current Market Value		
						U.K. £	U.S. $	Can. $
D6931	Mid	Doulton	5"	1992	Current	32.50	—	—

ATHOS

THE THREE MUSKETEERS, ONE OF FOUR,
NOW PART OF THE CHARACTERS FROM LITERATURE, ONE OF 11

Under the banner of "All for one and one for all," Athos was one of the original musketeers in the 19th-century novel by Alexandre Dumas. First issued as one of four in the Three Musketeers Series, Athos is now incorporated into the larger series, Characters from Literature.

VARIATION No. 1:   Mould — Feathers along rim of hat
                      Colourway — Black hat; white feather; green tunic with gold trim

Athos
D 6439
©DOULTON & CO LIMITED 1955

BACKSTAMP A

Athos
(One of the "Three Musketeers")
D 6452
COPR 1955
DOULTON & CO LIMITED
Rd No 677528
Rd No 34106
Rd No 7245
Rd No 290/55

BACKSTAMP B

Designer: Max Henk
Handle: Upper half of a sword
Colourway: Black hat; white feather; green tunic with gold trim

Backstamps: A. Doulton
                 B. Doulton /One of the Three Musketeers
                 The wording "One of the Three Musketeers" was included in the early backstamp to
                 indicate that Athos was one of the famous Musketeers.

Doulton Number	Size	Backstamp	Height	Intro.	Discon.	Current Market Value U.K. £	U.S. $	Can. $
D6439	Large	Doulton	7 1/4"	1956	1991	75.00	150.00	165.00
D6439	Large	Doulton/One	7 1/4"	1956	1991	75.00	150.00	165.00
D6452	Small	Doulton/One	3 3/4"	1956	1991	40.00	90.00	100.00
D6509	Miniature	Doulton/One	2 1/2"	1960	1991	45.00	90.00	100.00

VARIATION No. 2:   Mould — Feather along rim of hat
Colourway — Purple hat; white feather; yellow tunic with purple trim

VARIATION No. 3:   Mould — Feathers above rim of hat
Colourway — Purple hat; white feather; yellow tunic with purple trim

There were two different moulds used in the production of the Jones colourway, variation 2 and variation 3. A total of 1,000 jugs were issued, but how many of each variation were produced is unknown.

VARIATION NO. 2   VARIATION NO. 3

Designer: Max Henk
Handle: Upper half of a sword
Colourway: Black hat; white feather;
yellow tunic with blue trim

Backstamp: **Doulton/Peter Jones China Ltd.**
Commissioned by Peter Jones China Ltd.,
England. Issued in 1988 in a limited
edition of 1,000.

Royal Doulton®
ATHOS
D 6827
Modelled by

© 1955 ROYAL DOULTON
NEW COLOURWAY 1988
SPECIAL COMMISSION 1000
PETER JONES CHINA
LEEDS AND WAKEFIELD

Doulton Number	Size	Variation	Height	Intro.	Discon.	Current Market Value		
						U.K. £	U.S. $	Can. $
D6827	Large	Var. 2	7 1/4"	1988	Ltd. ed.	95.00	225.00	250.00
D6827	Large	Var. 3	7 1/4"	1988	(incl. in above)	95.00	225.00	250.00

THE AUCTIONEER

THE COLLECTING WORLD,
ONE OF THREE

Commissioned by Kevin Francis Ceramics Ltd. (KFC), The Auctioneer jug was issued in 1988 in a limited edition of 5,000. Characteristic of Kevin Francis, this is a left-handed jug.

Original Concept by Kevin Pearson and Geoff Blower

Royal Doulton®
THE AUCTIONEER
D 6838
Modelled by

G Blower

A Special Edition of 5000
From "The Collecting World" series
Produced by Royal Doulton
for Kevin Francis Ceramics
© 1988 ROYAL DOULTON
AND KEVIN FRANCIS CERAMICS

Designer: Geoff Blower
Handle: Auctioneer's gavel and The Bather (HN687)
Colourway: Green coat and bow tie; light brown cap

Backstamp: Doulton / Kevin Francis

Doulton Number	Size	Backstamp	Height	Intro.	Discon.	Current Market Value U.K. £	U.S. $	Can. $
D6838	Large	Doulton/KFC	6 1/4"	1988	Sp. ed. (1991)	95.00	275.00	295.00

AULD MAC

A song by Sir Harry Lauder, a 20th-century singer and comedian, called "Bang Went Saxpence," inspired this piece. In it a Scotsman named Mac found the prices too high in London because every time he made a move, "bang went saxpence," which is incised on the back of his tam, below "Auld Mac."

"OWD MAC"   "AULD MAC"

"Owd Mac."

Rd Nº 821283.
REG⁰ in AUSTRALIA

BACKSTAMP A

Auld Mac
D.5823

BACKSTAMP B

Designer: Harry Fenton
Handle: A brier
Colourway: Green tam; brown coat

Backstamps: A. Doulton/"Owd Mac"
"Owd Mac" was incised in the tam and printed in the backstamp, c. 1937.
B. Doulton/Auld Mac
"Auld Mac" was incised in the tam in 1938, but "Owd Mac" continued in the backstamp until c.1940.
C. Doulton/Auld Mac
"Auld Mac" was incised in the tam and printed in the backstamp.

Doulton Number	Size	Backstamp	Height	Intro.	Discon.	Current Market Value U.K. £	U.S. $	Can. $
D5823	Large	A. "Owd"/"Owd"	6 1/4"	1937	c. 1937	375.00	750.00	750.00
D5823	Large	B. "Auld/Owd"	6 1/4"	1938	1940	165.00	375.00	400.00
D5823	Large	C. "Auld/Auld"	6 1/4"	1940	1986	75.00	140.00	160.00
D5824	Small	A. "Owd"/"Owd"	3 1/4"	1937	1937	200.00	500.00	500.00
D5824	Small	B. "Auld/Owd"	3 1/4"	1938	1940	80.00	225.00	240.00
D5824	Small	C. "Auld/Auld"	3 1/4"	1940	1985	40.00	90.00	100.00
D6253	Miniature	C. "Auld/Auld"	2 1/4"	1946	1985	40.00	85.00	90.00
D6257	Tiny	C. "Auld/Auld"	1 1/4"	1946	1960	150.00	300.00	300.00

Auld Mac Derivatives

Doulton Number	Item	Height	Intro.	Discon.	Current Market Value U.K. £	U.S. $	Can. $
D5889	Musical jug	6 1/4"	1938	c. 1939	500.00	1,200.00	1,250.00
D6006	Ash bowl	3"	1938	1960	100.00	200.00	225.00

Note: The musical jug plays the tune "The Campbells are Coming."

AUXILIARY FIREMAN

HEROES OF THE BLITZ,
ONE OF THREE

Large numbers of volunteer firemen were needed to assist the regular firemen during the World War II bombing of London and other cities of Great Britain. It was through the courage of the Auxiliary Fire Service (A.F.S.) that many of the fires of the air raids were held in check. The Heroes of the Blitz set of jugs was commissioned by Lawleys By Post in a limited edition of 9,500 sets.

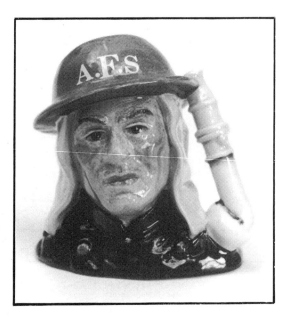

Designer: Stanley J. Taylor
Handle: Hose and nozzle
Colourway: Black jacket; grey helmet with white initials "A.F.S."

Backstamp: Doulton

Doulton Number	Size	Backstamp	Height	Intro.	Discon.	Current Market Value U.K. £	U.S. $	Can. $
D6887	Small	Doulton	4"	1991	Ltd. ed.	90.00	190.00	210.00

BACCHUS

In Greek and Roman mythology, Bacchus was the god of wine and nature, inspiring men and women to appreciate music and poetry. "Bacchanalia," the harvest celebrations to honour him, were reputed to be such orgies of excess that the Roman government had them banned.

Some of the earlier versions of the miniature jug had the leaves on the vine handle painted green. There is no current premium value for this variety.

Bacchus
D 6505
COPR 1958
DOULTON & CO LIMITED
Rd No 889570
Rd No 38226
Rd No 8036
Rd No 423/58

BACKSTAMP A

CITY OF
STOKE-ON-TRENT
JUBILEE YEAR
1959-1960
WITH THE COMPLIMENTS OF
LORD MAYOR AND LADY MAYORESS
ALDERMAN HAROLD CLOWES O.B.E. J.P
AND
MISS CHRISTINE CLOWES

BACKSTAMP B

Designer: Max Henk
Handle: Grapevine
Colourway: Maroon robes; green leaves and purple grapes adorn the head

Backstamps: A. Doulton
B. Doulton / City of Stoke-on-Trent Jubilee Year 1959 - 1960
With the compliments of Lord Mayor and Lady Mayoress Alderman Harold Clowes,
O.B.E., J.P. and Miss Christine Clowes

Doulton Number	Size	Backstamp	Height	Intro.	Discon.	Current Market Value U.K. £	U.S. $	Can. $
D6499	Large	Doulton	7"	1959	1991	70.00	140.00	160.00
D6499	Large	Doulton/City	7"	1959	1960		Rare	
D6505	Small	Doulton	4"	1959	1991	40.00	75.00	85.00
D6521	Miniature	Doulton	2 1/2"	1960	1991	35.00	70.00	75.00

Bacchus Derivative

Doulton Number	Item	Height	Intro.	Discon.	Current Market Value U.K. £	U.S. $	Can. $
D6505	Table lighter	3 1/2"	1964	1974	150.00	475.00	475.00

BAHAMAS POLICEMAN

This jug was commissioned by Island Galleria, Nassau, Bahamas, in a special edition of 1,000 jugs. The D number 6912 is also the numerical designation of The Snake Charmer.

Royal Doulton®

BAHAMAS POLICEMAN
D 6912
Modelled by

William K. Harper

© 1991 ROYAL DOULTON

ISLAND GALLERIA

An Island Galleria Exclusive

Designer: William K. Harper
Handle: Tassle
Colourway: White and red

Backstamp: Doulton/Island Galleria

Doulton Number	Size	Backstamp	Height	Intro.	Discon.	Current Market Value U.K. £	U.S. $	Can. $
D6912	Large	Doulton/Island	7"	1992	Sp. ed.	150.00	300.00	325.00

BASEBALL PLAYER

Only two of these jugs are known to exist, and each is different. They are test pieces and were never put into production.

STYLE ONE: HANDLE — BAT AND BALL

VARIATION No. 1: Colourway — Blue-green jersey; red sleeves and cap

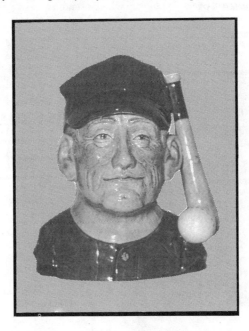

Designer: David Biggs   **Backstamp:** Doulton
Handle: Bat and ball
Colourway: Blue-green jersey; red sleeves and cap

Doulton Number	Size	Variation	Height	Intro.	Discon.	U.K. £	Current Market Value U.S. $	Can. $
D6624	Large	Var. 1	7 1/2"	1970	1970		Extremely rare	

VARIATION No. 2: Colourway — Striped blue and black jersey and cap

Doulton Number	Size	Variation	Height	Intro.	Discon.	U.K. £	Current Market Value U.S. $	Can. $
D6624	Large	Var. 2	7 1/2"	1970	1970		Extremely rare	

THE BASEBALL PLAYER

CHARACTERS FROM LIFE,
ONE OF SEVEN

STYLE TWO: HANDLE — BALL, BAT AND GLOVE

VARIATION No. 1: General baseball player — blue cap with lion and crown insignia

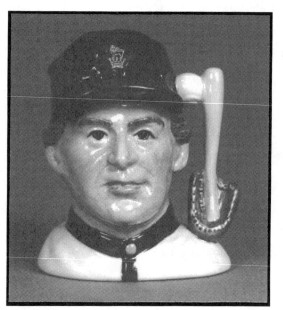

BACKSTAMP A

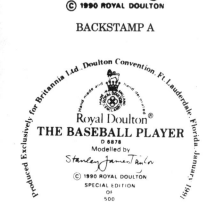

BACKSTAMP B

Designer: Stanley J. Taylor	**Backstamps: A.** Doulton
Handle: Ball, bat and glove	For general issue, 1991.
Colourway: Dark blue cap; white jersey	**B.** Doulton / Britannia Limited
with blue trim	Commissioned by Britannia Limited
	to celebrate the fifth anniversary of
	their Doulton Convention and Sale,
	January 1991. Issued in a special
	edition of 500 pieces.

Doulton Number	Size	Backstamp	Height	Intro.	Discon.	Current Market Value U.K. £	U.S. $	Can. $
D6878	Small	Doulton	4 1/4"	1991	Current	65.00	115.00	110.00
D6878	Small	Doulton/Britannia	4 1/4"	1991	Sp. ed.	95.00	225.00	250.00

VARIATION No. 2: Toronto Blue Jays — blue cap with Toronto Blue Jays insignia

This character jug was issued to commemorate the Toronto Blue Jays, winner of the 1992 and 1993 World Series of baseball. It was produced in limited edition of 2,500 worldwide.

Designer: Stanley J. Taylor
Handle: Ball, bat and glove
Colourway: Blue cap; white jersey with blue trim

Backstamp: Doulton/MLBPA/Blue Jays

Doulton Number	Size	Backstamp	Height	Intro.	Discon.	Current Market Value U.K. £	U.S. $	Can. $
D6973	Small	Doulton	4 1/4"	1994	Ltd. ed.	75.00	125.00	150.00

VARIATION No. 3:   Philadelphia

Produced to celebrate the 125th anniversary of Strawbridge and Clothier in Philadelphia, this jug was available only through that retailer. It was issued in a limited edition of 2,500 pieces.

Designer: Stanley J. Taylor
Handle: Ball, bat and glove
Colourway: Red cap; white jersey with red stripes

Backstamp: Doulton
"New Colourway 1993"

Doulton Number	Size	Backstamp	Height	Intro.	Discon.	Current Market Value U.K. £	U.S. $	Can. $
D6957	Small	Doulton	4 1/4"	1993	Current	95.00	225.00	250.00

BEEFEATER (WITH KEYS)

PROTOTYPE

This jug was designed for a proposed commission by PWC Publishing. The head was from the standard Beefeater jug, originally modelled by Harry Fenton, and Harry Sales remodelled the keys from Simon the Cellarer to form the handle. Due to cost and quantity requirements, the project was not continued.

Variation 3 was not returned to Doulton and is now in a U.S. collection.

VARIATION No. 1: Colourway — Grey keys; blue hat

VARIATION No. 2: Colourway — Yellow keys; blue hat; name highlighted in yellow

VARIATION No. 3: Colourway — Yellow keys; black hat with on-glaze red and blue band

Designer: Head — Harry Fenton
Keys — Remodelled by Harry Sales
Handle: See colourway variations above
Colourway: Scarlet tunic; white ruff; black hat

Backstamp: Doulton

Doulton Number	Size	Variation	Height	Intro.	Discon.	Current Market Value		
						U.K. £	U.S. $	Can. $
D —	Large	Var. 1	6 1/2"	1988	1988		Unique	
D —	Large	Var. 2	6 1/2"	1988	1988		Unique	

BEEFEATER

THE LONDON COLLECTION, ONE OF TEN

The Yeomen of the Guard and warders of the Tower of London are colloquially referred to as Beefeaters. The name "Beefeater" came from a visiting Grand Duke who was astonished by the large amounts of beef eaten by the Yeoman Guards. The monarch's cypher, GR, at the base of the handle is an abbreviation of George Rex, for King George VI. After his death in 1953, the cypher was changed to ER (Elizabeth Regina), for Queen Elizabeth II.

VARIATION No. 1: Handle — Pink with a "GR" cypher

Designer: Harry Fenton/Robert Tabbenor	**Backstamp:**	Doulton / "Beefeaters"
Handle: Pink with a "GR" cypher		The pluralized name was used on all
Colourway: Black hat; white ruff; pink tunic		three sizes of jugs from 1947 through 1953.

Doulton Number	Size	Variation	Height	Intro.	Discon.	Current Market Value U.K. £	U.S. $	Can. $
D6206	Large	Var. 1	6 1/2"	1947	1953	100.00	300.00	275.00
D6233	Small	Var. 1	3 1/4"	1947	1953	65.00	140.00	150.00
D6251	Miniature	Var. 1	2 1/2"	1947	1953	60.00	140.00	135.00

VARIATION No. 2:   Handle — Yellow with a "GR" cypher

Backstamp: Doulton / "Beefeaters"

Doulton Number	Size	Variation	Height	Intro.	Discon.	Current Market Value U.K. £	U.S. $	Can. $
D6206	Large	Var. 2	6 1/2"	1947	1947	1,000.00	3,500.00	3,500.00
D6233	Small	Var. 2	3 1/4"	1947	1947	900.00	2,250.00	2,250.00

VARIATION No. 3:   Handle — Pink with an "ER" cypher

BACKSTAMP A   BACKSTAMP B   BACKSTAMP B   BACKSTAMP C

Backstamps: A. Doulton/"Beefeaters"
The plural name was found only on early versions of the "ER" jugs.
B. Doulton/Beefeater
In late 1953 the backstamp was adjusted and the singular "Beefeater" name was incorporated.
C. Doulton/Beefeater
Fired in the last firing of a traditional Bottle Oven 1978 Longton Stoke-on-Trent, England

Doulton Number	Size	Variation	Height	Intro.	Discon.	Current Market Value U.K. £	U.S. $	Can. $
D6206	Large	Var. 3A	6 1/2"	1953	1953	60.00	195.00	150.00
D6206	Large	Var. 3B	6 1/2"	1953	1987	55.00	165.00	135.00
D6206	Large	Var. 3C	6 1/2"	1978	1978		Rare	
D6233	Small	Var. 3A	3 1/4"	1953	1953	40.00	140.00	90.00
D6233	Small	Var. 3B	3 1/4"	1953	1987	35.00	70.00	75.00
D6251	Miniature	Var. 3A	2 1/2"	1953	1953	35.00	70.00	75.00
D6251	Miniature	Var. 3B	2 1/2"	1953	1987	35.00	70.00	75.00

VARIATION No. 4:

VARIATION NO. 3   VARIATION NO. 2   VARIATION NO. 4

Designer: Harry Fenton
Modeller: Robert Tabbenor
Handle: Scarlet with an "ER" cypher
Colourway: Black hat; white ruff; scarlet tunic

Backstamps: A. Doulton/"Beefeater"
B. Doulton/Royal Doulton International Collectors Club
In 1988 Robert Tabbenor miniaturized Fenton's design of 1947 and created a tiny Beefeater, which
was offered for sale to the members of the RDICC.

Doulton Number	Size	Variation	Height	Intro.	Discon.	Current Market Value U.K. £	U.S. $	Can. $
D6206	Large	Var. 4A	6 1/2"	1987	Current	49.95	125.00	175.00
D6233	Small	Var. 4A	3 1/4"	1987	Current	25.00	69.50	110.00
D6251	Miniature	Var. 4A	2 1/2"	1987	1991	35.00	65.00	75.00
D6806	Tiny	Var. 4B	1 1/2"	1988	1988	75.00	195.00	175.00

Beefeater Derivative

Doulton Number	Item	Height	Intro.	Discon.	Current Market Value U.K. £	U.S. $	Can. $
D6233	Table lighter	3 1/2"	1958	1973	150.00	275.00	300.00

BENJAMIN FRANKLIN

An American publicist, scientist and statesman, Ben Franklin (1706-1790) was a signatory to the peace between Britain and the U.S.A. following the War of Independence. In 1748 he left his printing business to his foreman and devoted his life to science. His most famous discovery, that lightning is electricity, was accomplished with the simple objects of a knife and a key. It lead to the invention of the lightning rod, still used today to divert lightning harmlessly into the ground.

This jug was modelled for "The Queen's Table," Royal Doulton's exhibit at the United Kingdom Showcase at Walt Disney's Epcot Center in Orlando, Florida. It was sold exclusively to Epcot tourists visiting the exhibition during 1982, then released for general sale in 1983.

Royal Doulton
Benjamin Franklin
D.6695
Hand made and Hand decorated
© ROYAL DOULTON
TABLEWARE LTD. 1982

Designer: Eric Griffiths
Handle: A kite and key
Colourway: Black coat; white shirt; blue scarf

Backstamp: Doulton

Doulton Number	Size	Backstamp	Height	Intro.	Discon.	Current Market Value U.K. £	U.S. $	Can. $
D6695	Small	Doulton	4"	1982	1989	50.00	140.00	160.00

BETSY TROTWOOD

CHARLES DICKENS COMMEMORATIVE SET,
DICKENS TINIES, ONE OF 12

In Dickens's novel *David Copperfield*, Betsy is David's curt, yet loving, aunt.

The 12 jugs in this set were issued to commemorate the 170th anniversary of the birth of Charles Dickens, and each came with a certificate of authenticity. A mahogany display shelf completes the set. The set was first sold by Lawleys By Post in the U.K. from 1982 to 1988, and from 1985 in North America and Australia.

Betsy Trotwood
D 6685

Designer: Michael Abberley
Handle: Plain
Colourway: Yellow, white and black

Backstamp: Doulton

Doulton Number	Size	Backstamp	Height	Intro.	Discon.	U.K. £	U.S. $	Can. $
						Current Market Value		
D6685	Tiny	Doulton	1 1/2"	1982	1989	35.00	65.00	75.00
		Display stand for 12 tinies				65.00	45.00	50.00

BILL SIKES

One of Dickens's most memorable characters is the infamous Bill Sikes, a character from *Oliver Twist*. This jug was commissioned by Lawleys By Post in a limited edition of 2,500.

Designer: William K. Harper
Handle: Pistol and dog "Bull's-eye"
Colourway: Beige hat; green jacket; red scarf

Backstamp: Doulton

Doulton Number	Size	Backstamp	Height	Intro.	Discon.	Current Market Value U.K. £	Current Market Value U.S. $	Current Market Value Can. $
D6981	Large	Doulton	7"	1994	Ltd. ed	85.00	—	—

BILL SYKES

CHARLES DICKENS COMMEMORATIVE SET,
DICKENS TINIES, ONE OF 12

In Dickens's *Oliver Twist*, Sykes is a cruel cohort of Fagin and his band of child thieves.

The 12 jugs in this set were issued to commemorate the 170th anniversary of the birth of Charles Dickens, and each came with a certificate of authenticity. A mahogany display shelf completes the set. The set was first sold by Lawleys By Post in the U.K. from 1982 to 1988, and from 1985 in North America and Australia.

Bill Sykes
D 6684

Designer: Michael Abberley
Handle: Plain
Colourway: Green and dark blue

Backstamp: Doulton

Doulton Number	Size	Backstamp	Height	Intro.	Discon.	Current Market Value U.K. £	U.S. $	Can. $
D6684	Tiny	Doulton	1 1/2"	1982	1989	35.00	60.00	70.00
		Display stand for 12 tinies				65.00	45.00	50.00

BLACKSMITH

PROTOTYPE

This large prototype of the Blacksmith jug has older features, a different hat and a different hair style. Only one copy is known to exist.

Designer: David Biggs
Handle: Hammer, anvil and pliers
Colourway: Beige, white and black

Backstamp: Doulton

Doulton Number	Size	Backstamp	Height	Intro.	Discon.	Current Market Value U.K. £	U.S. $	Can. $
Not issued	Large	Doulton	7 1/4"	c. 1963		Unique		

BLACKSMITH

CHARACTERS FROM WILLIAMSBURG,
ONE OF EIGHT

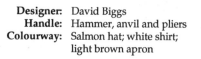

Designer: David Biggs
Handle: Hammer, anvil and pliers
Colourway: Salmon hat; white shirt;
light brown apron

Backstamp: Doulton

Doulton Number	Size	Backstamp	Height	Intro.	Discon.	Current Market Value		
						U.K. £	U.S. $	Can. $
D6571	Large	Doulton	7 1/4"	1963	1983	90.00	160.00	175.00
D6578	Small	Doulton	4"	1963	1983	50.00	110.00	125.00
D6585	Miniature	Doulton	2 1/2"	1963	1983	45.00	100.00	110.00

BONNIE PRINCE CHARLIE

James II's grandson, the "Young Pretender" (1720-1788), was born Charles Edward Stuart in Rome. He became the hopeful leader of the Jacobites, adherents to the Stuart line, and led them in an unsuccessful uprising in 1745. After being defeated at Culloden Moor in 1746, he escaped to France with the help of Flora McDonald. Charles roamed Europe, a drunkard, until settling in Rome where he passed the remainder of his life.

Royal Doulton®
BONNIE PRINCE CHARLIE
D 6858
Modelled by
Stanley James Taylor.
© 1989 ROYAL DOULTON

Designer:	Stanley J. Taylor
Handle:	Crown atop thistles
Colourway:	Blue plaid tam; red coat trimmed with yellow collar; white ruffles at the neck

Backstamp: Doulton

Doulton Number	Size	Backstamp	Height	Intro.	Discon.	Current Market Value U.K. £	U.S. $	Can. $
D6858	Large	Doulton	6 1/2"	1990	1994	85.00	225.00	250.00

BOOTMAKER

PROTOTYPE

This large-size prototype of the Bootmaker jug has younger features and different hair, handle and hat designs. Only one copy is known to exist.

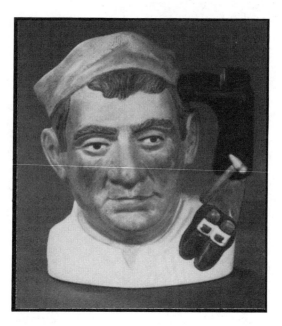

Designer: David Biggs
Handle: A boot and hammer, with a pair of shoes at the base
Colourway: Beige cap; white shirt; black shoes

Backstamp: Doulton

Doulton Number	Size	Backstamp	Height	Intro.	Discon.	Current Market Value		
						U.K. £	U.S. $	Can. $
Not issued	Large	Doulton	7 1/2"	c. 1963			Unique	

BOOTMAKER

CHARACTERS FROM WILLIAMSBURG,
ONE OF EIGHT

Designer: David Biggs
Handle: A boot and hammer, with a pair of shoes at the base
Colourway: Salmon cap; white shirt

Character Jugs from Williamsburg
Bootmaker
D 6572
COPR 1962
DOULTON & CO. LIMITED
Rd No 906342
Rd No 43449
Rd No 9228
Rd No 282-62

Backstamp: Doulton

Doulton Number	Size	Backstamp	Height	Intro.	Discon.	Current Market Value		
						U.K. £	U.S. $	Can. $
D6572	Large	Doulton	7 1/2"	1963	1983	85.00	160.00	175.00
D6579	Small	Doulton	4"	1963	1983	50.00	120.00	130.00
D6586	Miniature	Doulton	2 1/2"	1963	1983	45.00	100.00	110.00

BOWLS PLAYER

CHARACTERS FROM LIFE,
ONE OF SEVEN

Bowls is a British game played on a flat green in lanes. Sir Francis Drake is reputed to have been playing bowls when the Spanish Armada was sighted in the English Channel.

Royal Doulton®
THE BOWLS PLAYER
D 6896
Modelled by
Stanley James Taylor
© 1991 ROYAL DOULTON

Designer: Stanley J. Taylor
Handle: Bowl, jack and measure
Colourway: White and yellow

Backstamp: Doulton

Doulton Number	Size	Backstamp	Height	Intro.	Discon.	Current Market Value		
						U.K. £	U.S. $	Can. $
D6896	Small	Doulton	4"	1991	Current	29.95	82.50	120.00

BUFFALO BILL

William Frederick Cody (1846-1917) was a scout, plainsman, soldier in the Civil War, hotelier, rancher and showman. His expert marksmanship as a buffalo hunter earned him his nickname Buffalo Bill. In 1883, Cody and others formed "Buffalo Bill's Wild West Show," a theatrical shooting exhibition, which became very successful and travelled through the U.S. and Europe.

STYLE ONE: "W.F. CODY BUFFALO BILL"

This jug was piloted but never put into production, and only three jugs are known to exist. "W.F. Cody Buffalo Bill" is incised on the right shoulder in raised letters.

Designer: Unknown
Handle: A rifle and buffalo head
Colourway: Brown hat; grey moustache and goatee

Backstamp: Doulton

Doulton Number	Size	Backstamp	Height	Intro.	Discon.	Current Market Value U.K. £	U.S. $	Can. $
D —	Large	Doulton	7 1/2"		Unknown	Extremely rare		

BUFFALO BILL

THE WILD WEST COLLECTION,
ONE OF SIX

STYLE TWO: BUFFALO BILL

Designer: Robert Tabbenor   **Backstamp:** Doulton
Handle: Buffalo head and horn
Colourway: Light brown hat and buckskin jacket

Doulton Number	Size	Backstamp	Height	Intro.	Discon.	Current Market Value U.K. £	U.S. $	Can. $
D6735	Mid	Doulton	5 1/2"	1985	1989	60.00	140.00	150.00

THE BUSKER

PROTOTYPE

The prototype of The Busker jug had a one-man band for the handle; however, this was too complex for production and was replaced by a concertina.

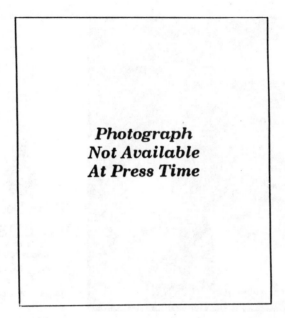

*Photograph
Not Available
At Press Time*

Designer: Stanley J. Taylor
Handle: One-man band
Colourway: Grey cap; green coat; yellow scarf

Backstamp: Doulton

Doulton Number	Size	Backstamp	Height	Intro.	Discon.	Current Market Value		
						U.K. £	U.S. $	Can. $
—	Large	Doulton	6 1/2"	c.1988			Unique	

THE BUSKER

THE LONDON COLLECTION,
ONE OF TEN

From its roots with the early wandering minstrels, entertaining in public places for money is still a way for artists to support themselves while gaining public exposure for their work.

Royal Doulton®
THE BUSKER
D 6775
Modelled by
Stanley James Taylor.
© 1987 ROYAL DOULTON

Designer: Stanley J. Taylor
Handle: An open concertina
Colourway: Grey cap; green coat; yellow scarf

Backstamp: Doulton

Doulton Number	Size	Backstamp	Height	Intro.	Discon.	Current Market Value U.K. £	U.S. $	Can. $
D6775	Large	Doulton	6 1/2"	1988	1991	90.00	225.00	250.00

BUZFUZ

This is an excellent example of the literary character designs of early character jugs. In Dickens's *Pickwick Papers*, Sergeant Buzfuz was the counsel of Mrs. Bardell in the breach of promise suit she brought against Mr. Pickwick.

Designer: Leslie Harradine / Harry Fenton
Handle: Plain
Colourway: White collar; brown waistcoat;
dark green coat; black robe

Backstamp: Doulton

Doulton Number	Size	Backstamp	Height	Intro.	Discon.	Current Market Value U.K. £	U.S. $	Can. $
D5838	Mid	Doulton	5 1/2"	1938	1948	145.00	275.00	295.00
D5838	Small	Doulton	4"	1948	1960	75.00	160.00	175.00

Buzfuz Derivatives

Doulton Number	Item	Height	Intro.	Discon.	Current Market Value U.K. £	U.S. $	Can. $
D5838	Table lighter	3 1/2"	1958	1959	150.00	400.00	400.00
D6048	Bust	3"	1939	1960	75.00	140.00	150.00

CABINET MAKER

CHARACTERS FROM WILLIAMSBURG,
ONE OF EIGHT

In 1981 it was announced that a new jug in the Williamsburg series, the Cabinet Maker, would be produced. The series was cancelled in 1983, however, so it was not put into production at that time.

The decision was made to put the jug into production in 1995 and to launch it the at the 15th anniversary convention of the Royal Doulton International Collectors Club, held at Williamsburg. It was issued in a special edition of 1,500 pieces.

Designer: Michael Abberley   **Backstamp:** Doulton
Handle: Brace
Colourway: Red, white and brown

Doulton Number	Size	Backstamp	Height	Intro.	Discon.	Current Market Value		
						U.K. £	U.S. $	Can. $
D6659	Large	Doulton	7 1/2"	1979	1979		Prototype	
D7010	Large	Doulton	7 1/2"	1995	Sp. ed.	—	235.00	—

CAPT AHAB

Captain Ahab sailed the whaler, *Pequod*, in Herman Melville's great 19th-century American classic, *Moby Dick*. He lost a leg and then his life in pursuit of the great white whale, who triumphed in the chase and sunk his ship.

Capt Ahab
D 6522
COPR 1958
DOULTON & CO LIMITED
Rd No 889571
Rd No 38227
Rd No 8037
Rd No 422/58

Designer: Garry Sharpe
Handle: A grey whale
Colourway: Blue cap; black coat; white sweater

Backstamp: Doulton

Doulton Number	Size	Backstamp	Height	Intro.	Discon.	Current Market Value U.K. £	U.S. $	Can. $
D6500	Large	Doulton	7"	1959	1984	80.00	175.00	185.00
D6506	Small	Doulton	4"	1959	1984	50.00	100.00	110.00
D6522	Miniature	Doulton	2 1/2"	1960	1984	40.00	95.00	100.00

Capt Ahab Derivative

Doulton Number	Item	Height	Intro.	Discon.	Current Market Value U.K. £	U.S. $	Can. $
D6506	Table lighter	3 1/2"	1964	1973	175.00	500.00	500.00

CAPTAIN BLIGH

This jug of the year for 1995 commemorates Captain Bligh and the *Mutiny on the Bounty*. In 1789 the crew of the *Bounty*, under the leadership of Christian Fletcher, mutinied and set Bligh adrift in an open boat. He survived a 3,500-mile voyage before reaching land.

Royal Doulton®
CHARACTER JUG OF THE YEAR 1995
CAPTAIN BLIGH
D 6967
Modelled by

Stanley James Taylor

© 1994 ROYAL DOULTON

Designer: Stanley J. Taylor
Handle: Navigation chart; palm tree and "Bligh of the Bounty"
Colourway: Black, cream, green, red and brown

Backstamp: Doulton

Doulton Number	Size	Backstamp	Height	Intro.	Discon.	Current Market Value U.K. £	U.S. $	Can. $
D6967	Large	Doulton	7"	1995	1995	89.95	200.00	295.00

CAP'N CUTTLE

The wonderful characters of Dickens's novels were the inspiration for many early jug designs. Captain Edward Cuttle was an eccentric English gentleman in *Dombey and Son* (1846), who is best known for saying, "When found, make a note of it."

Designer: Leslie Harradine / Harry Fenton
Handle: Plain
Colourway: Blue-black coat; grey-green hat; white collar; green bow tie

Backstamp: Doulton

Doulton Number	Size	Backstamp	Height	Intro.	Discon.	Current Market Value		
						U.K. £	U.S. $	Can. $
D5842	Mid	Doulton	5 1/2"	1938	1948	150.00	275.00	295.00
D5842	Small	Doulton	4"	1948	1960	75.00	160.00	175.00

Cap'n Cuttle Derivative

Doulton Number	Item	Height	Intro.	Discon.	Current Market Value		
					U.K. £	U.S. $	Can. $
D5842	Table lighter	3 1/2"	1958	1959	150.00	400.00	400.00

CAPT HENRY MORGAN

A privateer and pirate leader in the West Indies, Morgan (1635-1688) also carried out commissions from the British authorities. His attack on Panama in 1671 violated a peace treaty between England and Spain. Sent to England to stand trial, he was instead knighted and became Lieutenant Governor of Jamaica, where he remained until his death.

Capt Henry Morgan
D 6467
COPR 1957
DOULTON & CO LIMITED
Rd No 886231
Rd No 37211
Rd No 7853
Rd No 388/57

Designer: Garry Sharpe
Handle: Sails of a ship
Colourway: Black tricorn; blue collar trimmed with gold

Backstamp: Doulton

Doulton Number	Size	Backstamp	Height	Intro.	Discon.	Current Market Value U.K. £	U.S. $	Can. $
D6467	Large	Doulton	6 3/4"	1958	1982	85.00	160.00	175.00
D6469	Small	Doulton	3 1/2"	1958	1982	55.00	95.00	110.00
D6510	Miniature	Doulton	2 1/2"	1960	1982	50.00	85.00	100.00

CAPT HOOK

Captain Hook is the nemesis of Peter Pan in J.M. Barrie's famous story. Peter Pan cut off Hook's hand and fed it to a crocodile, who liked it so much he followed the captain around in hopes of eating the rest of him. Hook managed to keep eluding his predator because the crocodile had accidentally swallowed a clock that ticked inside him and ruined the element of surprise.

STYLE ONE: HANDLE — CROCODILE AND CLOCK

Backstamp: Doulton

Designer: Max Henk / David Biggs
Handle: An alligator and clock
Colourway: Blue tricorn trimmed with yellow;
green coat trimmed with yellow;
white ruffles at the neck

Doulton Number	Size	Backstamp	Height	Intro.	Discon.	Current Market Value		
						U.K. £	U.S. $	Can. $
D6597	Large	Doulton	7 1/4"	1965	1971	350.00	850.00	850.00
D6601	Small	Doulton	4"	1965	1971	225.00	500.00	500.00
D6605	Miniature	Doulton	2 1/2"	1965	1971	250.00	550.00	550.00

CAPTAIN HOOK

This was the character jug of the year for 1994.

STYLE TWO: HANDLE — SILVER HOOK AND CROCODILE

Royal Doulton®
CHARACTER JUG OF THE YEAR 1994
CAPTAIN HOOK
D 6947
Modelled by

© 1993 ROYAL DOULTON

Designer: Martyn C. R. Alcock
Handle: Crocodile, silver hook
Colourway: Black, scarlet and grey

Backstamp: Doulton

Doulton Number	Size	Backstamp	Height	Intro.	Discon.	Current Market Value		
						U.K. £	U.S. $	Can. $
D6947	Large	Doulton	7 1/2"	1994	1994	90.00	.00	300.00

CAROLER

CHRISTMAS MINIATURES SERIES,
ONE OF FIVE

This is the fifth in the Christmas Series of jugs. Issued during 1995, the jug was commissioned and sold by Royal Doulton (U.S.A.) Limited in America, and was made available worldwide through the Royal Doulton International Collectors Club.

Designer: Martyn C. R. Alcock
Handle: Sheet music and lantern
Colourway:

Backstamp: Doulton

Doulton Number	Size	Backstamp	Height	Intro.	Discon.	Current Market Value		
						U.K. £	U.S. $	Can. $
D7007	Miniature	Doulton	2 1/2"	1995	1995	—	75.00	—

THE CARDINAL

This jug has minor colour variations in the hair. The earliest jugs had brown hair, and later jugs either grey or white hair. This jug was produced with and without pink highlighting on the raised character name.

The Cardinal

Backstamp: Doulton

Designer: Charles Noke
Handle: Tassle
Colourway: Scarlet robes; Purple handle

Doulton Number	Size	Backstamp	Height	Intro.	Discon.	U.K. £	U.S. $	Can. $
						Current Market Value		
D5614	Large	Doulton	6 1/2"	1936	1960	95.00	225.00	235.00
D6033	Small	Doulton	3 1/2"	1939	1960	60.00	125.00	135.00
D6129	Miniature	Doulton	2 1/4"	1940	1960	55.00	100.00	110.00
D6258	Tiny	Doulton	1 1/2"	1947	1960	150.00	350.00	365.00

CATHERINE OF ARAGON

HENRY VIII AND HIS SIX WIVES, ONE OF EIGHT

Daughter of Ferdinand and Isabella of Spain, Catherine (1485-1536) was married to Arthur, Prince of Wales, in a political arrangement between the two countries. When Arthur died shortly after their wedding, she married Henry VIII to continue the arrangement. This first marriage for Henry lasted 24 years, until he became restless at the lack of a male heir and sought out Anne Boleyn. In 1527 Henry attempted to have his marriage annulled, a move that led to his excommunication by the Pope and, eventually, to the English Reformation. Catherine was banished from the royal court and lived until the age of 50, unhappy and lonely.

Designer: Alan Maslankowski
Handle: A tower
Colourway: Red, gold, black and white

Backstamp: Doulton

Doulton Number	Size	Backstamp	Height	Intro.	Discon.	Current Market Value U.K. £	U.S. $	Can. $
D6643	Large	Doulton	7"	1975	1989	85.00	185.00	200.00
D6657	Small	Doulton	4"	1981	1989	60.00	140.00	150.00
D6658	Miniature	Doulton	2 3/4"	1981	1989	50.00	140.00	150.00

CATHERINE HOWARD

HENRY VIII AND HIS SIX WIVES,
ONE OF EIGHT

Niece to the Duke of Norfolk, Catherine Howard (1521-1542) became Henry VIII's fifth wife on July 28, 1540, in a marriage arranged by her family. In 1541 Henry accused her of adultery and had her beheaded at the Tower of London.

Royal Doulton
CATHERINE HOWARD
D6645
Modelled by

Peter A Gee.

© ROYAL DOULTON TABLEWARE
LIMITED 1977

Designer: Peter Gee

Handle: An axe

Colourway: Brown, gold and white

Backstamp: Doulton

Doulton Number	Size	Backstamp	Height	Intro.	Discon.	Current Market Value U.K. £	U.S. $	Can. $
D6645	Large	Doulton	7"	1978	1989	85.00	275.00	295.00
D6692	Small	Doulton	4"	1984	1989	65.00	225.00	235.00
D6693	Miniature	Doulton	2 1/2"	1984	1989	60.00	250.00	265.00

CATHERINE PARR

HENRY VIII AND HIS SIX WIVES,
ONE OF EIGHT

Catherine Parr (1512-1548) became Henry VIII's last wife on July 12, 1543, after being twice widowed. She came to wield considerable power in the royal court, serving for a time as Queen regent in 1544 and overseeing the start of Edward VI's reign. After Henry's death in 1547, she married Baron Seymour of Sudeley, but died during childbirth the following year.

Royal Doulton®
CATHERINE PARR
D 6752
©1980 ROYAL DOULTON (UK)

Royal Doulton
CATHERINE PARR
D 6664
Modelled by

© ROYAL DOULTON TABLEWARE
LIMITED 1980

Designer: Michael Abberley
Handle: Bible and pulpit
Colourway: Black, brown and gold

Backstamp: Doulton

Doulton Number	Size	Backstamp	Height	Intro.	Discon.	Current Market Value U.K. £	U.S. $	Can. $
D6664	Large	Doulton	6 3/4"	1981	1989	95.00	275.00	295.00
D6751	Small	Doulton	4"	1987	1989	85.00	250.00	265.00
D6752	Miniature	Doulton	2 1/2"	1987	1989	110.00	275.00	290.00

THE CAVALIER

The cavaliers were Royalist soldiers who fought for Charles I during the English Civil War. They became known for their gallantry and haughtiness, an attitude still described as "cavalier."

STYLE ONE: CAVALIER WITH GOATEE

Designer: Harry Fenton
Handle: Handle of a sword
Colourway: Green hat; white ruff

Backstamp: Doulton

Doulton Number	Size	Backstamp	Height	Intro.	Discon.	Current Market Value		
						U.K. £	U.S. $	Can. $
D6114	Large	Doulton	7"	1940	1950	1,650.00	4,500.00	4,500.00

THE CAVALIER

This jug was originally listed in Royal Doulton's product guide as the Laughing Cavalier, presumably after the famous Frans Hals painting.

STYLE TWO: CAVALIER WITHOUT GOATEE

Slight colour changes, along with alterations to the ruff and removal of the goatee, occurred in 1950.

Designer: Harry Fenton
Handle: Handle of a sword
Colourway: Green hat; white ruff

Backstamp: Doulton

Doulton Number	Size	Backstamp	Height	Intro.	Discon.	Current Market Value U.K. £	U.S. $	Can. $
D6114	Large	Doulton	7"	1950	1960	100.00	225.00	235.00
D6173	Small	Doulton	3 1/4"	1941	1960	60.00	110.00	120.00

CELTIC (FOOTBALL CLUB)

THE FOOTBALL SUPPORTERS,
ONE OF NINE

Designer: Stanley J. Taylor
Handle: Team coloured scarf
Colourway: Green and white uniform

Backstamp: Doulton

Doulton Number	Size	Backstamp	Height	Intro.	Discon.	Current Market Value		
						U.K. £	U.S. $	Can. $
D6925	Mid	Doulton	5"	1992	Current	32.50	—	—

CHARLES I

ENGLISH CIVIL WAR SERIES,
ONE OF TWO

Commissioned by Lawleys By Post, Charles I (1600-1649) and his companion jug, Oliver Cromwell (1599-1659), form a pair which are being issued in a limited edition of 2,500. See page 355 for the Oliver Cromwell jug.

Designer: William K. Harper
Handle: Crown and bible against a red sash
Colourway: Black hat; maroon and purple jacket; cream collar

Backstamp: Doulton

Doulton Number	Size	Backstamp	Height	Intro.	Discon.	Current Market Value U.K. £	U.S. $	Can. $
D6985	Small	Doulton	4 1/2"	1995	Ltd. ed.	50.00	—	—

CHARLES DICKENS

CHARLES DICKENS COMMEMORATIVE SET, DICKENS TINIES, ONE OF 12

The 12 jugs in this set were issued to commemorate the 170th anniversary of the birth of Charles Dickens, and each one comes with a certificate of authenticity. A mahogany display shelf completes the set. The set was first sold by Lawleys By Post in the U.K. from 1982 to 1988, and from 1985 in North America and Australia.

STYLE ONE: HANDLE — PLAIN

Charles Dickens D 6676

Designer: Eric Griffiths	**Backstamp:** Doulton
Handle: Plain	
Colourway: Grey and black	

Doulton Number	Size	Backstamp	Height	Intro.	Discon.	Current Market Value		
						U.K. £	U.S. $	Can. $
D6676	Tiny	Doulton	1 1/2"	1982	1989	60.00	165.00	175.00
		Display stand for 12 tinies				65.00	45.00	50.00

CHARLES DICKENS

ROYAL DOULTON INTERNATIONAL COLLECTORS CLUB

The Charles Dickens jug was commissioned by the Royal Doulton International Collectors Club in a limited edition of 7,500 pieces.

STYLE TWO: HANDLE — QUILL PEN AND INK POT

CHARLES DICKENS
" *Whatever the word 'great' means,*
Dickens was what it means".
J. K. Chesterton.
EXCLUSIVELY FOR
COLLECTORS CLUB
LIMITED EDITION OF 7,500

THIS IS N° **963**

© 1991 ROYAL DOULTON
MODELLED BY

Designer: William K. Harper
Handle: Quill pen and ink pot, the book
"The Old Curiosity Shop"
Colourway: Black and olive green

Backstamp: Doulton/RDICC

Doulton Number	Size	Backstamp	Height	Intro.	Discon.	Current Market Value U.K. £	U.S. $	Can. $
D6901	Small	Doulton/RDICC	4"	1991	Ltd. ed.	75.00	140.00	150.00

CHARLES DICKENS

The 125th anniversary of the death of Charles Dickens is being commemorated in 1995 with a two-handled jug of Dickens, in a limited edition of 2,500.

STYLE THREE: TWO-HANDLED JUG

Royal Doulton®

Charles Dickens

D 6939

Modelled by

William K. Harper

© 1993 ROYAL DOULTON
LIMITED EDITION OF 2,500

THIS IS No. 129

Designer: William K. Harper
Handle: Six of Dickens characters:
Oliver Twist, Sairey Gamp, Ebenezer Scrooge,
Little Nell, Mr. Pickwick and Little Dorritt
Colourway: Green, black, yellow and brown

Backstamp: Doulton

Doulton Number	Size	Backstamp	Height	Intro.	Discon.	Current Market Value U.K. £	U.S. $	Can. $
D6939	Large	Doulton	7"	1995	Ltd. ed.	250.00	500.00	675.00

CHARLIE CHAPLIN

Issued in 1993 in a limited edition of 5,000, this jug was available through Lawleys By Post.

Designer: William K. Harper
Handle: Cane
Colourway: Black hat and jacket with green, white and
black striped tie

Backstamp: Doulton

Doulton Number	Size	Backstamp	Height	Intro.	Discon.	Current Market Value U.K. £	U.S. $	Can. $
D6949	Large	Doulton	7 1/4"	1993	Ltd. ed.	80.00	—	—

CHELSEA PENSIONER

THE LONDON COLLECTION,
ONE OF TEN

Charles II founded the Royal Hospital in Chelsea for "worthy old soldiers broken in the wars." It was built by Christopher Wren and completed in 1692. Each year on Founders Day, the opening of the hospital is celebrated by the soldiers in full dress uniform, as worn by the gentleman depicted on this jug.

Royal Doulton®

CHELSEA PENSIONER

D 6817

Modelled by

Stanley James Taylor.

© 1988 ROYAL DOULTON

Designer: Stanley J. Taylor
Handle: Medals of honour
Colourway: Black tricorn trimmed with gold; scarlet tunic; black collar

Backstamp: A. Doulton
For general issue, 1989.

BACKSTAMP B   BACKSTAMP C   BACKSTAMP D

Pre-released in the U.S.A. in 1988 at the following four stores in a limited edition of 1,000 pieces, with 250 jugs per store:

Backstamps: B. Doulton / Joseph Horne's / To commemorate the First Anniversary of the opening of the Royal Doulton Room Joseph Horne's, Pittsburgh, Pennsylvania, U.S.A.

C. Doulton / D. H. Holme's / To commemorate the First Anniversary of the opening of the Royal Doulton Room D. H. Holme's, New Orleans, Louisiana, U.S.A.

D. Doulton / Higbee Company / To commemorate the Third Anniversary of the opening of the Royal Doulton Room The Higbee Company, Cleveland, Ohio, U.S.A.

E. Doulton / Strawbridge and Clothier / To commemorate the Second Anniversary of the opening of the Royal Doulton Room Strawbridge and Clothier, Philadelphia, Pennsylvania, U.S.A.

Doulton Number	Size	Backstamp	Height	Intro.	Discon.	Current Market Value U.K. £	U.S. $	Can. $
D6817	Large	Var. A	6 1/2"	1989	1991	75.00	225.00	250.00
D6830	Large	Var. B	6 1/2"	1988	Ltd. ed.	160.00	275.00	300.00
D6831	Large	Var. C	6 1/2"	1988	Ltd. ed.	160.00	275.00	300.00
D6832	Large	Var. D	6 1/2"	1988	Ltd. ed.	160.00	275.00	300.00
D6833	Large	Var. E	6 1/2"	1988	Ltd. ed.	160.00	275.00	300.00

CHIEF SITTING BULL
GEORGE ARMSTRONG CUSTER

THE ANTAGONISTS' COLLECTION (TWO-FACED JUG),
ONE OF FOUR

Chief Sitting Bull (1831-1890) of the Sioux Indians spent his life working for the right of his people to own and control their land. He was shot by the Indian police on a questionable charge of resisting arrest.

George Armstrong Custer (1839-1876) was the youngest general in the U.S. Army. He first saw action in the Civil War and was later stationed in the Dakota Territory during the gold rush on Sioux Land. In 1876 he led an attack against an Indian encampment at Little Big Horn. Sitting Bull and his men outnumbered Custer's regiment and easily defeated them, leaving no survivors.

This jug was issued in a limited edition of 9,500 pieces.

VARIATION No. 1: Colourway — Multi-coloured; Sitting Bull has grey eyes.

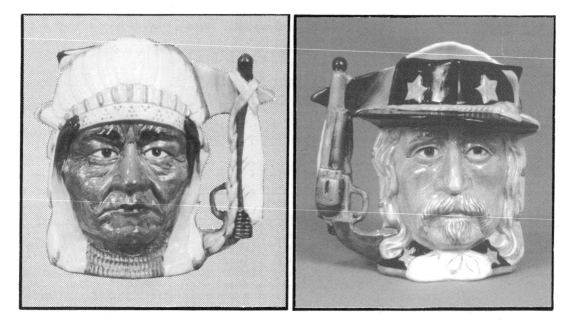

Designer: Michael Abberley	**Backstamp:** Doulton
Handle: Sitting Bull—tomahawk; Custer—pistol	
Colourway: Multi-coloured; Sitting Bull has grey eyes	

Doulton Number	Size	Variation	Height	Intro.	Discon.	Current Market Value U.K. £	U.S. $	Can. $
D6712	Large	Var. 1	7"	1984	Ltd. ed.	150.00	275.00	300.00

VARIATION No. 2: Colourway — Multi-coloured; Sitting Bull has brown eyes

VARIATION NO. 2   VARIATION NO. 1
BROWN EYES   GREY EYES

Doulton Number	Size	Variation	Height	Intro.	Discon.	Current Market Value U.K. £	U.S. $	Can. $
D6712	Large	Var. 2	7"	1984	1989	140.00	250.00	265.00

CHRISTOPHER COLUMBUS

STYLE ONE: HANDLE — MAP OF THE NEW WORLD

Designer: Stanley J. Taylor   **Backstamp:** Doulton
Handle: Map of the New World
Colourway: Dark blue and white

Doulton Number	Size	Backstamp	Height	Intro.	Discon.	Current Market Value		
						U.K. £	U.S. $	Can. $
D6891	Large	Doulton	7"	1991	Current	59.95	125.00	220.00

CHRISTOPHER COLUMBUS

ROYAL DOULTON INTERNATIONAL COLLECTORS CLUB

This jug was issued to recognize the 500th anniversary of Columbus's voyage to America in 1492. It was created exclusively for the Royal Doulton International Collectors Club and was issued in a limited edition of 7,500. The jug was exhibited in the British Pavillion at Expo '92 in Seville, Spain.

STYLE TWO: HANDLE — THE SHIP *SANTA MARIA*

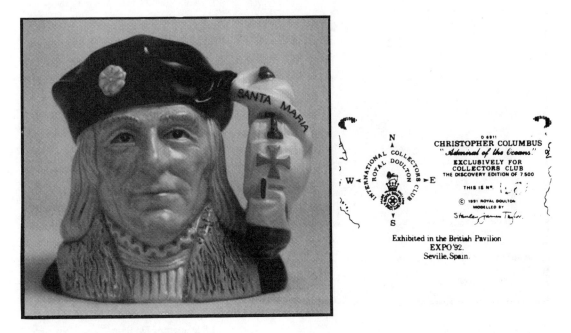

Designer: Stanley J. Taylor
Handle: The ship *Santa Maria*
Colourway: Brown, light brown, grey and cream

Backstamp: Doulton / RDICC / Christopher Columbus "Admiral of the Oceans." Exclusively For Collectors Club The Discovery Edition of 7,500

Doulton Number	Size	Backstamp	Height	Intro.	Discon.	Current Market Value U.K. £	U.S. $	Can. $
D6911	Small	Doulton/RDICC	3 1/2"	1992	Ltd. ed.	60.00	165.00	175.00

CHURCHILL

Sir Winston Leonard Spencer Churchill (1874-1965) was first lord of the Admiralty, Home Secretary and Prime Minister on three occasions. As Prime Minister during World War II, he led Britain to victory and captured the spirit of the Allies with his famous radio broadcasts. He was awarded the Nobel Prize for Literature in 1953.

VARIATION No. 1:   With an inscription on the base
Colourway — Cream with two black handles

WINSTON SPENCER CHURCHILL
PRIME MINISTER
OF BRITAIN
— 1940 —
THIS LOVING CUP WAS MADE
DURING THE "BATTLE OF BRITAIN"
AS A TRIBUTE TO A GREAT LEADER

modelled by NOKE

Designer: Charles Noke
Handle: Plain
Colourway: Cream; two black handles

Backstamp: Doulton

Doulton Number	Size	Variation	Height	Intro.	Discon.	Current Market Value U.K. £	U.S. $	Can. $
D6170	Large	Doulton	6 1/2"	1940	1941	3,500.00	9,000.00	7,000.00

Note: For Sir Winston Churchill, see page 432. For Winston Churchill, see page 472.

VARIATION No. 2: Modelling portrays a young Churchill
Colourway — Very lightly coloured overall, with two grey handles
Without inscription on base; green Doulton backstamp

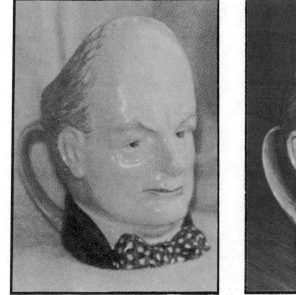 

VARIATION NO. 2   VARIATION NO. 3

Doulton Number	Size	Variation	Height	Intro.	Discon.	Current Market Value U.K. £	U.S. $	Can. $
D6170	Large	Var. 2	6 1/2"	Unknown			Extremely rare	

VARIATION No. 3: Modelling portrays a young Churchill
Colourway — Fully decorated in natural colours, with two dark brown handles
No inscription on base

Doulton Number	Size	Variation	Height	Intro.	Discon.	Current Market Value U.K. £	U.S. $	Can. $
D6170	Large	Var. 3	6 1/2"	Unknown			Extremely rare	

CITY GENT

THE LONDON COLLECTION,
ONE OF TEN

Royal Doulton®

CITY GENT

D 6815

Modelled by

Stanley James Taylor

© 1988 ROYAL DOULTON

Designer: Stanley J. Taylor
Handle: Umbrella handle
Colourway: Black and grey hat;
black coat; white shirt; grey tie

Backstamp: Doulton

Doulton Number	Size	Backstamp	Height	Intro.	Discon.	Current Market Value		
						U.K. £	U.S. $	Can. $
D6815	Large	Doulton	7"	1988	1991	75.00	225.00	250.00

CLARK GABLE

THE CELEBRITY COLLECTION,
ONE OF SIX

An Ohio native, Clark Gable (1901-1960) worked in a tire factory and as a lumberjack before he took up acting. He began his career in 1930 and appeared in over seventy films. He won an Academy Award in 1934 for his performance in *It Happened One Night*, but is perhaps best remembered as Rhett Butler in *Gone With the Wind*.

This jug was issued in the U.S.A. prior to approval from the Gable estate and had to be withdrawn when permission was denied. A small number of jugs are known to exist.

Backstamp: Doulton

Designer: Stanley J. Taylor
Handle: Movie camera entwined in film
Colourway: Brown; light brown suit; tan tie

Doulton Number	Size	Backstamp	Height	Intro.	Discon.	Current Market Value U.K. £	U.S. $	Can. $
D6709	Large	Doulton	7"	1984	1984	2,000.00	4,500.00	4,000.00

THE CLOWN

There are three recognised variations of The Clown without hat, those with red, brown or white hair.

STYLE ONE: CLOWN WITHOUT HAT

VARIATION No. 1:   Colourway — Red hair
Handle — Multi-coloured

The Clown.
COPR. 1930.
DOULTON & CO. LIMITED.
R⁹N⁰ 28163.
R⁹N⁰ 6207.
R⁹N⁰ 92/30.

Designer: Harry Fenton
Handle: Multi-coloured
Colourway: Red hair

Backstamp: Doulton

Doulton Number	Size	Colour	Height	Intro.	Discon.	Current Market Value U.K. £	U.S. $	Can. $
D5610	Large	Red hair	7 1/2"	1937	1942	1,350.00	4,300.00	4,000.00

VARIATION No. 2: Colourway — Brown hair
Handle — Plain brown

Doulton Number	Size	Colour	Height	Intro.	Discon.	Current Market Value		
						U.K. £	U.S. $	Can. $
D5610	Large	Brown hair	7 1/2"	c. 1937	1942	1,450.00	3,500.00	3,200.00

VARIATION No. 3: Colourway — White hair
Handle — Multi-coloured

Doulton Number	Size	Colour	Height	Intro.	Discon.	Current Market Value		
						U.K. £	U.S. $	Can. $
D6322	Large	White hair	7 1/2"	1951	1955	600.00	1,500.00	1,350.00

Note: A black-haired example exists on the market; however, its authencity as a factory release has not yet been determined.

THE CLOWN

THE CIRCUS,
ONE OF FOUR

STYLE TWO: CLOWN WITH HAT

Royal Doulton®
THE CLOWN
D 6834
Modelled by

Stanley James Taylor

© 1988 ROYAL DOULTON

Designer: Stanley J. Taylor
Handle: Gloved hand touching cap
Colourway: Green cap; yellow bow tie with black spots; red nose and mouth

Backstamp: Doulton

Doulton Number	Size	Backstamp	Height	Intro.	Discon.	Current Market Value U.K. £	U.S. $	Can. $
D6834	Large	Doulton	6 1/2"	1989	Current	69.95	175.00	275.00

THE COLLECTOR

THE COLLECTING WORLD,
ONE OF THREE

These jugs were commissioned by Kevin Francis Ceramics Ltd. (KFC). The large size was issued in 1988 in a special edition of 5,000 pieces, and the small size was issued in 1991 in a special edition of 1,500 pieces. Note the Kevin Francis characteristic of the left-handed jug.

Original Concept by Kevin Pearson and Geoff Blower

Royal Doulton•
THE COLLECTOR
D 6796
Modelled by
Stanley James Taylor
A Special Edition of 5000
From "The Collecting World" series
Produced by Royal Doulton
for Kevin Francis Ceramics
© 1987 ROYAL DOULTON
AND KEVIN FRANCIS CERAMICS

Designer: Stanley J. Taylor
Handle: A hand holding a Mephistopheles jug
Colourway: Black hat; dark green jacket; tan shirt

Backstamp: Doulton / Kevin Francis

Doulton Number	Size	Backstamp	Height	Intro.	Discon.	Current Market Value U.K. £	U.S. $	Can. $
D6796	Large	Doulton/KFC	7"	1988	Sp. ed.	85.00	300.00	325.00
D6906	Small	Doulton/KFC	4"	1991	Sp. ed.	65.00	175.00	195.00

CONFUCIUS

FLAMBÉ SERIES,
ONE OF TWO

Issued in a limited edition of 1,750, this is the second jug to be decorated in flambé.

Designer: Robert Tabbenor
Handle: Yin and Yang symbol and book of his
teachings, "The Analects"
Colourway: Flambé

Backstamp: Doulton

Doulton Number	Size	Backstamp	Height	Intro.	Discon.	Current Market Value		
						U.K. £	U.S. $	Can. $
D7003	Large	Doulton	7"	1995	Ltd. ed.	125.00	335.00	—

THE COOK AND THE CHESHIRE CAT

These are two characters from Lewis Carroll's *Alice's Adventures in Wonderland*.

Designer: William K. Harper
Handle: A Cheshire cat
Colourway: White mob cap trimmed with a blue bow

Backstamp: Doulton

Doulton Number	Size	Backstamp	Height	Intro.	Discon.	Current Market Value U.K. £	U.S. $	Can. $
D6842	Large	Doulton	7"	1990	1991	100.00	275.00	295.00

CYRANO DE BERGERAC

Designer: David Biggs
Handle: Sword, quill and letter
Colourway: Maroon jacket; white collar; black hat; white plume

Backstamp: Doulton

Doulton Number	Size	Backstamp	Height	Intro.	Discon.	Current Market Value		
						U.K. £	U.S. $	Can. $
D7004	Large	Doulton	7"	1995	Current	69.95	185.00	295.00

D'ARTAGNAN

THE THREE MUSKETEERS, ONE OF FOUR,
NOW PART OF THE CHARACTERS FROM LITERATURE, ONE OF 11

A character in Alexandre Dumas's lively 19th-century fiction, D'Artagnan came to Paris to join the celebrated band of Three Musketeers and share their adventures.

Designer: Stanley J. Taylor
Handle: An extension of the feathers
with a fleur-de-lis and sword
at the base
Colourway: Black hat trimmed with white
feathers; white lace collar

Backstamp: Doulton

Doulton Number	Size	Backstamp	Height	Intro.	Discon.	Current Market Value		
						U.K. £	U.S. $	Can. $
D6691	Large	Doulton	7 1/2"	1982	Current	59.95	125.00	175.00
D6764	Small	Doulton	4"	1987	Current	29.95	69.50	100.00
D6765	Miniature	Doulton	2 1/2"	1987	1991	45.00	110.00	125.00

DAVID COPPERFIELD

CHARLES DICKENS COMMEMORATIVE SET,
DICKENS TINIES, ONE OF 12

David Copperfield is the orphan protagonist in Dickens's novel, *David Copperfield*.

The 12 jugs in this set were issued to commemorate the 170th anniversary of the birth of Charles Dickens, and each came with a certificate of authenticity. A mahogany display shelf completes the set. The set was first sold by Lawleys By Post in the U.K. from 1982 to 1988, and from 1985 in North America and Australia.

David Copperfield
D.6680

Designer: Michael Abberley
Handle: Plain
Colourway: Dark blue and black

Backstamp: Doulton

Doulton Number	Size	Backstamp		Height	Intro.	Discon.	Current Market Value		
							U.K. £	U.S. $	Can. $
D6680	Tiny	Doulton	1 1/2"		1982	1989	40.00	60.00	70.00
		Display stand for 12 tinies					65.00	45.00	50.00

DAVY CROCKETT AND SANTA ANNA

THE ANTAGONISTS' COLLECTION (TWO-FACED JUG),
ONE OF FOUR

Davy Crockett (1786-1836) was a hunter and expert marksman, as well as a gregarious drinker. Antonio Lopez de Santa Anna (1795-1876) was a Mexican general who led troops on many missions into the U.S. He was finally defeated in Texas in 1837 and jailed for a year.

This jug was issued in 1985 in a limited edition of 9,500 pieces.

Designer: Michael Abberley
Handle: Crocket—Alamo, a horn, mission wall
Santa Anna—Sword, mission wall
Colourway: Yellow and brown

Royal Doulton
'The Antagonists'
Collection
D.6729
The Battle of the Alamo 1836
Davy Crockett/Antonio Lopez de Santa Anna
Hand made and Hand decorated
Designed by Michael Abberley

© ROYAL DOULTON (U.K.) 1984
Worldwide Limited Edition of 9,500
This is Number 393

Backstamp: Doulton

Doulton Number	Size	Backstamp	Height	Intro.	Discon.	Current Market Value U.K. £	U.S. $	Can. $
D6729	Large	Doulton	7"	1985	Ltd. ed.	95.00	225.00	235.00

DENNIS THE MENACE

Dennis the Menace is a cartoon character from the U.K. comic magazine, *The Beano*. At the present time, this jug is available exclusively in the U.K. market.

Designer: Simon Ward
Handle: A bag of peas, pea shooter, Gnasher the dog
Colourway: Red; black and green

Backstamp: Doulton

Doulton Number	Size	Backstamp	Height	Intro.	Discon.	Current Market Value U.K. £	U.S. $	Can. $
D7005	Large	Doulton	7"	1995	Current	69.95	—	—

DESPERATE DAN

Desperate Dan is a cartoon character from the U.K. comic "The Dandy." At the present time, this jug is available exclusively in the U.K. market.

Designer: Simon Ward
Handle: A cow pie, cactus and jug of Owl Hoot juice
Colourway: Red shirt; black vest; blue scarf; brown and black hat

Backstamp: Doulton

Doulton Number	Size	Backstamp	Height	Intro.	Discon.	Current Market Value U.K. £	U.S. $	Can. $
D7006	Large	Doulton	7"	1995	Current	69.95	—	—

DICK TURPIN

Dick Turpin (1705-1739) joined forces with fellow highwayman Tom King, whom he accidently shot. Before he died King betrayed him. Dick Turpin was hanged in 1739 for the murder of an Epping Forest gamekeeper.

The first style of the Dick Turpin jug has the mask up on the brim of the tricorn, and a pistol forms the handle. All of the sizes should have "R.T." inscribed on the pistol grip; however, it may be more obvious on certain jugs due to the casting variations. There is no premium value whether or not the "R.T." inscription is visible.

The tiny version was one of a set of six issued in 1994, in a limited edition of 2,500, to celebrate the diamond anniversary of the first character jug.

STYLE ONE: HANDLE — A PISTOL

Designer:	Charles Noke / Harry Fenton — Large	Backstamps:	A.	Doulton
	William K. Harper — Tiny		B.	Doulton / Bentalls /
Handle:	Pistol			Souvenir From Bentalls 1936
Colourway:	Brown hat; black mask up; green coat; white cravat			

Doulton Number	Size	Backstamp	Height	Intro.	Discon.	Current Market Value U.K. £	U.S. $	Can. $
D5485	Large	Doulton	6 1/2"	1935	1960	95.00	225.00	250.00
D5618	Small	Doulton	3 1/2"	1936	1960	55.00	100.00	110.00
D5618	Small	Doulton/Bentalls	3 1/2"	1936	1936	375.00	1,000.00	1,000.00
D6128	Miniature	Doulton	2 1/4"	1940	1960	45.00	90.00	100.00
D6951	Tiny	Doulton	1 1/2"	1994	Ltd. ed. (1994)	45.00	90.00	100.00

Dick Turpin Derivative

Doulton Number	Item	Height	Intro.	Discon.	Current Market Value U.K. £	U.S. $	Can. $
D5601	Match stand/ashtray	3"	1936	1960	95.00	225.00	240.00

DICK TURPIN

This second style of Dick Turpin has the mask covering the eyes, and the handle depicts a horse's head and neck.

STYLE TWO: HANDLE — NECK AND HEAD OF HORSE

Dick Turpin
D 6528
COPR 1959
DOULTON & CO LIMITED
Rd No 893841
Rd No 39649
Rd No 8313
Rd No 420/59

Designer: David Biggs
Handle: Head and neck of a horse
Colourway: Green tricorn; black mask over the eyes; red jacket

Backstamp: Doulton

Doulton Number	Size	Backstamp	Height	Intro.	Discon.	Current Market Value		
						U.K. £	U.S. $	Can. $
D6528	Large	Doulton	7"	1960	1981	75.00	160.00	175.00
D6535	Small	Doulton	3 3/4"	1960	1981	50.00	85.00	100.00
D6542	Miniature	Doulton	2 1/4"	1960	1981	50.00	85.00	100.00

DICK WHITTINGTON

The first Dick Whittington jug was styled on the character of a poor orphan boy who was employed in a London kitchen, as described in a play dated 1605. He gave his cat to his employer to sell to earn money, but then ran away to escape his evil employer's cook who mistreated him. The Bow Bells rang as he fled and seemed to say, "Turn back, Whittington, Lord Mayor of London." He obeyed and found that his cat had fetched a huge sum, making him a wealthy man.

Designer: Geoff Blower
Handle: A stick and handkerchief
Colourway: Dark green cap and robes

Backstamp: Doulton

Doulton Number	Size	Backstamp	Height	Intro.	Discon.	Current Market Value		
						U.K. £	U.S. $	Can. $
D6375	Large	Doulton	6 1/2"	1953	1960	250.00	600.00	650.00

DICK WHITTINGTON, LORD MAYOR OF LONDON

Richard Whittington (1358-1423), in actual fact, made his fortune as a textile dealer. He entered London politics as a councilman and rose to become the Lord Mayor of London in 1397, an office he held three times.

This jug was commissioned by the Guild of Specialist China and Glass Retailers and issued in 1989 in a limited edition of 5,000 pieces.

Designer: William K. Harper

Handle: Handle is of a signpost to London, the Bow Bells are above the signpost and a sack of gold is at the base

Colourway: Blue tricorn hat trimmed with white feathers; blue coat trimmed with white fur; yellow chain of office

Backstamp: Doulton/Guild

Doulton Number	Size	Backstamp	Height	Intro.	Discon.	Current Market Value		
						U.K. £	U.S. $	Can. $
D6846	Large	Doulton/Guild	7 1/2"	1989	Ltd. ed. (1991)	75.00	275.00	295.00

DOC HOLLIDAY

THE WILD WEST COLLECTION,
ONE OF SIX

The son of a lawyer, John Henry Holliday (1852-1887) worked as a dentist in Baltimore, Maryland. At the age of 20 he learned he had tuberculosis and moved west to a warmer climate to prolong his life. He became adept at using firearms and the bowie knife and became known for his wild gambling, brawls and shootouts. He survived the famous gunfight at the O.K. Corral, but died in a sanatorium at age 35.

Designer: Stanley J. Taylor
Handle: Pistol in a holster and dice
Colourway: Black and grey hat; black coat

Backstamp: Doulton

Doulton Number	Size	Backstamp	Height	Intro.	Discon.	Current Market Value		
						U.K. £	U.S. $	Can. $
D6731	Mid	Doulton	5 1/2"	1985	1989	60.00	40.00	150.00

DON QUIXOTE

CHARACTERS FROM LITERATURE, ONE OF 11

Don Quixote is the hero of the novel by Cervantes, a satirical parody of the chivalrous knight. Don Quixote leads a life of adventure, capturing many hearts along the way.

The helmet colour of the jugs varies from dark grey to light grey, with no difference in value.

"Don Quixote".
D 6455
COPR 1956
DOULTON & CO LIMITED
Rd Nº 881509
Rd Nº 35705
Rd Nº 7560
Rd Nº 332 56

Designer: Geoff Blower
Handle: A feather with a shield at the base
Colourway: Blue-grey helmet; dark green robes

Backstamp: Doulton

Doulton Number	Size	Backstamp	Height	Intro.	Discon.	Current Market Value		
						U.K. £	U.S. $	Can. $
D6455	Large	Doulton	7 1/4"	1957	1991	75.00	175.00	195.00
D6460	Small	Doulton	3 1/4"	1957	1991	50.00	100.00	115.00
D6511	Miniature	Doulton	2 1/2"	1960	1991	45.00	90.00	100.00

DRAKE

Sir Francis Drake (1540-1596) was an English navigator and admiral. He was Queen Elizabeth I's right hand against the Spanish, going on many plundering expeditions in the Spanish West Indies. On one of these voyages, between 1577 and 1580, Drake became the first Englishman to sail around the world. He also repelled the Spanish Armada sent to invade England.

STYLE ONE: WITHOUT HAT

VARIATION No. 1: Colourway - White ruff; red-brown coat
The raised lettering "Sir Francis Drake" on the back of the coat is painted over

REGISTRATION
APPLIED FOR

Designer: Harry Fenton
Handle: Plain
Colourway: White ruff; red-brown coat

Backstamp: Doulton

Doulton Number	Size	Backstamp	Height	Intro.	Discon.	Current Market Value U.K. £	U.S. $	Can. $
D6115	Large	Doulton	5 3/4"	1940	1941	1,500.00	4,500.00	4,000.00

VARIATION No. 2: Colourway — White ruff; green coat
The raised lettering "Sir Francis Drake" on the back of the coat is painted white, highlighting the name

"Drake."
Rᵈ Nº838085.

Doulton Number	Size	Backstamp	Height	Intro.	Discon.	Current Market Value		
						U.K. £	U.S. $	Can. $
D6115	Large	Doulton	5 3/4"	1940	1941		Extremely rare	

DRACE

STYLE TWO: WITH HAT

Designer: Harry Fenton
Handle: Rope
Colourway: Brown hat; green robes; white ruff;
brown drum at back of handle alongside ruff

Backstamp: Doulton

Doulton Number	Size	Backstamp	Height	Intro.	Discon.	Current Market Value U.K. £	U.S. $	Can. $
D6115	Large	Doulton	5 3/4"	1940	1960	95.00	225.00	250.00
D6174	Small	Doulton	3 1/4"	1941	1960	60.00	110.00	125.00

DUKE OF WELLINGTON

THE GREAT GENERALS COLLECTION,
ONE OF THREE

Arthur Wellesley (1769-1852), first Duke of Wellington, was a British general and statesman. He led the British forces in the defeat of Napoleon at Waterloo in 1815 and also served as Prime Minister from 1828 to 1830.

This jug was commissioned by UK International Ceramics Ltd., in a special edition. The backstamp states that 5,000 were made, but according to UK International Ceramics, only 3,500 were made available for sale.

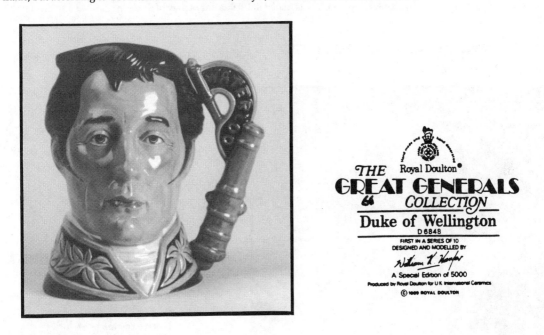

Designer: William K. Harper
Handle: Cannon above a banner reading "Waterloo"
Colourway: Blue and gold

Backstamp: Doulton/UK International Ceramics

Doulton Number	Size	Backstamp	Height	Intro.	Discon.	Current Market Value U.K. £	U.S. $	Can. $
D6848	Large	Doulton/UK Int'l	7 1/4"	1989	Sp. ed.	120.00	225.00	250.00

Note: For Wellington see page 468.

EARL MOUNTBATTEN OF BURMA

HEROIC LEADERS,
ONE OF THREE

A British naval and military leader, Louis Francis Albert Victor Nicholas Mountbatten (1900-1979) was the last viceroy of India. Mountbatten was governor general of the Dominion of India from 1947 to 1948, relinquishing power to native rule in 1948. Upon his retirement from the navy in 1959, he became the principal military adviser to the Ministry of Defence. He was killed when a bomb exploded his fishing boat off the coast of Ireland.

This jug was commissioned by Lawleys By Post. It was issued in 1989 as one of a set of three, in a limited edition of 9,500 pieces.

STYLE ONE: HANDLE — NAVAL ENSIGN

Designer: Stanley J. Taylor
Handle: Naval ensign
Colourway: White naval uniform trimmed with gold

Backstamp: Doulton

Doulton Number	Size	Backstamp	Height	Intro.	Discon.	Current Market Value U.K. £	U.S. $	Can. $
D6851	Small	Doulton	3 1/4"	1990	Ltd. ed. (1991)	95.00	190.00	210.00

EARL MOUNTBATTEN OF BURMA

This was the first large-size character jug to be commissioned by the Royal Doulton International Collectors Club and was issued in a limited edition of 5,000 jugs.

STYLE TWO: HANDLE — ANCHOR AND INTERTWINED ROPE

Designer: Stanley J. Taylor
Handle: Anchor and intertwined rope
Colourway: Yellow, black and white

Backstamp: Doulton/Royal Doulton International Collectors Club

Doulton Number	Size	Backstamp	Height	Intro.	Discon.	Current Market Value U.K. £	U.S. $	Can. $
D6944	Large	Doulton/RDICC	7"	1993	Ltd. ed.	150.00	300.00	325.00

THE ELEPHANT TRAINER

THE CIRCUS,
ONE OF FOUR

Royal Doulton®
THE ELEPHANT TRAINER
D 6841
Modelled by
Stanley James Taylor
© 1989 ROYAL DOULTON

BACKSTAMP A

Designer: Stanley J. Taylor
Handle: Head of an elephant
Colourway: Orange turban; black coat trimmed
with green and yellow

Backstamps A. Doulton
General issue, 1990.
B. Doulton / The Higbee Company /
To commemorate the Fourth Anniversary of the opening of The Royal Doulton Room
The Higbee Company, Cleveland, Ohio, U.S.A. Commissioned by the Higbee Company,
Cleveland, Ohio. Issued in 1989 in a limited edition of 250 pieces.
C. Doulton/Royal Doulton Rooms USA Strawbridge and Clothier, Hornes, Holmes /
To commemorate the anniversary of the opening of the Royal Doulton Rooms in the
United States of America. Issued in a limited edition of 250.

Doulton Number	Size	Backstamp	Height	Intro.	Discon.	Current Market Value U.K. £	U.S. $	Can. $
D6841	Large	Doulton	7"	1990	Current	95.00	275.00	300.00
D6856	Large	Higbee	7"	1989	Ltd. ed.	225.00	350.00	375.00
D6857	Large	Strawbridge	7"	1989	Ltd. ed.	225.00	350.00	375.00

ELF

CHRISTMAS MINIATURES SERIES,
ONE OF SIX

The Elf miniature character jug was specially commissioned for the U.S. market. It was designed to compliment the miniature Caroler (D7007), Mrs. Claus (D6922), Santa Claus (D6900) and Snowman (D6972). Although commissioned for the U.S. market, the jug is also available in other countries through the Royal Doulton International Collectors Club.

Royal Doulton®
ELF
D 6942
© 1993 ROYAL DOULTON

Designer: William K. Harper
Handle: Holly Wreath
Colourway: Green

Backstamp: Doulton

Doulton Number	Size	Backstamp	Height	Intro.	Discon.	Current Market Value U.K. £	U.S. $	Can. $
D6942	Miniature	Doulton	2 3/4"	1993	Current	50.00	85.00	100.00

ELVIS PRESLEY

THE CELEBRITY COLLECTION

PROTOTYPE

Elvis Aaron Presley (1935-1977), the "King of Rock 'n' Roll," was the most popular artist in the history of American rock music. After his debut in 1955, he appeared in 33 films, as well as on numerous albums. This jug was not issued due to copyright problems, and while at least two prototypes are known to exist, none are known to be in private collections.

Designer: Stanley J. Taylor
Handle: Guitar and strap
Colourway: Black hair; white shirt with gold trim

Backstamp: Doulton

Doulton Number	Size	Backstamp	Height	Intro.	Discon.	Current Market Value U.K. £	U.S. $	Can. $
D6730	Large	Doulton	7 1/4"	1987	1987		Extremely rare	

THE ENGINE DRIVER

JOURNEY THROUGH BRITAIN,
ONE OF FOUR

Each jug in the Journey Through Britain series was given a specially designed backstamp relating to the subject of the jug. The backstamp on the Engine Driver has the wording within the outline of a locomotive engine. It was issued through Lawleys By Post in a limited edition of 5,000 pieces.

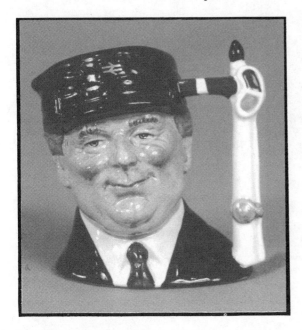

Designer: Stanley J. Taylor	**Backstamp:** Doulton
Handle: A railway signal	
Colourway: Black cap and coat; white shirt	

Doulton Number	Size	Backstamp	Height	Intro.	Discon.	Current Market Value U.K. £	U.S. $	Can. $
D6823	Small	Doulton	4"	1988	Ltd. ed. (1991)	75.00	225.00	235.00

EVERTON (FOOTBALL CLUB)

THE FOOTBALL SUPPORTERS,
ONE OF NINE

Royal Doulton®
FOOTBALL SUPPORTER'S
CHARACTER JUG.
D 6926
Modelled by
Stanley James Taylor
© 1992 ROYAL DOULTON
¨EVERTON¨

Designer: Stanley J. Taylor
Handle: Team coloured scarf
Colourway: Blue and white uniform

Backstamp: Doulton

Doulton Number	Size	Backstamp	Height	Intro.	Discon.	Current Market Value U.K. £	U.S. $	Can. $
D6926	Mid	Doulton	5"	1992	Current	32.50	—	—

FAGIN

CHARLES DICKENS COMMEMORATIVE SET,
DICKENS TINIES, ONE OF 12

In Dickens's novel, *Oliver Twist*, Fagin leads a band of child thieves.

The 12 jugs in this set were issued to commemorate the 170th anniversary of the birth of Charles Dickens, and each came with a certificate of authenticity. A mahogany display shelf completes the set. The set was first sold by Lawleys By Post in the U.K. from 1982 to 1988, and from 1985 in North America and Australia.

Fagin
D. 6679

Designer: Robert Tabbenor
Handle: Plain
Colourway: Orange and brown

Backstamp: Doulton

Doulton Number	Size	Backstamp	Height	Intro.	Discon.	Current Market Value U.K. £	Current Market Value U.S. $	Current Market Value Can. $
D6679	Tiny	Doulton	1 1/2"	1982	1989	40.00	85.00	95.00
		Display stand for 12 tinies				65.00	45.00	50.00

THE FALCONER

Once called the sport of kings, falconry is the art of training birds of prey for the hunt. The sport began in China more than 3,000 years ago and still enjoys popularity in Europe and North America.

VARIATION No. 1: Colourway — Green with black and white striped fur hat; green coat; grey and white falcon

Designer: Max Henk
Handle: A falcon
Colourway: Green with black and white striped fur hat; green coat; grey and white falcon

The Falconer
D 6540
COPR 1959
DOULTON & CO LIMITED
Rd No 893846
Rd No 39654
Rd No 8318
Rd No 415/59
Backstamp: Doulton

Doulton Number	Size	Backstamp	Height	Intro.	Discon.	Current Market Value U.K. £	U.S. $	Can. $
D6533	Large	Doulton	7 1/2"	1960	1991	70.00	160.00	175.00
D6540	Small	Doulton	3 3/4"	1960	1991	40.00	100.00	115.00
D6547	Miniature	Doulton	2 3/4"	1960	1991	40.00	75.00	90.00

VARIATION No. 2: Colourway — Dark green and brown striped fur hat; dark brown coat; ginger beard; brown falcon

Backstamp: Doulton/Joseph Horne Company /
Celebrating the opening of The Royal Doulton Room, Hornes, Pittsburgh, Pennsylvania, U.S.A.
Specially commissioned from Royal Doulton by the Joseph Horne Company, Pittsburgh, Pennsylvania,
U.S.A. Issued in 1987 in a limited edition of 250 pieces.

Doulton Number	Size	Backstamp	Height	Intro.	Discon.	Current Market Value U.K. £	U.S. $	Can. $
D6798	Large	Doulton/Horne	7 1/2"	1987	Ltd. ed.	225.00	400.00	400.00

VARIATION No. 3:   Colourway — Black with maroon and white striped fur hat; red-brown coat; brown falcon

Royal Doulton®
THE FALCONER
D 8800
Modelled by

© 1959 ROYAL DOULTON
NEW COLOURWAY 1987
SPECIAL COMMISSION 1000
PETER JONES COLLECTION
LEEDS AND WAKEFIELD

Backstamp: Doulton / Peter Jones China Ltd /
New Colourway 1987 Special Commission 1000 Peter Jones Collection Leeds and Wakefield
Commissioned by Peter Jones China Ltd, Leeds and Wakefield, England. Issued in 1987 in a
special edition of 1,000 pieces.

Doulton Number	Size	Backstamp	Height	Intro.	Discon.	Current Market Value		
						U.K. £	U.S. $	Can. $
D6800	Large	Doulton/Jones	7 1/2"	1987	Sp. ed.	85.00	275.00	295.00

FALSTAFF

CHARACTERS FROM LITERATURE,
ONE OF 11

Sir John Falstaff is a fat, good-humoured braggart who figures in Shakespeare's *Henry IV* and *The Merry Wives of Windsor*. A trial piece exists in a red and dark green colourway, but it was not released for sale.

VARIATION No. 1: Colourway — Rose tunic; black hat trimmed with rose plumes; grey beard

Falstaff
D 6287
COPR 1949
DOULTON & CO LIMITED

Designer: Harry Fenton
Handle: Plain
Colourway: Rose tunic; black hat trimmed with rose plumes; grey beard

Backstamp: Doulton

Doulton Number	Size	Backstamp	Height	Intro.	Discon.	Current Market Value U.K. £	U.S. $	Can. $
D6287	Large	Doulton	6"	1950	Current	49.95	150.00	175.00
D6385	Small	Doulton	3 1/2"	1950	Current	25.00	82.50	100.00
D6519	Miniature	Doulton	2 1/2"	1960	1991	35.00	70.00	85.00

VARIATION No. 2:
Colourway — Yellow tunic; black hat trimmed with yellow plumes; brown beard

Produced Exclusively for U.K. Fairs Ltd. in a Special Edition of 1500

Royal Doulton®
FALSTAFF
D 6795
Modelled by

H. FENTON

© 1949 ROYAL DOULTON
NEW COLOURWAY 1987

Backstamp: Doulton/U.K. Fairs Ltd.
Produced exclusively for U.K. Fairs Ltd. in a special edition of 1,500.

Doulton Number	Size	Backstamp	Height	Intro.	Discon.	Current Market Value U.K. £	U.S. $	Can. $
D6797	Large	Doulton/ U.K. Fairs	6"	1987	Sp. ed.	95.00	225.00	250.00

Falstaff Derivatives

Doulton Number	Item	Height	Intro.	Discon.	Current Market Value U.K. £	U.S. $	Can. $
D6385	Table lighter	4 1/2"	1958	1973	150.00	200.00	225.00
D6854	Teapot	Unknown	1989	1991	100.00	250.00	275.00

FARMER JOHN

STYLE ONE: HANDLE — INSIDE JUG

"Farmer John".
Rᵈ N° 820500.
REGᵈIN AUSTRALIA
Coleman's Compliments

BACKSTAMP B

Designer: Charles Noke
Handle: Brown handle set within the neck of the jug
Colourway: Brown

Backstamps: A. Doulton
B. Doulton/Coleman's/ Coleman's Compliments

Doulton Number	Size	Backstamp	Height	Intro.	Discon.	Current Market Value U.K. £	U.S. $	Can. $
D5788	Large	Doulton	6 1/2"	1938	1960	100.00	250.00	275.00
D5788	Large	Doulton/Coleman's	6 1/2"	1938	1938	1,000.00	2,200.00	2,200.00
D5789	Small	Doulton	3 1/4"	1938	1960	65.00	140.00	150.00

FARMER JOHN

STYLE TWO: HANDLE — OUTSIDE JUG

Designer: Charles Noke
Handle: Brown handle set at the top of the neck.
Colourway: Brown

Backstamp: Doulton

Doulton Number	Size	Backstamp	Height	Intro.	Discon.	Current Market Value U.K. £	U.S. $	Can. $
D5788	Large	Doulton	6 1/2"	1938	1960	95.00	225.00	250.00
D5789	Small	Doulton	3 1/4"	1938	1960	60.00	110.00	125.00

Farmer John Derivative

Doulton Number	Item	Height	Intro.	Discon.	Current Market Value U.K. £	U.S. $	Can. $
D6007	Ash bowl	3"	1939	1960	100.00	175.00	195.00

FAT BOY

Another wonderful Dickens's character, Joe, the Fat Boy, was the lazy glutton who worked as servant to Mr. Wardle in *The Pickwick Papers*.

Designer: Leslie Harradine/Harry Fenton **Backstamp:** Doulton
Handle: Plain
Colourway: Blue shirt; white scarf

Doulton Number	Size	Backstamp	Height	Intro.	Discon.	Current Market Value U.K. £	U.S. $	Can. $
D5840	Mid	Doulton	5"	1938	1948	135.00	350.00	375.00
D5840	Small	Doulton	4"	1948	1960	70.00	200.00	225.00
D6139	Miniature	Doulton	2 1/2"	1940	1960	55.00	110.00	125.00
D6142	Tiny	Doulton	1 1/2"	1940	1960	75.00	160.00	175.00

Fat Boy Derivative

Doulton Number	Item	Height	Intro.	Discon.	Current Market Value U.K. £	U.S. $	Can. $
M59	Napkin ring	3 1/2"	1935	1939	225.00	750.00	750.00

FIELD MARSHALL MONTGOMERY

Issued for the 50th anniversary of Montgomery's victory over Rommel in North Africa in 1942, this jug was produced in a limited edition of 2,500 pieces worldwide.

Royal Doulton®

FIELD MARSHAL

MONTGOMERY

D 6908

The El Alamein Edition
• • •
A Limited Edition of 2,500
MODELLED BY

Stanley James Taylor.

THIS IS No. 1930

© 1991 ROYAL DOULTON

Designer: Stanley J. Taylor
Handle: Baton, oak leaves, "El Alamein"
Colourway: Black beret; khaki uniform; purple and cream baton

Backstamp: Doulton

Doulton Number	Size	Backstamp	Height	Intro.	Discon.	Current Market Value U.K. £	U.S. $	Can. $
D6908	Large	Doulton	6 1/2"	1992	Ltd. ed.	100.00	275.00	300.00

Note: For Monty see page 333. For Viscount Montgomery of Alamein see page 464.

THE FIREMAN

Launched exclusively by Griffith Pottery House in 1983, The Fireman jug was then released into the general range in 1984. Varieties of the handle exist, with the nozzle ranging from dark orange to light yellow, but there is no premium value for these colourway variations.

An error in this jug exists. The red background of the helmet badge was not applied during painting, resulting in a white badge. This curiousity piece has very little premium value.

STYLE ONE: HANDLE — NOZZLE OF FIRE HOSE

Royal Doulton
The Fireman
D 6697
Hand made and Hand decorated
Designed by Jerry D. Griffith
Modelled by Robert Tabbenor
ⓒ ROYAL DOULTON
TABLEWARE LTD 1982

BACKSTAMP C

Designer: Robert Tabbenor
Handle: Nozzle of fire hose
Colourway: Black, brown and red helmet badge

Backstamps: A. Doulton/Hand made and Hand decorated
No credits
B. Doulton/Hand made and Hand decorated
Modelled by Robert Tabbenor
C. Doulton/Hand made and Hand decorated
Designed by Jerry D. Griffith/Modelled by
Robert Tabbenor

Doulton Number	Size	Backstamp	Height	Intro.	Discon.	Current Market Value U.K. £	U.S. $	Can. $
D6697	Large	A. Doulton	7 1/4"	1984	1991	85.00	225.00	250.00
D6697	Large	B. Doulton	7 1/4"	1984	1991	75.00	225.00	250.00
D6697	Large	C. Doulton	7 1/4"	1983	1991	75.00	225.00	250.00

THE FIREMAN

JOURNEY THROUGH BRITAIN,
ONE OF FOUR

As with the other pieces in this series, the wording of the backstamp is contained within a design connected to the subject. This design is a coiled hose. Issued through Lawleys By Post in 1988, this jug was produced in a limited edition of 5,000 pieces.

STYLE TWO: HANDLE — AXE AND FIRE HOSE

Designer: Stanley J. Taylor
Handle: An axe and fire hose
Colourway: Yellow helmet; dark blue jacket

Backstamp: Doulton

Doulton Number	Size	Backstamp	Height	Intro.	Discon.	Current Market Value U.K. £	U.S. $	Can. $
D6839	Small	Doulton	4 1/4"	1989	Ltd. ed. (1991)	75.00	200.00	215.00

THE FORTUNE TELLER

STYLE ONE: HANDLE — SIGNS OF THE ZODIAC

The Fortune Teller
D.6497
COPR 1958
DOULTON & CO LIMITED
Rd No 889568
Rd No 38224
Rd No 8034
Rd No 425,58

Designer: Garry Sharpe
Handle: Zodiac design
Colourway: Green scarf around head; black shawl;
purple handle

Backstamp: Doulton

Doulton Number	Size	Backstamp	Height	Intro.	Discon.	Current Market Value U.K. £	U.S. $	Can. $
D6497	Large	Doulton	6 3/4"	1959	1967	300.00	850.00	850.00
D6503	Small	Doulton	3 3/4"	1959	1967	225.00	500.00	500.00
D6523	Miniature	Doulton	2 1/2"	1960	1967	250.00	525.00	525.00

THE FORTUNE TELLER

Beginning in 1991, one jug was selected as the character jug of the year, produced for one year only and issued with a certificate of authenticity. The Fortune Teller was the character jug of the year for 1991.

STYLE TWO: HANDLE — TAROT CARDS

Royal Doulton®
CHARACTER JUG OF THE YEAR
THE FORTUNE TELLER
D 6874
Modelled by

Stanley James Taylor

This special edition will only
be available during the year
1991
© 1990 ROYAL DOULTON

Designer: Stanley J. Taylor
Handle: Bandana and tarot cards
Colourway: Orange polka-dot bandana;
light blue shirt

Backstamp: Doulton/Character Jug of the Year

Doulton Number	Size	Backstamp	Height	Intro.	Discon.	Current Market Value		
						U.K. £	**U.S. $**	**Can. $**
D6874	Large	Jug of the Year	7"	1991	1991	125.00	300.00	325.00

FRANCIS ROSSI

STATUS QUO,
ONE OF TWO

Produced in a limited edition of 2,500 pieces, the Francis Rossi jug was issued in conjunction with a jug for Rick Parfitt, both frontmen for Status Quo, a U.K. band. The jug handle of the Parfitt jug is on the left, and the handle is on the right on the Rossi jug, so they may be displayed as a pair.

Designer:	Martyn C. R. Alcock	**Backstamp:** Doulton
Handle:	Green guitar	Signed "Francis Rossi" and
Colourway:	Black, white and brown	Phantom Music Ltd.

Doulton Number	Size	Backstamp	Height	Intro.	Discon.	Current Market Value U.K. £	U.S. $	Can. $
D6961	Small	Doulton	5"	1993	Ltd. ed.	50.00	75.00	100.00

FRIAR TUCK

Fat and jolly and fond of drink, Friar Tuck joined the legendary Robin Hood and his band of rogues in Sherwood Forest as they robbed the rich to feed the poor in rural England.

Friar Tuck.
COPR.1950.
DOULTON &CO.LIMITED.
Rᵈ Nᵒ 862066.
Rᵈ Nᵖ 28162.
Rᵈ Nᵖ 6206.
Rᵈ Nᵒ 95/50.

Designer: Harry Fenton
Handle: Tree trunk
Colourway: Light and dark brown robes;
green oak leaves

Backstamp: Doulton

Doulton Number	Size	Backstamp	Height	Intro.	Discon.	Current Market Value		
						U.K. £	U.S. $	Can. $
D6321	Large	Doulton	7"	1951	1960	250.00	650.00	675.00

GAOLER

CHARACTERS FROM WILLIAMSBURG,
ONE OF EIGHT

Character Jugs from Williamsburg®

Gaoler
D 6 5 7 0
COPR 1962
DOULTON & CO LIMITED
Rd No 906340
Rd No 43447
Rd No 9226
Rd No 284/62

Designer: David Biggs
Handle: Two keys
Colourway: Black tricorn; white shirt; red vest

Backstamp: Doulton

Doulton Number	Size	Backstamp	Height	Intro.	Discon.	Current Market Value		
						U.K. £	U.S. $	Can. $
D6570	Large	Doulton	7"	1963	1983	85.00	160.00	175.00
D6577	Small	Doulton	3 3/4"	1963	1983	55.00	110.00	125.00
D6584	Miniature	Doulton	2 3/4"	1963	1983	50.00	100.00	115.00

THE GARDENER

STYLE ONE: HANDLE — A SPADE AND VEGETABLES

VARIATION No. 1: Colourway — Red scarf; red striped shirt; brown hat

The Gardener
D.6630
©DOULTON & CO. LIMITED 1972
REGISTRATION APPLIED FOR

Designer: David Biggs
Handle: A spade with carrots and a marrow at the base
Colourway: Red scarf; red striped shirt; brown hat
Backstamp: Doulton

Doulton Number	Size	Backstamp	Height	Intro.	Discon.	Current Market Value U.K. £	U.S. $	Can. $
D6630	Large	Doulton	7 3/4"	1971	1971	Extremely rare		

VARIATION No. 2: Colourway — Yellow scarf; white shirt; light brown hat

Doulton Number	Size	Backstamp	Height	Intro.	Discon.	Current Market Value U.K. £	U.S. $	Can. $
D6630	Large	Doulton	7 3/4"	1973	1981	150.00	275.00	300.00
D6634	Small	Doulton	4"	1973	1981	100.00	125.00	135.00
D6638	Miniature	Doulton	2 3/4"	1973	1981	90.00	140.00	150.00

THE GARDENER

CHARACTERS FROM LIFE,
ONE OF SEVEN

STYLE TWO: HANDLE — A RED FLOWERING POTTED PLANT

Designer: Stanley J. Taylor
Handle: A potted plant
Colourway: Beige hat; green sweater; beige shirt
Backstamp: Doulton

Royal Doulton®

THE GARDENER
D 6867
Modelled by

Stanley James Taylor

© 1990 ROYAL DOULTON

VARIATION No. 1:   Mould — Younger face with hair in front

Doulton Number	Size	Variation	Height	Intro.	Discon.	Current Market Value U.K. £	U.S. $	Can. $
D6867	Large	Var. 1	7 1/4"	1990	1991	75.00	225.00	250.00

VARIATION No. 2:   Mould — Older face without hair in front

Doulton Number	Size	Variation	Height	Intro.	Discon.	Current Market Value U.K. £	U.S. $	Can. $
D6868	Small	Var. 2	4"	1990	Current	29.95	82.50	100.00

GENERAL EISENHOWER

THE GREAT GENERALS COLLECTION,
ONE OF THREE

This jug was issued by U.K. International Ceramics in a limited edition of 1,000. It commemorates the 50th anniversary of the U.S. Army's landing in Africa on November 7 and 8, 1942.

Designer:	William K. Harper
Handle:	Face — Shield "S.H.A.E.F."
	Back — U.S. flag
	Both rest on tin helmet
Colourway:	Brown uniform; cream shield;
	red and white stars and stripes

Backstamp: Doulton/U.K. International Ceramics

Doulton Number	Size	Backstamp	Height	Intro.	Discon.	Current Market Value U.K. £	U.S. $	Can. $
D6937	Large	Doulton/UK Int'l	7"	1993	Sp. ed.	195.00	350.00	375.00

GENERAL GORDON

THE GREAT GENERALS COLLECTION,
ONE OF THREE

Charles George Gordon (1833-1885) was known as "Chinese Gordon" after he commanded the Chinese forces against Taiping rebels in 1863. As governor general of the Sudan, he was instrumental in closing down the slave trade. In 1884 he was ordered to rescue Egyptian garrisons there, was beseiged at Khartoum and killed.

The jug was commissioned by U.K. International Ceramics and issued in 1991 in a special edition of 1,500 pieces.

Designer: William K. Harper
Handle: Camel's head and neck with Khartoum ensign
Colourway: Red, blue and gold

Backstamp: Doulton/U.K. International Ceramics

Doulton Number	Size	Backstamp	Height	Intro.	Discon.	Current Market Value U.K. £	U.S. $	Can. $
D6869	Large	Doulton/UK Int'l	7 1/4"	1991	Sp. ed. (1991)	125.00	300.00	325.00

GENIE

MYSTICAL CHARACTERS,
ONE OF THREE

Popularized through legend, the genie is said to reside in a magic lantern and to become the servant of whoever frees him.

Royal Doulton®
THE GENIE
D 6892
Modelled by

Stanley James Taylor

© 1991 ROYAL DOULTON

Designer: Stanley J. Taylor
Handle: Lamp and flame
Colourway: Grey, black, red and yellow

Backstamp: Doulton

Doulton Number	Size	Backstamp	Height	Intro.	Discon.	Current Market Value U.K. £	U.S. $	Can. $
D6892	Large	Doulton	7"	1991	1991	150.00	350.00	375.00

GEORGE III AND GEORGE WASHINGTON

THE ANTAGONISTS' COLLECTION (TWO-FACED JUG),
ONE OF FOUR

George Washington (1732-1799), as commander-in-chief of the American States, led the U.S. to victory in the War of Independence. In 1789 he became the first president of the United States, governing for two terms until 1797.

King George III (1738-1820) ruled Great Britain from 1760 until his death. He led his country in the war against the American States, which he lost in 1776.

This jug was issued in 1986 in a limited edition of 9,500.

Designer: Michael Abberley
Handle: George Washington —
Declaration of Independence
George III — A cannon
Colourway: Red crown; black hat

Royal Doulton®
'The Antagonists'
Collection
D. 6749
The Siege of Yorktown 1781
George III/George Washington
Hand made and Hand decorated ·
Designed by Michael Abberley

© 1985 ROYAL DOULTON (UK)
Worldwide Limited Edition of 9,500
This is Number 3895

Backstamp: Doulton

Doulton Number	Size	Backstamp	Height	Intro.	Discon.	Current Market Value U.K. £	U.S. $	Can. $
D6749	Large	Doulton	7 1/4"	1986	Ltd. ed. (1991)	100.00	225.00	250.00

GEORGE HARRISON

THE BEATLES,
ONE OF FOUR

One of the members of the legendary rock band, the Beatles, George Harrison was born in 1943 in Liverpool, England. He is a guitar player and song writer, and since the break-up of the Beatles in 1970, Harrison has pursued a solo career.

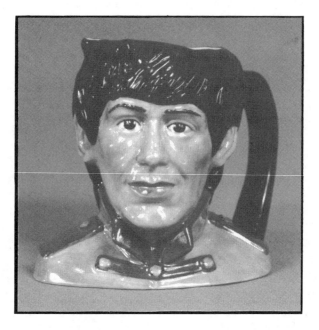

Designer: Stanley J. Taylor
Handle: Plain
Colourway: Green tunic; orange collar and epaulettes

Backstamp: Doulton

Doulton Number	Size	Backstamp	Height	Intro.	Discon.	Current Market Value U.K. £	U.S. $	Can. $
D6727	Mid	Doulton	5 1/2"	1984	1991	75.00	165.00	175.00

GEORGE TINWORTH

ROYAL DOULTON INTERNATIONAL COLLECTORS CLUB

This jug was created exclusively for the Royal Doulton International Collectors Club.

Designer: William K. Harper
Handle: Tinworth sculptures
Colourway: Browns, black and grey

Backstamp: Doulton

Doulton Number	Size	Backstamp	Height	Intro.	Discon.	Current Market Value		
						U.K. £	**U.S. $**	**Can. $**
D7000	Small	Doulton	4 1/4"	1995	1996	39.95	99.00	135.00

GEORGE WASHINGTON

As commander-in-chief of the American States, George Washington (1732-1799) led them to victory in the War of Independence. In 1789 he became the first President of the United States, governing for two terms until 1797. This jug was issued to celebrate the 250th anniversary of Washington's birth.

STYLE ONE: HANDLE — DECLARATION OF INDEPENDENCE

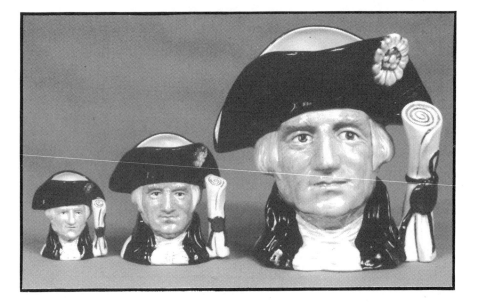

Designer: Stanley J. Taylor
Handle: Declaration of Independence
Colourway: Black hat and coat; beige shirt

Backstamps: A. Doulton.
   B. Doulton/George Washington 1732-1799/
   First Issued in 1982 to Celebrate the
   250th Anniversary of his Birth
   C. Doulton/George Washington/
   To Commemorate the 200th Anniversary
   of the Election of the First President
   of the United States of America

© ROYAL DOULTON
TABLEWARE LTD 1982
D6669

George Washington
1732 - 1799
First Issued in 1982 to Celebrate
the 250th Anniversary of his Birth

BACKSTAMP B

Doulton Number	Size	Backstamp	Height	Intro.	Discon.	Current Market Value U.K. £	U.S. $	Can. $
D6669	Large	A	7 1/2"	1982	1994	65.00	200.00	175.00
D6669	Large	B	7 1/2"	1989	1989	110.00	200.00	225.00
D6824	Small	A	4"	1989	1991	40.00	95.00	100.00
D6824	Small	B	4"	1989	1989	50.00	95.00	100.00
D6825	Miniature	C	2 1/2"	1989	1991	50.00	140.00	150.00

GEORGE WASHINGTON

PRESIDENTIAL SERIES,
ONE OF THREE

The George Washington jug was issued in a limited edition of 2,500.

STYLE TWO: HANDLE — AXE, CHERRIES, LEAVES AND SCROLL

Designer: Stanley J. Taylor
Handle: Axe, cherries and leaves with scroll reading
"To the memory of the man, first in war, first
in peace, first in the hearts of his countrymen"
Colourway: Green, cream and red

Backstamp: Doulton

Doulton Number	Size	Backstamp	Height	Intro.	Discon.	Current Market Value		
						U.K. £	U.S. $	Can. $
D6965	Large	Doulton	7"	1995	Ltd. ed.	—	200.00	—

GERONIMO

THE WILD WEST COLLECTION,
ONE OF SIX

Geronimo (1829-1909) was the last leader of the Apache Indians while they were still independent of American colonial rule. Although he fought many battles to protect the freedom of his people, in 1886 he surrendered to General Nelson Miles, and Apache territory became the state of Arizona.

Designer: Stanley J. Taylor
Handle: Indian game pieces
Colourway: Black, red and white

Backstamp: Doulton

Doulton Number	Size	Backstamp	Height	Intro.	Discon.	Current Market Value		
						U.K. £	U.S. $	Can. $
D6733	Mid	Doulton	5 1/2"	1985	1989	85.00	250.00	265.00

GLADIATOR

From about 246 B.C., gladiatorial games were a popular form of entertainment for Roman audiences. The gladiators were most often slaves or prisoners condemned to fight, which they did to the death using sword, spear or trident. The most famous gladiator of the period was Spartacus, a slave who led an unsuccessful rebellion against Rome. Emperor Honorius banned the brutal games in 404 A.D.

Gladiator
D 6550
COPR 1960
DOULTON & CO LIMITED
Rd No 897939
Rd No 40889
Rd No 8598
Rd No 548 A⁄60

Designer: Max Henk
Handle: A dagger and shield
Colourway: Brown helmet; grey armour

Backstamp: Doulton

Doulton Number	Size	Backstamp	Height	Intro.	Discon.	Current Market Value U.K. £	U.S. $	Can. $
D6550	Large	Doulton	7 3/4"	1961	1967	350.00	950.00	950.00
D6553	Small	Doulton	4 1/4"	1961	1967	250.00	600.00	600.00
D6556	Miniature	Doulton	2 3/4"	1961	1967	250.00	575.00	575.00

GLENN MILLER

This jug commemorates the 50th anniversary of the disappearance of Glenn Miller in an airplane over the Bay of Biscay in 1944. Glenn wears his uniform and a pair of metal glasses. The backstamp includes his date of birth and death.

Royal Doulton®
GLENN MILLER
D 6970
Modelled by

William K. Harper

© 1994 ROYAL DOULTON
1904 – 1944

Designer: William K. Harper
Handle: Song sheet for "Moonlight Serenade"
Colourway: Browns and beige

Backstamps: A: Doulton
Dates of Miller's birth and death included.
B: Doulton
Without dates.

Doulton Number	Size	Backstamp	Height	Intro.	Discon.	Current Market Value U.K. £	U.S. $	Can. $
D6970	Large	Doulton/dates	7 1/2"	1994	1994	150.00	300.00	425.00
D6970	Large	Doulton	7 1/2"	1995	Current	99.95	270.00	380.00

GOLFER

The Golfer character jug was modelled in the likeness of W. J. Carey, the former chairman of Doulton U.S.A.

STYLE ONE: HANDLE — GOLD BAG AND CLUBS

VARIATION No. 1: Colourway — Blue cap; brown sweater; brown golf bag

Royal Doulton

GOLFER
D 6623
Modelled by

David B Biggs

© ROYAL DOULTON TABLEWARE
LIMITED 1970

Designer: David Biggs
Handle: A golf bag and clubs
Colourway: Blue cap; brown sweater; brown golf bag

Backstamp: Doulton

Doulton Number	Size	Backstamp	Height	Intro.	Discon.	Current Market Value		
						U.K. £	U.S. $	Can. $
D6623	Large	Doulton	7"	1971	Current	49.95	125.00	175.00
D6756	Small	Doulton	4 1/2"	1987	1990	40.00	90.00	100.00
D6757	Miniature	Doulton	2 1/2"	1987	1991	45.00	95.00	110.00

VARIATION No. 2:   Colourway — Dark blue cap; blue striped sweater; light brown golf bag

Backstamp: Doulton / John Sinclair
Commissioned by John Sinclair, Sheffield, England. Issued in 1987 in a limited edition of 1,000 pieces.

Doulton Number	Size	Backstamp	Height	Intro.	Discon.	Current Market Value		
						U.K. £	U.S. $	Can. $
D6787	Large	Doulton/Sinclair	7"	1987	Ltd. ed.	75.00	225.00	235.00

THE GOLFER / THE MODERN GOLFER

CHARACTERS FROM LIFE,
ONE OF SEVEN

In the United States, the Royal Doulton product list carries this jug as "The Modern Golfer."

STYLE TWO: HANDLE — 18TH-HOLE FLAG, BALL, TEE AND GOLF CLUB

Royal Doulton ®
THE GOLFER
D 6865
Modelled by

Stanley James Taylor

© 1990 ROYAL DOULTON

Designer: Stanley J. Taylor
Handle: Golf club, 18th-hole flag,
 ball and tee
Colourway: Yellow sweater; green sun visor

Backstamp: Doulton

Doulton Number	Size	Backstamp	Height	Intro.	Discon.	Current Market Value U.K. £	U.S. $	Can. $
D6865	Small	Doulton	4"	1990	Current	29.95	82.50	100.00

GONDOLIER

The shallow, long craft the gondolier pilots through Venetian canals must be painted all black, according to ancient law. When not ferrying or serenading lovers on moonlight rides, the gondolier moors his gondola to a brightly striped pole by the waterside.

Gondolier
D 6589
COPR 1963
DOULTON & CO LIMITED
Rd No 913139
Rd No 45357
Rd No 9682
Rd No 812/63

Designer: David Biggs
Handle: Gondola
Colourway: Yellow hat; blue and white t-shirt; maroon and white pole

Backstamp: Doulton

Doulton Number	Size	Backstamp	Height	Intro.	Discon.	Current Market Value		
						U.K. £	U.S. $	Can. $
D6589	Large	Doulton	8"	1964	1969	350.00	900.00	900.00
D6592	Small	Doulton	4"	1964	1969	225.00	600.00	625.00
D6595	Miniature	Doulton	2 1/2"	1964	1969	250.00	550.00	575.00

GONE AWAY

This very British huntsman looks ready to give the traditional call signalling the loss of the quarry. His prey, the fox, has won this round!

Gone Away
D 6531
COPR 1959
DOULTON & CO LIMITED
Rd No 893844
Rd No 39659
Rd No 8316
Rd No 417/59

Designer: Garry Sharpe
Handle: A fox
Colourway: Red jacket; black cap

Backstamp: Doulton

Doulton Number	Size	Backstamp	Height	Intro.	Discon.	Current Market Value U.K. £	U.S. $	Can. $
D6531	Large	Doulton	7 1/4"	1960	1982	80.00	200.00	215.00
D6538	Small	Doulton	3 3/4	1960	1982	50.00	100.00	115.00
D6545	Miniature	Doulton	2 1/2"	1960	1982	40.00	110.00	125.00

THE GRADUATE (MALE)

Royal Doulton®
THE GRADUATE
D 6916
Modelled by
Stanley James Taylor
© 1991 ROYAL DOULTON

Designer: Stanley J. Taylor
Handle: Diploma
Colourway: Black and white

Backstamp: Doulton

Doulton Number	Size	Backstamp	Height	Intro.	Discon.	Current Market Value		
						U.K. £	U.S. $	Can. $
D6916	Small	Doulton	3 1/2"	1991	Current	29.95	69.50	115.00

GRANNY

PROTOTYPE

This early coloured prototype of the toothless Granny proved too expensive to produce. Only one copy is known to exist.

Granny
D 5521

Designer: Harry Fenton
Handle: Plain
Colourway: Yellows

Backstamp: Doulton

Doulton Number	Size	Backstamp	Height	Intro.	Discon.	Current Market Value		
						U.K. £	U.S. $	Can. $
D5521	Large	Doulton	6 1/4"	1935	Unknown		Unique	

GRANNY

STYLE ONE: TOOTHLESS GRANNY

The wimple on this style does not show between the hat and the hair at the front of the head. There is no tooth showing between the lips.

Granny
D 6384

Designer: Harry Fenton
Handle: Plain
Colourway: Dark green and white

Backstamp: Doulton

Doulton Number	Size	Backstamp	Height	Intro.	Discon.	Current Market Value U.K. £	U.S. $	Can. $
D5521	Large	Doulton	6 1/4"	1935	1941	450.00	1,200.00	1,200.00
D6384	Small	Doulton	3 1/4"	1935	Unknown		Extremely rare	

GRANNY

STYLE TWO: GRANNY WITH ONE TOOTH SHOWING

The wimple on this style shows in waves under most of the hat.

The tiny version of Granny was one of a set of six tinies issued in 1994, in a limited edition of 2,500, to celebrate the diamond anniversary of the first character jug. The set was sold out within the first year. Other tinies in this set are Dick Turpin, the Jester, John Barleycorn, Parson Brown and Simon the Cellarer.

Designer: Harry Fenton, large size; Max Henk, small and miniature sizes; William K. Harper, tiny size

Handle: Pink, blue, green and cream tied yarn

Colourway: Dark grey and white

Backstamp: Doulton

Doulton Number	Size	Backstamp	Height	Intro.	Discon.	Current Market Value U.K. £	U.S. $	Can. $
D5521	Large	Doulton	6 1/4"	1941	1983	80.00	160.00	175.00
D6384	Small	Doulton	3 1/4"	1953	1983	50.00	95.00	110.00
D6520	Miniature	Doulton	2 1/4"	1960	1983	50.00	110.00	125.00
D6954	Tiny	Doulton	1 1/2"	1994	Ltd. ed. (1994)	45.00	90.00	100.00

Granny Derivative

Doulton Number	Item	Height	Intro.	Discon.	Current Market Value U.K. £	U.S. $	Can. $
D —	Table lighter	3 1/2"	Unknown		Extremely rare		

GROUCHO MARX

PROTOTYPE

This design, with two of the Marx Brothers peering out from behind the cigar, was never put into production due to the complicated handle. Only one is known to exist.

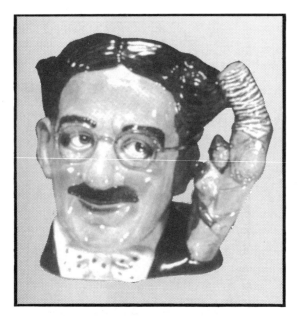

Designer: Stanley J. Taylor
Handle: Cigar with two other Marx Brothers
Colourway: Plain jacket, spotted bow tie

Backstamp: Doulton

Doulton Number	Size	Variation	Height	Intro.	Discon.	Current Market Value U.K. £	U.S. $	Can. $
D6710	Large	Prototype	7"	c.1984			Unique	

GROUCHO MARX

THE CELEBRITY COLLECTION,
ONE OF SIX

Julius Marx (1895-1977) was one of four brothers who became stars of American comedy. The Marx Brothers were known for their crazy slapstick antics and hilarious puns. Groucho led the gang, always smoking his trademark cigar.

VARIATION No. 1:   Colourway — Plain jacket; spotted bow tie

Designer: Stanley J. Taylor
Handle: Cigar
Colourway: Plain jacket; spotted bow tie

Backstamp: Doulton

Doulton Number	Size	Variation	Height	Intro.	Discon.	Current Market Value U.K. £	Current Market Value U.S. $	Current Market Value Can. $
D6710	Large	Var. 1	7"	1984	1988	95.00	200.00	225.00

VARIATION No. 2:   Colourway — Plaid jacket

Doulton Number	Size	Variation	Height	Intro.	Discon.	Current Market Value U.K. £	Current Market Value U.S. $	Current Market Value Can. $
D6710	Large	Var. 2	7"	Unknown			Extremely rare	

GUARDSMAN

CHARACTERS FROM WILLIAMSBURG,
ONE OF EIGHT

STYLE ONE: TRICORN HAT WITH PIKE

Character Jugs from Williamsburg®

Guardsman
D 6575
COPR 1962
DOULTON & CO LIMITED
Rd No 906338
Rd No 43445
Rd No 9224
Rd No 286/62

Designer: Max Henk
Handle: Pike
Colourway: Dark blue and yellow hat and jacket

Backstamp: Doulton

Doulton Number	Size	Backstamp	Height	Intro.	Discon.	Current Market Value U.K. £	U.S. $	Can. $
D6568	Large	Doulton	6 3/4"	1963	1983	95.00	200.00	225.00
D6575	Small	Doulton	4 1/4"	1963	1983	65.00	140.00	150.00
D6582	Miniature	Doulton	2 1/2"	1963	1983	55.00	140.00	150.00

THE GUARDSMAN

PROTOTYPE

This was the original design of The Guardsman jug, a prototype with the Union Jack flag.

Designer: Stanley J. Taylor
Handle: A sword draped with the Union Jack
Colourway: Red tunic; black bearskin hat

Backstamp: Doulton

Doulton Number	Size	Variation	Height	Intro.	Discon.	Current Market Value U.K. £	U.S. $	Can. $
D —	Large	Prototype	8"	Unknown			Extremely rare	

THE GUARDSMAN

THE LONDON COLLECTION,
ONE OF TEN

Long a fixture in London, the guardsman is easily identified by his tall bearskin hat and scarlet uniform. Today he still stands outside Buckingham Palace to protect the Queen.

STYLE TWO: BEARSKIN HAT WITH SWORD

Designer: Stanley J. Taylor
Handle: Sword with draped brown flag
Colourway: Red tunic; black bearskin hat

Royal Doulton®

THE GUARDSMAN
D 6755
Modelled by
Stanley James Taylor
© 1986 ROYAL DOULTON

Backstamp: Doulton

Doulton Number	Size	Backstamp	Height	Intro.	Discon.	Current Market Value		
						U.K. £	U.S. $	Can. $
D6755	Large	Doulton	8"	1986	Current	55.00	125.00	175.00
D6771	Small	Doulton	4"	1987	Current	29.95	69.50	100.00
D6772	Miniature	Doulton	2 1/2"	1987	1991	40.00	70.00	80.00

GULLIVER

Jonathon Swift satirized society's leading men and institutions in his book, *Gulliver's Travels*, published in 1726. In it Gulliver the traveller sails to foreign lands, surviving shipwrecks, giants and the tiny people of Lilliput.

Gulliver
D 6560
COPR 1961
DOULTON & CO LIMITED
Rd No 902091
Rd No 42143
Rd No 8926
Rd No R 85/61

Designer: David Biggs
Handle: Castle tower with two Lilliputians in the turret
Colourway: Dark blue and grey hat; blue jacket; grey handle

Backstamp: Doulton

Doulton Number	Size	Backstamp	Height	Intro.	Discon.	Current Market Value U.K. £	U.S. $	Can. $
D6560	Large	Doulton	7 1/2"	1962	1967	350.00	950.00	950.00
D6563	Small	Doulton	4"	1962	1967	250.00	600.00	600.00
D6566	Miniature	Doulton	2 1/2"	1962	1967	245.00	550.00	550.00

GUNSMITH

PROTOTYPE

This prototype has a different hat, hair style and handle from the design that was issued. Only one jug is known to exist.

Designer: David Biggs
Handle: Stock of a musket and flintlock
Colourway: Black hat; cream shirt;
light brown apron

Backstamp: Doulton

Doulton Number	Size	Backstamp	Height	Intro.	Discon.	Current Market Value U.K. £	U.S. $	Can. $
D —	Large	Doulton	7 1/4"	c. 1963			Unique	

GUNSMITH

CHARACTERS FROM WILLIAMSBURG, ONE OF EIGHT

Character Jugs from Williamsburg
Gunsmith
D 6573
COPR 1962
DOULTON & CO LIMITED
Rd No 906898
Rd No 43583
Rd No 9284
Rd No 322/82

Designer: David Biggs
Handle: Stock of a musket
Colourway: Black hat; cream shirt; light brown apron

Backstamp: Doulton

Doulton Number	Size	Backstamp	Height	Intro.	Discon.	Current Market Value U.K. £	U.S. $	Can. $
D6573	Large	Doulton	7 1/4"	1963	1983	90.00	160.00	175.00
D6580	Small	Doulton	3 1/2"	1963	1983	60.00	115.00	125.00
D6587	Miniature	Doulton	2 1/2"	1963	1983	50.00	100.00	110.00

GUY FAWKES

Guy Fawkes (1570-1606) was part of the infamous "Gunpowder Plot," a plan by Catholic rebels to blow up the British Houses of Parliament and King James I on November 5, 1605. The conspiracy was leaked by a letter to Lord Monteagle, and Guy Fawkes was arrested and hanged. Every year on November 5, Guy Fawkes Day is celebrated with fireworks and the burning of Fawkes in effigy.

VARIATION No. 1:   Colourway — Black hat; red band; white collar on black coat

Royal Doulton®
GUY FAWKES
D 6861
Modelled by

William K. Harper

© 1990 ROYAL DOULTON

Designer: William K. Harper
Handle: A lantern above a barrel of gunpowder
Colourway: Black hat; red band; white collar; black coat

Backstamp: Doulton

Doulton Number	Size	Backstamp	Height	Intro.	Discon.	Current Market Value U.K. £	U.S. $	Can. $
D6861	Large	Doulton	7"	1990	Current	49.95	125.00	275.00

VARIATION No. 2:   Colourway — Black hat; orange band; white collar on black coat

Designer: William K. Harper	**Backstamp:** Doulton / Canadian Art and
Handle: A lantern above a barrel	Collectables Show
of gunpowder	Pre-release was limited to 750 for the Third
Colourway: Black hat; orange band;	Annual Canadian Doulton Show and
white collar; black coat	Sale in conjuction with the 1990
	Canadian Collectables Showcase,
	May 5 and 6, 1990, Durham, Ontario.

| Doulton | | | | | | Current Market Value | | |
Number	Size	Backstamp	Height	Intro.	Discon.	U.K. £	U.S. $	Can. $
D6861	Large	Doulton/Can.	7"	1990	Ltd. ed.	120.00	225.00	250.00

HAMLET

THE SHAKESPEAREAN COLLECTION, ONE OF SIX

Probably Shakespeare's most famous play, *Hamlet, Prince of Denmark,* was first performed between 1599 and 1602. Hamlet became the quintessential tragic hero, driven by conscience and familial obligation to avenge his father's murder.

© ROYAL DOULTON TABLEWARE LIMITED 1982
D 6672

The
Shakespearean
Collection
HAMLET
A series of hand-made, hand-decorated Character Jugs by
Royal Doulton

Designer: Michael Abberley
Handle: A dagger and skull join the feather of the cap
Colourway: Black cap and robes; blond hair; grey feather

Backstamp: Doulton

Doulton Number	Size	Backstamp	Height	Intro.	Discon.	Current Market Value U.K. £	U.S. $	Can. $
D6672	Large	Doulton	7 1/4"	1982	1989	90.00	175.00	195.00

THE HAMPSHIRE CRICKETER

The Hampshire Cricketer jug was developed and sold by the Hampshire Cricket Club to celebrate the centenary of the Hampshire cricket grounds. It was issued in 1985 in a limited edition of 5,000 pieces.

Designer: Harry Sales
Handle: Cricket bat
Colourway: Navy blue cap; cream sweater with navy and yellow stripes

Backstamp: Doulton/Hampshire Cricket Club

Doulton Number	Size	Backstamp	Height	Intro.	Discon.	Current Market Value		
						U.K. £	U.S. $	Can. $
D6739	Small	Doulton/ Hampshire	5"	1985	Ltd. ed. (1991)	60.00	160.00	175.00

HARDY

LAUREL AND HARDY SERIES,
ONE OF TWO

The Hardy jug was commissioned by Lawleys By Post and issued in a limited edition of 3,500.

Designer: William K. Harper
Handle: Early movie camera
Colourway: Light brown

Backstamp: Doulton

Doulton Number	Size	Backstamp	Height	Intro.	Discon.	Current Market Value U.K. £	U.S. $	Can. $
D7009	Small	Doulton	5"	1995	Ltd. ed.	99.00 (set of two jugs)		

HENRY V

THE SHAKESPEAREAN COLLECTION,
ONE OF SIX

King Henry V (1387-1422) renewed the Hundred Years' War against France, and at the Battle of Agincourt in 1415, he won one of the most famous victories in English history. Henry married the daughter of King Charles VI of France and by the Treaty of Troyes became heir to the French throne.

VARIATION No. 1:   Handle — Embossed
Colourway — Yellow crown with gold, turquoise and red design

© ROYAL DOULTON TABLEWARE LIMITED 1982
D 6671

The
Shakespearean
Collection

HENRY V̱

A series of hand-made, hand-decorated Character Jugs by
Royal Doulton

Designer:	Robert Tabbenor
Handle:	Royal Ensign
Colourway:	Yellow crown with gold, turquoise and red design

Backstamp: Doulton

Doulton Number	Size	Variation	Height	Intro.	Discon.	Current Market Value U.K. £	Current Market Value U.S. $	Current Market Value Can. $
D6671	Large	Var. 1	7 1/4"	1982	c. 1984	165.00	350.00	375.00

VARIATION No. 2: Handle — Embossed
Colourway — Yellow crown; some blue colouring; no red or gold
This jug is actually a factory second, marked and sold as such.
One of the steps used when firing and painting the jugs was
missed. Hundreds are known to exist.

Doulton Number	Size	Variation	Height	Intro.	Discon.	Current Market Value		
						U.K. £	U.S. $	Can. $
D6671	Large	Var. 2	7 1/4"	Unknown		600.00	4,500.00	1,500.00

VARIATION No. 3: Handle — Decorated with a decal
Colourway — Yellow crown with gold, blue and red design

Doulton Number	Size	Variation	Height	Intro.	Discon.	Current Market Value		
						U.K. £	U.S. $	Can. $
D6671	Large	Var. 3	7 1/4"	c.1984	1989	90.00	175.00	195.00

HENRY VIII

HENRY VIII AND HIS SIX WIVES,
ONE OF EIGHT

Henry VIII (1491-1547) was king of Great Britain from 1509 to 1547, during which time his infamous private life changed the course of history. Attempting to produce a male heir to the throne, he married six times, was excommunicated by the Pope for divorce and founded the Church of England.

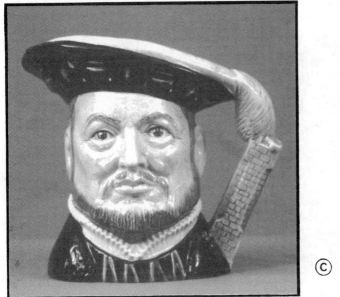

HENRY VIII
D 6642
Ⓒ ROYAL DOULTON
TABLEWARE LTD 1975

Designer: Eric Griffiths
Handle: A tower joins the feather in the hat
Colourway: Black and gold hat; white plume; brown and maroon tunic

Backstamp: Doulton

Doulton Number	Size	Backstamp	Height	Intro.	Discon.	Current Market Value U.K. £	U.S. $	Can. $
D6642	Large	Doulton	6 1/2"	1975	Current	49.95	125.00	175.00
D6647	Small	Doulton	3 3/4"	1979	Current	25.00	69.50	100.00
D6648	Miniature	Doulton	2 3/4"	1979	1991	50.00	110.00	120.00

Note: For King Henry VIII, see page 293.

HOME GUARD

HEROES OF THE BLITZ,
ONE OF THREE

In the early part of World War II, young and old joined the Home Guard to protect the country from what was perceived as an imminent invasion by the German army, allowing the regular army to be used elsewhere. The Heroes of the Blitz series was available only from Lawleys By Post, in a limited edition of 9,500.

Designer: Stanley J. Taylor
Handle: Sten gun with hand grenade
Colourway: Khaki uniform and cap

Backstamp: Doulton

Doulton Number	Size	Variation	Height	Intro.	Discon.	Current Market Value U.K. £	U.S. $	Can. $
D6886	Small	Doulton	4"	1991	Ltd. ed.	85.00	200.00	225.00

HUMPHREY BOGART

THE CELEBRITY COLLECTION

PROTOTYPE

Humphrey DeForest Bogart began his acting career in 1920 and enjoyed a prolific career, winning an Academy Award in 1952 for his performance in *The African Queen*. His best-known role, however, was that of Rick in *Casablanca*. The jug could not be issued due to copyright problems and is not known to be in private collections.

Designer: Eric Griffiths
Handle: Movie camera pointing right
Colourway: Black hat; brown coat;
black bow tie

Backstamp: Doulton

Doulton Number	Size	Variation	Height	Intro.	Discon.	Current Market Value U.K. £	U.S. $	Can. $
D —	Large	Prototype	7"		Unknown		Extremely rare	

IZAAK WALTON

The English writer Izaak Walton (1593-1683) is best known for his book *The Compleat Angler, or Contemplative Man's Recreation*. First published in 1653, this work became the most famous book written on the sport of fishing.

TO COMMEMORATE THI
300ᵗʰ ANNIVERSARY
OF THE
COMPLEAT ANGLER
1653 - 1953

IZAAK WALTON
D. 6404
COPR.1953.
DOULTON&CO LIMITED
R.N: 871560
R.N: 31804
R.N: 6825
R.N: 237/53

BACKSTAMP A

CITY OF
STOKE-ON-TRENT
JUBILEE YEAR
1959-1960
WITH THE COMPLIMENTS OF
LORD MAYOR AND LADY MAYORESS
ALDERMAN HAROLD CLOWES O.B.E. J.P
AND
MISS CHRISTINE CLOWES

BACKSTAMP B

Designer: Geoff Blower
Handle: A fishing rod resting on a tree trunk
Colourway: Brown hat and coat; white collar

Backstamps:
A. Doulton
B. Doulton/City of Stoke-on-Trent Jubilee Year 1959-1960/
With the compliments of Lord Mayor and Lady Mayoress
Alderman Harold Clowes, O.B.E., J.P. and Miss Christine Clowes

Doulton Number	Size	Backstamp	Height	Intro.	Discon.	Current Market Value U.K. £	Current Market Value U.S. $	Current Market Value Can. $
D6404	Large	Doulton	7"	1953	1982	85.00	160.00	175.00
D6404	Large	Doulton/City	7"	1959	1960		Extremely rare	

JANE SEYMOUR

HENRY VIII AND HIS SIX WIVES,
ONE OF EIGHT

While serving as lady-in-waiting to both Catherine of Aragon and Anne Boleyn, Jane Seymour (1509-1537) attracted the attention of Henry VIII. She refused any proposal from the King except marriage, a factor leading to the trial of Anne. Two weeks after Anne Boleyn was beheaded, Jane Seymour became the third wife of Henry VIII, and the only one to bear him a male heir. She died shortly after Edward was born, and was the only wife to be buried at Henry's side.

Designer: Large size — Michael Abberley
Small and miniature sizes — Peter Gee
Handle: A mandolin
Colourway: Black and gold

Royal Doulton®
JANE SEYMOUR
D 6746
Designed by M Abberley
Modelled by
Peter A Gee
© 1978 ROYAL DOULTON (UK)
Backstamp: Doulton

Doulton Number	Size	Backstamp	Height	Intro.	Discon.	Current Market Value U.K. £	U.S. $	Can. $
D6646	Large	Doulton	7 1/4"	1979	1990	85.00	200.00	215.00
D6746	Small	Doulton	4 1/4"	1986	1990	50.00	125.00	135.00
D6747	Miniature	Doulton	2 3/4"	1986	1990	60.00	175.00	185.00

JARGE

Jarge, the coloquial version of George, is a typical country bumpkin, with his polka-dot scarf and the piece of straw in his teeth.

"Jarge."

COPR 1949
DOULTON & CO LIMITED.
RdNo 857577.
RdNo 5904.
RdNo 76/49.

Designer: Harry Fenton
Handle: The scarf extends upwards to the cap
Colourway: Green cap; white scarf with
red polka-dots

Backstamp: Doulton

Doulton Number	Size	Backstamp	Height	Intro.	Discon.	Current Market Value		
						U.K. £	U.S. $	Can. $
D6288	Large	Doulton	6 1/2"	1950	1960	250.00	475.00	500.00
D6295	Small	Doulton	3 1/2"	1950	1960	125.00	275.00	300.00

JESTER

The tiny version of the Jester was one of a set of six tinies issued in 1994, in a limited edition of 2,500. Other tinies in this set, modelled by William K Harper, are Dick Turpin, John Barleycorn, Granny, Parson Brown and Simon the Cellarer. The original issue price was £150.00. The green and yellow colouring on either side of the hat may be reversed as a preference of the painter. Minor variations of this nature do not command a price differential.

JESTER
BACKSTAMP A

BACKSTAMP B

SHEFFIELD &
ROTHERHAM
BACKSTAMP C

Designer: Charles Noke
Handle: Plain
Colourway: Brown, green and yellow

Backstamps:
    A. Doulton
    B. Doulton/Bentalls/Souvenir From Bentalls. 1936.
       Commissioned by Bentalls as an advertising piece.
    C. Doulton/Darley/Souvenir from Darley & Son, Sheffield & Rotherham

Doulton Number	Size	Backstamp	Height	Intro.	Discon.	Current Market Value U.K. £	U.S. $	Can. $
D5556	Small	Doulton	3 1/8"	1936	1960	85.00	175.00	190.00
D5556	Small	Doulton/Bentalls	3 1/8"	1936	1936	395.00	1,000.00	1,000.00
D5556	Small	Doulton/Darley	3 1/8"	1936	1936	395.00	1,000.00	1,000.00
D6953	Tiny	Doulton	1 1/2"	1994	Ltd. ed. (1994)	45.00	90.00	100.00

Jester Derivative

Doulton Number	Item	Height	Intro.	Discon.	Current Market Value U.K. £	U.S. $	Can. $
D6111	Wall pocket	7 1/4"	1940	1941	1,100.00	3,000.00	3,000.00

JIMMY DURANTE

THE CELEBRITY COLLECTION,
ONE OF SIX

James Francis Durante (1893-1980) began his entertaining career playing the piano, but it was his singing and clowning that brought him fame in Vaudeville theatre, night clubs, films, radio and television. Using his large nose as the object of jokes, Durante earned his nickname "Schnozzle."

by Royal Doulton
A hand-made, hand-decorated series
JIMMY DURANTE ⊚
Goodnight Mrs Calabash
wherever you are

Designer: David Biggs
Handle: A piano keyboard
Colourway: Grey and black cap; yellow jacket; cream shirt

Backstamp: Doulton

Doulton Number	Size	Backstamp	Height	Intro.	Discon.	Current Market Value		
						U.K. £	U.S. $	Can. $
D6708	Large	Doulton	7 1/2"	1985	1988	85.00	200.00	225.00

JOCKEY

Small and miniature sized jugs of the Jockey were test piloted but not produced. A small pilot jug is known to exist.

STYLE ONE: GOGGLES RESTING ON HIS CHEST
HANDLE — WINNING POLE

Jockey
D 6625
COPR 1970
DOULTON & CO LIMITED
Rd No 949548
Rd No 57981
Rd No 12388
Rd No 917/70

Designer: David Biggs
Handle: The winning pole
Colourway: Red and yellow striped cap
and racing jersey

Backstamp: Doulton

Doulton Number	Size	Backstamp	Height	Intro.	Discon.	Current Market Value		
						U.K. £	U.S. $	Can. $
D6625	Large	Doulton	7 3/4"	1971	1975	275.00	500.00	550.00
D6629	Small	Doulton	4"	1974	1974		Unique	

THE JOCKEY

CHARACTER JUGS FROM LIFE,
ONE OF SEVEN

STYLE TWO: GOGGLES RESTING ON CAP
HANDLE — WINNING POLE AND HORSE HEAD

Royal Doulton®
THE JOCKEY
D 6877
Modelled by

© 1990 ROYAL DOULTON

Designer: Stanley J. Taylor
Handle: Head of a horse and the winning pole
Colourway: Beige riding cap; yellow and
black racing jersey

Backstamp: Doulton

Doulton Number	Size	Backstamp	Height	Intro.	Discon.	Current Market Value		
						U.K. £	U.S. $	Can. $
D6877	Small	Doulton	4"	1991	Current	29.95	69.50	110.00

JOHN BARLEYCORN

John Barleycorn is the personification of barley, the grain source of malt liquor. This character jug was the first design created by Charles Noke in 1934.

STYLE ONE: HANDLE — INSIDE JUG, 1934 TO 1939

JOHN BARLEYCORN.

BACKSTAMP A

12

R^tN^o782778

Coleman's Compliments

D 5327

BACKSTAMP B

Designer: Charles Noke
Handle: Plain brown
Colourway: Brown rim with light brown body

Backstamps: A. Doulton
B. Doulton/Coleman's/
Coleman's Compliments
This large-size jug was commissioned by Coleman's as an advertising piece.
C. Doulton/Salt River Cement Works/
With Compliments From Salt River Cement Works
This large-size jug was commissioned by Salt River Cement Works as an advertising piece.

Doulton Number	Size	Backstamp	Height	Intro.	Discon.	Current Market Value U.K. £	U.S. $	Can. $
D5327	Large	Doulton	6 1/2"	1934	1939	100.00	275.00	295.00
D5327	Large	Doulton/Coleman's	6 1/2"	1938	1939	750.00	2,250.00	2,000.00
D5327	Large	Doulton/Salt River	6 1/2"	Unknown		1,000.00	3,000.00	2,500.00
D5735	Small	Doulton	3 1/2"	1937	1939	70.00	140.00	150.00
D6041	Mini	Doulton	2 1/2"	Unknown		Extremely rare		

JOHN BARLEYCORN

STYLE TWO: HANDLE — OUTSIDE JUG, 1939 TO 1994

VARIATION No. 1: Handle — Brown shading

The tiny version of John Barleycorn was one of a set of six tinies issued in 1994, in a limited edition of 2,500, to celebrate the diamond anniversary of the first character jug. The set, modelled by William K. Harper, was sold out within the first year. Other tinies in this set are Dick Turpin, The Jester, Granny, Parson Brown and Simon the Cellarer. The original issue price was £150.00 for the complete set with a display stand.

Designer: Charles Noke
Handle: Plain, brown shading
Colourway: Brown rim; light brown face

Backstamp: Doulton

Doulton Number	Size	Backstamp	Height	Intro.	Discon.	Current Market Value U.K. £	U.S. $	Can. $
D5327	Large	Doulton	6 1/2"	1939	1960	95.00	250.00	265.00
D5735	Small	Doulton	3 1/2"	1939	1960	65.00	140.00	150.00
D6041	Miniature	Doulton	2 1/2"	1939	1960	60.00	110.00	125.00
D6952	Tiny	Doulton	1 1/4"	1994	Ltd. ed. (1994)	45.00	90.00	100.00

VARIATION No. 2: Handle — Black shading
Issued from 1978 to 1982, this jug was similar to the previous variation, but a new mould had to be made because the original was not available. This special exhibition jug, modelled by Michael Abberley and limited to 7,500 pieces, was sold at Royal Doulton events.

JOHN BARLEYCORN
D.5327
SPECIAL EXHIBITION REPRODUCTION
LIMITED TO 7,500 PIECES
THIS IS NUMBER 249

Designer: Charles Noke
Modeller: Michael Abberley
Handle: Plain, black shading
Colourway: Brown rim; light brown face

Backstamp: Doulton / Special Exhibition Reproduction
Limited to 7,500 Pieces

Doulton Number	Size	Backstamp	Height	Intro.	Discon.	Current Market Value		
						U.K. £	U.S. $	Can. $
D5327	Large	Doulton/Special	6"	1978	Ltd. ed.	165.00	225.00	250.00

John Barleycorn Derivative

Doulton Number	Item		Height	Intro.	Discon.	Current Market Value		
						U.K. £	U.S. $	Can. $
D5602	Ash bowl		4"	1936	1960	100.00	225.00	250.00

JOHN BARLEYCORN

Commissioned by American Express to form part of a 12-tankard set from various manufacturers, John Barleycorn was sold to between 500 and 600 card members.

STYLE THREE: BLUE HAT WITH BARLEY EARS

Royal Doulton®
JOHN BARLEYCORN
TANKARD
D 8780
*Specially Commissioned
by*
AMERICAN EXPRESS
Modelled by
Stanley James Taylor
© 1987 ROYAL DOULTON

Designer: Stanley J. Taylor
Handle: Twisted barley stalk
Colourway: Pale blue cap; light brown barley ears

Backstamp: Doulton/American Express

Doulton Number	Size	Backstamp	Height	Intro.	Discon.	Current Market Value U.K. £	U.S. $	Can. $
D6780	Mid	Doulton/Amex	5 1/2"	1988	Sp. ed.	200.00	425.00	450.00

JOHN DOULTON

ROYAL DOULTON INTERNATIONAL COLLECTORS CLUB

John Doulton (1793-1873) served a seven-year apprenticeship in the pottery industry as a thrower before fortune smiled on him and he was able to buy into a pottery partnership. In 1815 he bought a one-third share of a stoneware pot-house in Vauxhall Walk, Lambeth, and the company of Doulton and Watts was born.

To honour John Doulton, the Royal Doulton International Collectors Club made this jug available to all their original charter members in 1980.

This first style of this jug has the time shown on "Big Ben" as 8 o'clock.

STYLE ONE: TIME SHOWN ON BIG BEN IS EIGHT O'CLOCK

D 6656
JOHN DOULTON
1793 · 1873
EXCLUSIVELY FOR
COLLECTORS CLUB
ⓒ ROYAL DOULTON
TABLEWARE LTD 1980

Designer: Eric Griffiths
Handle: The tower of Big Ben
Colourway: White cravat; Big Ben is grey

Backstamp: Doulton/RDICC

Doulton Number	Size	Backstamp	Height	Intro.	Discon.	Current Market Value U.K. £	U.S. $	Can. $
D6656	Small	Doulton/RDICC	4 1/4"	1980	c. 1982	75.00	165.00	175.00

JOHN DOULTON

ROYAL DOULTON INTERNATIONAL COLLECTORS CLUB

Starting in 1981 each new member joining the Royal Doulton International Collectors Club had the opportunity of purchasing the John Doulton jug; however, the time now shown on Big Ben is two o'clock.

STYLE TWO: TIME SHOWN ON BIG BEN IS TWO O'CLOCK

JOHN DOULTON
1793 - 1873
EXCLUSIVELY FOR
COLLECTORS CLUB
© ROYAL DOULTON
TABLEWARE LTD 1980

Designer: Eric Griffiths
Handle: The tower of Big Ben
Colourway: Yellow cravat; Big Ben is light brown

Backstamp: Doulton/RDICC

Doulton Number	Size	Backstamp	Height	Intro.	Discon.	Current Market Value U.K. £	U.S. $	Can. $
D6656	Small	Doulton/RDICC	4 1/4"	1981	1994	40.00	75.00	85.00

JOHN GILPIN

PROTOTYPE

"The Diverting History of John Gilpin" is an 18th-century poem by Cowper. In it Gilpin, a "linen draper bold" and his wife go to Edmonton to celebrate their 20th wedding anniversary. His horse runs out of control, however, and John careers ten miles beyond Edmonton and back again.

Designer: David Biggs
Handle: Brown wood sign post reading "Edmonton"
Colourway: Dark green hat; maroon coat

Backstamp: Doulton

Doulton Number	Size	Backstamp	Height	Intro.	Discon.	Current Market Value		
						U.K. £	U.S. $	Can. $
D —	Large	Doulton	7"	1968	1968	Extremely rare. Only two known.		

JOHN LENNON

THE BEATLES,
ONE OF FOUR

John Winston Lennon (1940-1980) played guitar and wrote songs for the Beatles until the group disbanded in 1970. With his wife Yoko Ono, Lennon pursued a successful solo career until his tragic assassination in 1980.

VARIATION No. 1:   Colourway — Turquoise jacket with maroon collar and epaulettes

Royal Doulton
THE BEATLES
John Lennon
D 6725
Modelled by

© ROYAL DOULTON TABLEWARE
LIMITED 198?

Designer: Stanley J. Taylor
Handle: Plain
Colourway: Turquoise jacket with
maroon collar and epaulettes

Backstamp: Doulton

Doulton Number	Size	Backstamp	Height	Intro.	Discon.	Current Market Value		
						U.K. £	U.S. $	Can. $
D6725	Mid	Doulton	5 1/2"	1984	1991	75.00	165.00	175.00

VARIATION No. 2:   Colourway — Red jacket with yellow collar and epaulettes

Backstamp: Doulton/John Sinclair/
New Colourway Special Edition of 1000 for John Sinclair, Sheffield
Commissioned by John Sinclair, Sheffield. Issued in 1987 in a limited edition of 1,000 pieces.

Doulton Number	Size	Backstamp	Height	Intro.	Discon.	Current Market Value U.K. £	U.S. $	Can. $
D6797	Mid	Doulton/Sinclair	5 1/2"	1987	Ltd. ed.	125.00	275.00	295.00

JOHN PEEL

John Peel (1776-1854) was a famous English huntsman, known for his enthusiasm, skill and hospitality. Fond of drink, he hosted large, popular post-hunt celebrations. Peel has been immortalized in the song "D'ye ken John Peel," written by John Woodcock Graves.

VARIATION No. 1:   Colourway — Grey handle

"John Peel."
Rᵈ№809559.

Designer: Harry Fenton
Handle: Riding crop, with hunting horn forming top of handle
Colourway: Dark grey hat; maroon coat; dark blue bow tie

Backstamp: Doulton

Doulton Number	Size	Variation	Height	Intro.	Discon.	Current Market Value U.K. £	U.S. $	Can. $
D5612	Large	Var. 1	6 1/2"	1936	1960	100.00	250.00	275.00
D5731	Small	Var. 1	3 1/2"	1937	1960	65.00	120.00	135.00
D6130	Miniature	Var. 1	2 1/4"	1940	1960	55.00	100.00	115.00
D6259	Tiny	Var. 1	1 1/4"	1947	1960	130.00	325.00	350.00

VARIATION No. 2:   Colourway — Black and orange handle

Doulton Number	Size	Variation	Height	Intro.	Discon.	Current Market Value U.K. £	U.S. $	Can. $
D5612	Large	Var. 2	6 1/2"	Unknown		95.00	275.00	295.00
D6130	Miniature	Var. 2	2 1/4"	c.1942	Unknown	65.00	135.00	150.00

JOHN SHORTER

Commissioned by the Character and Toby Jug Collectors Society of Australia, this depiction of Australian retailer John Shorter was released in 1991 in a limited edition of 1,500 pieces.

Royal Doulton®
JOHN SHORTER
D.6890
Modelled by

William K. Harper

© 1990 ROYAL DOULTON
Specially commissioned from Royal Doulton
by the Character and Toby Jug Collectors Society
of Australia to commemorate
the 10th anniversary of the Society 1980 – 1990.
ISSUED IN A WORLDWIDE
LIMITED EDITION OF 1,500
THIS IS Nº **372**

Designer: William K. Harper
Handle: A kangaroo and joey
Colourway: Grey hair; black jacket; maroon and white polka-dot bow tie

Backstamp: Doulton/CJCSA

Doulton Number	Size	Backstamp	Height	Intro.	Discon.	Current Market Value		
						U.K. £	U.S. $	Can. $
D6880	Small	Doulton/CJCSA	4 1/4"	1991	Ltd. ed. (1991)	100.00	250.00	225.00

JOHNNY APPLESEED

John Chapman (1774-1845) was an American pioneer who sold and gave saplings and apple seeds to colonizing families. He travelled the eastern U.S., sowing apple orchards and tending his trees. After his death, Chapman became the hero of many legends.

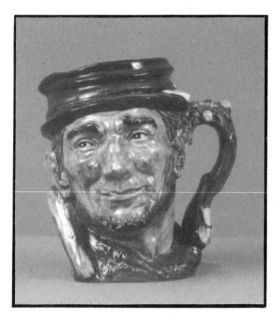

Johnny Appleseed
D.6372
COPR.1952.
DOULTON & CO.LIMITED
R⁴Nº 868196
R⁹Nº 98801
R!Nº 30304
R⁹Nº 6647.

Designer: Harry Fenton
Handle: An apple tree and knapsack
Colourway: Maroon and grey cap; brown robes

Backstamp: Doulton

Doulton Number	Size	Backstamp	Height	Intro.	Discon.	Current Market Value		
						U.K. £	U.S. $	Can. $
D6372	Large	Doulton	6"	1953	1969	250.00	525.00	575.00

THE JUGGLER

THE CIRCUS,
ONE OF FOUR

Royal Doulton®

THE JUGGLER
D 6835
Modelled by

Stanley James Taylor

© 1988 ROYAL DOULTON

Designer: Stanley J. Taylor
Handle: Skittles and balls
Colourway: Brown hair; yellow, blue and red tunic;
dark green head band

Backstamp: Doulton

Doulton Number	Size	Backstamp	Height	Intro.	Discon.	Current Market Value		
						U.K. £	U.S. $	Can. $
D6835	Large	Doulton	6 1/2"	1989	1991	95.00	250.00	265.00

KING ARTHUR AND GUINEVERE

THE STAR-CROSSED LOVERS COLLECTION (TWO-FACED JUG),
ONE OF FOUR

Arthur is the legendary fifth-century King of Britain, known for his courage and honesty. His 12 knights, with whom he ruled and planned his campaigns, sat at a round table, so that none had precedence. His best friend, the knight Lancelot, betrayed him by falling in love with his beautiful wife Guinevere. Arthur died at Camelford in a battle against his usurping nephew Mordred.

This jug was issued in 1989 in a limited edition of 9,500.

Designer: Stanley J. Taylor
Handle: King Arthur — Sword
Guinevere — Chalice
Colourway: Blue-grey, yellow and white

Royal Doulton®
THE
STAR-CROSSED LOVERS
COLLECTION
King Arthur & Guinevere
D 6836
Modelled by Stanley James Taylor

Worldwide Limited Edition of 9,500.
This is Number 792
© 1988 Royal Doulton

Backstamp: Doulton

Doulton Number	Size	Backstamp	Height	Intro.	Discon.	Current Market Value		
						U.K. £	U.S. $	Can. $
D6836	Large	Doulton	6 1/2"	1989	Ltd. ed. (1991)	115.00	275.00	295.00

KING CHARLES I

This jug was issued in a limited edition of 2,500 to commemorate the 350th anniversary of the English Civil War. It is unusual in the sense that it is the first three-handled character jug ever produced by Doulton. On Charles's left Oliver Cromwell forms the handle, on his right, Queen Henrietta. The third handle, at the King's back and not seen in the photo below, is a plume.

Royal Doulton®
KING CHARLES I
D 6917
Modelled by

William K. Harper

ⓒ 1992 ROYAL DOULTON
LIMITED EDITION OF 2,500
THIS IS Nº 1931
To commemorate the 350th
Anniversary of the start of
the English Civil War, 1642

Designer: William K. Harper
Handle: Three handles (see above)
Colourway: Black, yellow and red

Backstamp: Doulton

Doulton Number	Size	Backstamp	Height	Intro.	Discon.	Current Market Value		
						U.K. £	U.S. $	Can. $
D6917	Large	Doulton	7"	1992	Ltd. ed. (1993)	250.00	550.00	600.00

Note: For Charles I see page 169.

KING EDWARD VII

ROYAL DOULTON INTERNATIONAL COLLECTORS CLUB EXCLUSIVE

In this jug, King Edward VII is shown wearing a crown and all his finery. The handle comprises the traditional Royal Doulton backstamp of the crown and lion. This piece had a limited edition of 2,500 and was issued exclusively for the Royal Doulton International Collectors Club.

King Edward VII
D.6923
EXCLUSIVELY FOR
COLLECTORS CLUB
Limited edition of
2,500
THIS IS NO
1586
MODELLED BY
William K. Harper
© 1992 Royal Doulton

Designer: William K. Harper
Handle: Lion and crown of the Doulton backstamp
Colourway: Red, gold, and white

Backstamp: Doulton/RDICC

Doulton Number	Size	Backstamp	Height	Intro.	Discon.	Current Market Value U.K. £	U.S. $	Can. $
D6923	Small	Doulton/RDICC	5 1/2"	1992	Ltd. ed.	150.00	350.00	375.00

Note: For Edward VII see page 295.

KING HENRY VIII

This is a two-handled jug and, strictly speaking, should be classified as a loving cup. It was issued in 1991 in a limited edition of 1,991 to commemorate the 500th anniversary of the birth of Henry VIII.

Designer: William K. Harper
Handle: Double handle, three wives on either side
Colourway: White and black with gold trim

Backstamp: Doulton

Doulton Number	Size	Backstamp	Height	Intro.	Discon.	Current Market Value U.K. £	U.S. $	Can. $
D6888	Large	Doulton	7"	1991	Ltd. ed. (1991)	425.00	1,350.00	1,350.00

Note: For Henry VIII see page 267.

KING PHILIP OF SPAIN

King of Spain during its most powerful and influential era, Philip (1527-1598) was a strong defender of Catholicism and leader of an anti-reformation movement against Protestant leaders, such as Queen Elizabeth I. He led a rebellion in the Netherlands and waged wars against the Ottoman Empire and England in the name of his cause. His attempted invasion of England in 1588 by the Spanish Armada was defeated in one of the most famous naval battles in history. Issued by Lawleys By Post in 1988, this jug is one of a pair (with Queen Elizabeth I) produced to celebrate the 400th anniversary of the defeat of the Spanish Armada. Both jugs are limited editions of 9,500 pieces.

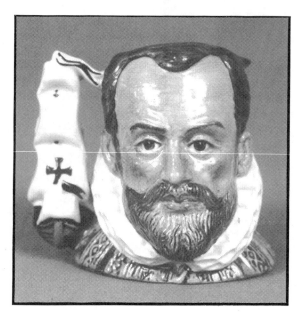

Designer: William K. Harper
Handle: Galleon sailing on the left
Colourway: Grey, white and brown

Backstamp: Doulton

Doulton Number	Size	Backstamp	Height	Intro.	Discon.	Current Market Value U.K. £	U.S. $	Can. $
D6822	Small	Doulton	4"	1988	Ltd. ed. (1991)	95.00	225.00	250.00

KINGS AND QUEENS OF THE REALM

This set of six tinies was issued by Lawleys By Post in a limited edition of 2,500 sets. Each set came with a wooden display stand and a certificate of authenticity.

Designer: William K. Harper

Handles: Henry VIII — Bible and lute
Victoria — Gold lion and crown
Elizabeth I — Orb and sceptre
Edward VII — Scroll reading "Entente Cordiale"
Henry V — Royal standard
Charles I — Crown and sceptre

Backstamp: Doulton

Colourways: Henry VIII — Black, white and gold
Victoria — Yellow, brown and silver
Elizabeth I — Green, yellow and brown
Edward VII — Gold, white and yellow
Henry V — Gold, maroon and yellow
Charles I — Black, yellow and red

Doulton Number	Name	Height	Intro.	Discon.	Current Market Value U.K. £	U.S. $	Can. $
D6990	Henry VIII	1 1/2"	1994	Ltd. ed.			
D6991	Victoria	1 1/2"	1994	Ltd. ed.			
D6992	Elizabeth I	1 1/2"	1994	Ltd. ed.	£195.00 (Complete set with stand)		
D6993	Edward VII	1 1/2"	1994	Ltd. ed.			
D6994	Henry V	1 1/2"	1994	Ltd. ed.			
D6995	Charles I	1 1/2"	1994	Ltd. ed.			

LAUREL

LAUREL AND HARDY SERIES,
ONE OF TWO

Commissioned by Lawleys By Post and produced in a limited edition of 3,500, this jug was issued as a partner to the Hardy jug.

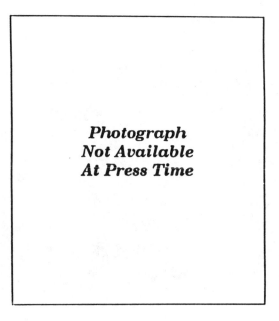

Designer: William K. Harper
Handle: Early movie camera
Colourway: Light brown

Backstamp: Doulton

Doulton Number	Size	Backstamp	Height	Intro.	Discon.	Current Market Value		
						U.K. £	U.S. $	Can. $
D7008	Small	Doulton	4"	1995	Ltd. ed.	99.00 (set of two jugs)		

THE LAWYER

The Lawyer
D 6498
COPR 1958
DOULTON & CO LIMITED
Rd No 889569
Rd No 38225
Rd No 8035
Rd No 424/58

Royal Doulton
THE LAWYER
D 6504
Modelled by

© ROYAL DOULTON TABLEWARE
LIMITED 1958

Designer: Max Henk
Handle: Green feather quill
Colourway: Grey wig; black robes; white shirt

Backstamp: Doulton

Doulton Number	Size	Backstamp	Height	Intro.	Discon.	Current Market Value U.K. £	U.S. $	Can. $
D6498	Large	Doulton	7"	1959	Current	49.95	125.00	175.00
D6504	Small	Doulton	4"	1959	Current	25.00	69.50	100.00
D6524	Miniature	Doulton	2 1/2"	1960	1991	40.00	85.00	95.00

The Lawyer Derivative

Doulton Number	Item	Height	Intro.	Discon.	Current Market Value U.K. £	U.S. $	Can. $
D6504	Table lighter	3 1/2"	1962	1974	150.00	350.00	375.00

LEEDS UNITED (FOOTBALL CLUB)

THE FOOTBALL SUPPORTERS,
ONE OF NINE

Royal Doulton®
FOOTBALL SUPPORTER'S
CHARACTER JUG.
D 6928
Modelled by

Stanley James Taylor

© 1992 ROYAL DOULTON
"LEEDS UNITED"

Designer: Stanley J. Taylor
Handle: Team coloured scarf
Colourway: White, blue and yellow uniform

Backstamp: Doulton

Doulton Number	Size	Backstamp	Height	Intro.	Discon.	Current Market Value U.K. £	Current Market Value U.S. $	Current Market Value Can. $
D6928	Mid	Doulton	5"	1992	Current	32.50	—	—

LEN HUTTON

Sir Leonard Hutton played for the Yorkshire County Cricket Club. The ribbon bearing the number 364, which is intertwined around the handle of the jug, represents his famous record innings against Australia at the Oval cricket grounds in 1938, a record which still stands in England today. The jug was commissioned by Lawleys By Post and was issued in a limited edition of 9,500. The first jug was presented to Her Royal Highness, the Duchess of Kent, who is patron of the Len Hutton 364 Appeal.

Designer: Stanley J. Taylor
Handle: Cricket bat, stumps and ball
Colourway: White shirt and sweater; black cap

Backstamp: Doulton

Doulton Number	Size	Backstamp	Height	Intro.	Discon.	Current Market Value U.K. £	U.S. $	Can. $
D6945	Mid	Doulton	4"	1993	Ltd. Ed.	75.00	200.00	225.00

LEPRECHAUN

This wizened little elf is a legendary Irish sprite with a mischievous nature. The Irish believed that leprechauns guarded hoards of treasure hidden at the end of rainbows.

BACKSTAMP A

BACKSTAMP C

Designer:	William K. Harper
Handle:	Rainbow with a sack of gold at the base
Colourway:	Green cap; brown coat
Backstamps:	A. Doulton For general release: large size — 1991, small size — 1992 B. Doulton/The Site of the Green Large size commissioned by the Site of the Green and issued in 1990 in a special edition of 500 pieces. C. Doulton/The Site of the Green Small size commissioned by the Site of the Green and issued in 1991 in a special edition of 500 pieces.

Doulton Number	Size	Backstamp	Height	Intro.	Discon.	Current Market Value U.K. £	U.S. $	Can. $
D6847	Large	Doulton	7 1/2"	1991	Current	59.95	205.00	245.00
D6847	Large	Doulton/Site	7 1/2"	1990	Sp. ed.	150.00	275.00	295.00
D6899	Small	Doulton	4 1/2"	1992	Current	29.95	69.50	120.00
D6899	Small	Doulton/Site	4 1/2"	1991	Sp. ed.	75.00	140.00	150.00

LITTLE MESTER MUSEUM PIECE

This jug was modelled on the likeness of Grinder Rowland Swindon, a grinder from Sheffield, England. It was commissioned by John Sinclair of Sheffield and issued in 1988 in a limited edition of 3,500 pieces. One thousand jugs were bought by the World Student Games to help launch the games in Sheffield.

Royal Doulton•
**LITTLE MESTER
MUSEUM PIECE**
D 6819
Modelled by
Stanley James Taylor.
© 1988 ROYAL DOULTON
SPECIAL EDITION OF 3,500
790

Designer:	Stanley J. Taylor
Handle:	Bowie knife and grinder
Colourway:	Black cap; blue jacket; white shirt; red scarf

Backstamp: Doulton

Doulton Number	Size	Backstamp	Height	Intro.	Discon.	Current Market Value U.K. £	U.S. $	Can. $
D6819	Large	Doulton	6 3/4"	1988	Sp. ed. (1991)	100.00	300.00	325.00

LITTLE NELL

CHARLES DICKENS COMMEMORATIVE SET,
DICKENS TINIES, ONE OF 12

Little Nell is the ill-fated protagonist in Dickens's *The Old Curiosity Shop*. The jug was issued to commemorate the 170th anniversary of the birth of Charles Dickens. There are 12 jugs in this set, each issued with a certificate of authenticity. A mahogany display shelf completes the set. The set was first sold by Lawleys By Post in the U.K. from 1982 to 1988, and from 1985 in North America and Australia.

Little Nell
D.6681

Designer: Michael Abberley
Handle: Plain
Colourway: Yellow and black

Backstamp: Doulton

Doulton						Current Market Value		
Number	Size	Backstamp	Height	Intro.	Discon.	U.K. £	U.S. $	Can. $
D6681	Tiny	Doulton	1 1/2"	1982	1989	40.00	70.00	80.00
		Display stand for 12 tinies				65.00	45.00	50.00

LIVERPOOL (FOOTBALL CLUB)

THE FOOTBALL SUPPORTERS,
ONE OF NINE

Royal Doulton®
FOOTBALL SUPPORTER'S
CHARACTER JUG.
D 6930
Modelled by

Stanley James Taylor

© 1992 ROYAL DOULTON
"LIVERPOOL"

Designer: Stanley J. Taylor
Handle: Team coloured scarf
Colourway: Red and white uniform

Backstamp: Doulton

Doulton Number	Size	Backstamp	Height	Intro.	Discon.	Current Market Value		
						U.K. £	U.S. $	Can. $
D6930	Mid	Doulton	5"	1992	Current	32.50	—	—

LIVERPOOL CENTENARY JUG (BILL SHANKLY)

Issued to commemorate the 100th anniversary of the Liverpool Football Club in 1992, this jug is a limited edition of 5,500.

LIVERPOOL CENTENARY JUG
D 6914

Specially Commissioned from

Royal Doulton®

by

LIVERPOOL F.C.
In celebration of
the clubs centenary
In 1992

Modelled by *William K. Harper*

© 1991 ROYAL DOULTON
A LIMITED EDITION OF 5,500
THIS IS N° 775

Designer: William K. Harper
Handle: Two footballs and flag
Colourway: Red jersey; white collar; gray hair

Backstamp: Doulton/Liverpool F.C.

Doulton Number	Size	Backstamp	Height	Intro.	Discon.	Current Market Value		
						U.K. £	U.S. $	Can. $
D6914	Small	Doulton/ Liverpool	3 1/2"	1992	Ltd. ed.	50.00	175.00	195.00

LOBSTER MAN

VARIATION No. 1:   Colourway — Dark blue jacket and cap; white fisherman's jersey

LOBSTER MAN
D 6652
COPR 1967
DOULTON & CO LIMITED

Designer: David Biggs
Handle: Lobster
Colourway: Dark blue jacket and cap;
white fisherman's jersey

Backstamp: Doulton

Doulton Number	Size	Variation	Height	Intro.	Discon.	Current Market Value U.K. £	U.S. $	Can. $
D6617	Large	Var. 1	7 1/2"	1968	1991	75.00	160.00	175.00
D6620	Small	Var. 1	3 3/4"	1968	1991	40.00	90.00	100.00
D6652	Miniature	Var. 1	2 3/4"	1980	1991	40.00	80.00	100.00

VARIATION No. 2:   Colourway — Dark blue jacket and cap; blue-grey fisherman's jersey

Doulton Number	Size	Variation	Height	Intro.	Discon.	Current Market Value U.K. £	U.S. $	Can. $
D6783	Large	Var. 2	8"	1987	1989	85.00	225.00	250.00

VARIATION No. 3:   Colourway — Light blue jacket

Doulton Number	Size	Variation	Height	Intro.	Discon.	Current Market Value U.K. £	U.S. $	Can. $
D —	Small	Var. 2	3 3/4"	1987	Unknown	75.00	150.00	165.00

THE LONDON 'BOBBY'

THE LONDON COLLECTION,
ONE OF TEN

VARIATION No. 1:   Hat badge embossed and hand painted

Royal Doulton®
THE LONDON 'BOBBY'
D 6744
Modelled by
Stanley James Taylor
© 1985 ROYAL DOULTON (UK)

Designer: Stanley J. Taylor
Handle: Tower of Big Ben and a whistle
Colourway: Black and white badge (see variations)

Backstamp: Doulton

Doulton Number	Size	Variation	Height	Intro.	Discon.	Current Market Value U.K. £	U.S. $	Can. $
D6744	Large	Var. 1	7"	1986	1987	100.00	350.00	365.00
D6762	Small	Var. 1	3 1/2"	1987	1987	75.00	175.00	195.00
D6763	Miniature	Var. 1	2 1/2"	1987	1987	65.00	225.00	235.00

VARIATION No. 2:   Hat badge decal decorated

Doulton Number	Size	Variation	Height	Intro.	Discon.	Current Market Value U.K. £	U.S. $	Can. $
D6744	Large	Var. 2	7 1/2"	1987	Current	55.00	125.00	175.00
D6762	Small	Var. 2	3 1/2"	1987	Current	29.95	69.50	100.00
D6763	Miniature	Var. 2	2 1/2"	1987	1991	45.00	100.00	110.00

LONG JOHN SILVER

CHARACTERS FROM LITERATURE,
ONE OF 11

This scoundrel and pirate from Robert Louis Stevenson's *Treasure Island* had a wooden leg and a parrot companion. Together with the boy-hero Jim Hawkins, he set sail in a hair-raising search for buried treasure.

VARIATION No. 1:   Colourway — Maroon shirt; green and grey parrot

Designer: Max Henk
Handle: A parrot
Colourway: Maroon shirt; green and grey parrot

˙ Long John Silver ˙
D.6335
COPR 1951.
DOULTON &CO LIMITED
R⁴Nº 864843.
R⁴Nº 29156.
R⁴Nº 6404.
R⁴Nº 112/51

Backstamp: Doulton

Doulton Number	Size	Backstamp	Height	Intro.	Discon.	Current Market Value		
						U.K. £	U.S. $	Can. $
D6335	Large	Doulton	7"	1952	Current	49.95	125.00	175.00
D6386	Small	Doulton	4"	1952	Current	25.00	69.50	100.00
D6512	Miniature	Doulton	2 1/2"	1960	1991	40.00	70.00	80.00

VARIATION No. 2: Colourway — Yellow shirt, yellow-green parrot

"LONG JOHN SILVER"
D 6799

Specially Commissioned
from
Royal Doulton®
by
D.H. HOLMES COMPANY LTD
Celebrating the opening of
The Royal Doulton Room
D.H. Holmes, New Orleans, Louisiana, U.S.A.
HAND MODELLED AND HAND DECORATED
A LIMITED EDITION OF 250
THIS IS NO. 91
© 1987 ROYAL DOULTON

Backstamp: Doulton/D. H. Holmes/
Specially Commissioned from Royal Doulton by D. H. Holmes Company Ltd./
Celebrating the opening of The Royal Doulton Room D. H. Holmes, New Orleans, Louisiana, U.S.A.
Commissioned by D. H. Holmes Company Ltd. and issued in 1987 in a limited edition of 250 pieces.

Doulton Number	Size	Backstamp	Height	Intro.	Discon.	Current Market Value U.K. £	U.S. $	Can. $
D6799	Large	Doulton/Holmes	7"	1987	Ltd. ed.	250.00	450.00	475.00

Long John Silver Derivatives

Doulton Number	Item	Height	Intro.	Discon.	Current Market Value U.K. £	U.S. $	Can. $
D6386	Lighter	3 1/2"	1958	1973	140.00	250.00	275.00
D6853	Teapot	7"	1990	1991	75.00	225.00	225.00

LORD MAYOR OF LONDON

THE LONDON COLLECTION,
ONE OF TEN

Designer: Stanley J. Taylor
Handle: Sceptre of office
Colourway: Black plume hat; red cloak;
yellow chain of office

Backstamp: Doulton

Doulton Number	Size	Backstamp	Height	Intro.	Discon.	Current Market Value U.K. £	U.S. $	Can. $
D6864	Large	Doulton	7 1/4"	1990	1991	95.00	225.00	250.00

LORD NELSON

Horatio Nelson (1758-1805), a member of the navy since the age of 12, was made commander-in-chief of his own fleet in 1803. He saw action in the West Indies and in Canada, but is best remembered for his defeat of the French and Spanish navies at the Battle of Trafalgar in 1805. Nelson died during the battle.

Designer: Geoff Blower
Handle: Plain
Colourway: Blue tricorn and jacket with gold trim; white cravat

Backstamps:
  A. Doulton
  B. Doulton/Battle of Trafalgar/
    Commemorating the 150th Anniversary of the Battle of Trafalgar 21st October 1955
    Commissioned for the Admiralty to commemorate the 150th anniversary of Nelson's
    victory at Trafalgar, October 21, 1955.
  C. Three of the jugs carry an added line to the backstamp, either "First Lord," "First Sea Lord"
    or "Secretary," the intention being that these three jugs would be held in perpetuity at the
    respective offices. However one of the elected officials left office with a jug, which later
    appeared on the market.

Doulton Number	Size	Backstamp	Height	Intro.	Discon.	Current Market Value U.K. £	U.S. $	Can. $
D6336	Large	A	7"	1952	1969	275.00	600.00	650.00
D6336	Large	B	7"	1955	1955	1,000.00	1,500.00	1,750.00
D6336	Large	C	7"	1955	1955	Only three issued and each with different backstamps.		

Note: For Nelson see page 344. For Vice-Admiral Nelson see page 461.

LOUIS ARMSTRONG

THE CELEBRITY COLLECTION,
ONE OF SIX

Daniel Louis "Satchmo" Armstrong (1900-1971) evolved from a self-taught cornet player to the first internationally famous soloist in jazz. He was well known for both his brilliant technique on the trumpet and for his deep throaty singing. Appearing in many live shows, Broadway musicals and films, Armstrong's music had a lasting influence on jazz.

© ROYAL DOULTON TABLEWARE LIMITED 1985
D 6707

THE CELEBRITY COLLECTION

by Royal Doulton
A hand-made, hand-decorated series
LOUIS ARMSTRONG ⊖
"Man, if you gotta ask, you'll never know"
(His reply when asked what Jazz was).

Louis Armstrong ⊖

Backstamp: Doulton

Designer: David Biggs
Handle: Trumpet and handkerchief
Colourway: Brown and pink

Doulton Number	Size	Backstamp	Height	Intro.	Discon.	Current Market Value U.K. £	U.S. $	Can. $
D6707	Large	Doulton	7 1/2"	1984	1988	95.00	225.00	240.00

LUMBERJACK

A small quantity of miniature Lumberjack prototypes are known to exist.

Royal Doulton backstamp crest

Lumberjack
D 6610
COPR 1966
DOULTON & CO LIMITED
Rd No 924807
Rd No 49146
Rd No 10601
Rd No 53/66

BACKSTAMP A

CANADIAN CENTENNIAL SERIES
1867 - 1967

The Lumberjack
D 6610
COPR 1966
DOULTON & CO LIMITED
Rd No 924807
Rd No 49146
Rd No 10601
Rd No 53/66

BACKSTAMP B

Designer: Max Henk
Handle: Tree trunk and axe
Colourway: Red cap; green jacket; pink sweater

Backstamps: A. Doulton
B. Doulton/Canadian Centenary/ Canadian Centennial Series 1867-1967 Available in North America during 1967 only.

Doulton Number	Size	Backstamp	Height	Intro.	Discon.	Current Market Value U.K. £	U.S. $	Can. $
D6610	Large	Doulton	7 1/4"	1967	1982	75.00	200.00	220.00
D6610	Large	Centenary	7 1/4"	1967	1967	150.00	350.00	375.00
D6613	Small	Doulton	3 1/2"	1967	1982	50.00	100.00	115.00
D —	Miniature	Doulton	2 1/2"	Unknown		Extremely rare		

Note: The Lumberjack is one of three jugs that received a special backstamp in 1967. The other two, the North American Indian and the Trapper, complete the three-jug Canadian Centennial Series.

MACBETH

THE SHAKESPEAREAN COLLECTION,
ONE OF SIX

First performed in 1606, this Shakespearean tragedy was based on Scottish history. With the help of his wife, Macbeth plots to usurp the throne. Three witches prophesy that he will succeed, but that the heirs of his enemy Banquo will one day rule the kingdom. In a series of grisly events, their dark predictons are fulfilled.

STYLE ONE: HANDLE — WITCHES FACING OUTWARD

The faces of the three witches on the outer side of the handle face outward (noses out). Only after the jug was in the initial stages of production did Doulton realize that the possibility of the handle being damaged during shipping was great, and thus the moulds were quickly modified resulting in the production of style two.

Designer: Michael Abberley
Handle: Three witches facing to the right
Colourway: Brown, yellow and green

Backstamp: Doulton

Doulton Number	Size	Backstamp	Height	Intro.	Discon.	Current Market Value U.K. £	U.S. $	Can. $
D6667	Large	Doulton	7 1/4"	1981	1981		Extremely rare	

MACBETH

THE SHAKESPEAREAN COLLECTION,
ONE OF SIX

STYLE TWO: HANDLE — WITCHES FACING INWARD

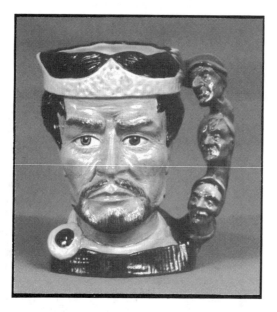

Designer: Michael Abberley
Handle: The faces of the three witches are on
the front of the handle facing forwards.
Colourway: Brown, yellow and grey

Backstamp: Doulton

Doulton Number	Size	Backstamp	Height	Intro.	Discon.	Current Market Value		
						U.K. £	**U.S. $**	**Can. $**
D6667	Large	Doulton	7 1/4"	1982	1989	85.00	175.00	195.00

MAD HATTER

ALICE IN WONDERLAND,
ONE OF SIX

A character from Lewis Carroll's *Alice's Adventures in Wonderland*, the Mad Hatter wears a watch that tells time in months, rather than in hours.

VARIATION No. 1:   Colourway — Black hat; dark red bow tie

Mad Hatter
D 6598
COPR 1970
DOULTON & CO LIMITED
Rd No 917231
Rd No 46577
Rd No 10000
Rd No 592/64

Designer: Max Henk
Handle: A dormouse above a pocket watch
Colourway: Black hat, dark red bow tie

Backstamp: Doulton

Doulton Number	Size	Variation	Height	Intro.	Discon.	Current Market Value U.K. £	U.S. $	Can. $
D6598	Large	Var. 1	7 1/4"	1965	1983	100.00	275.00	295.00
D6602	Small	Var. 1	3 3/4"	1965	1983	70.00	160.00	175.00
D6606	Miniature	Var. 1	2 1/2"	1965	1983	70.00	140.00	150.00

VARIATION No. 2: Colourway — Black hat; yellow bow tie

"MAD HATTER"
D.6748
Specially Commissioned from
Royal Doulton®
by
THE HIGBEE COMPANY 1985
Celebrating the opening of
The First Royal Doulton Room
Higbee's, Cleveland, U.S.A.
HAND MODELLED AND HAND DECORATED
A LIMITED EDITION OF 250
THIS IS NO. 224
© 1985 ROYAL DOULTON

BACKSTAMP A

Backstamps: A. Doulton / Higbee's
The large-size jug was commissioned by the Higbee Company to celebrate the opening of the first Royal Doulton Room. Issued on October 28, 1985, in a limited edition of 250 pieces.
B. Doulton/Higbee's
The small-size jug was commissioned by the Higbee Department Store to celebrate the second anniversary of the opening of the Royal Doulton Room. Issued in 1987 in a limited edition of 500 pieces.

Doulton Number	Size	Backstamp	Height	Intro.	Discon.	Current Market Value U.K. £	U.S. $	Can. $
D6748	Large	Doulton/Higbee	7"	1985	Ltd. ed.	450.00	950.00	950.00
D6790	Small	Doulton/Higbee	3 1/4"	1987	Ltd. ed.	150.00	275.00	300.00

MAE WEST

THE CELEBRITY COLLECTION, ONE OF SIX

From her screen debut in 1932, Mae West (1892-1980) became an instant hit. She is best known for portraying tough, sophisticated characters who loved luxury and men. The public adored her and her witty quips, the most famous of which appears on the base of the jug: "When I'm good, I'm very good. But when I'm bad, I'm better."

BACKSTAMP A

Designer:	Colin M. Davidson
Handle:	Umbrella with a bow tied around the handle
Colourway:	Yellow hair; white feather dress

Backstamps: A. Doulton
General issue, 1983.
B. Doulton/American Express/
Premier Edition for American Express
This series was first introduced in the U.S.A. as a promotional jug for the American Express Company. Approximately 500 jugs jugs were given the special backstamp and were available only to the North American market.

Doulton Number	Size	Backstamp	Height	Intro.	Discon.	Current Market Value U.K. £	U.S. $	Can. $
D6688	Large	Doulton	7"	1983	1986	100.00	225.00	250.00
D6688	Large	Doulton/Amex	7"	1983	1983	300.00	550.00	650.00

MANCHESTER UNITED (FOOTBALL CLUB)

THE FOOTBALL SUPPORTERS,
ONE OF NINE

Designer: Stanley J. Taylor
Handle: Team coloured scarf
Colourway: Red, white and black uniform

Backstamp: Doulton

Doulton Number	Size	Backstamp	Height	Intro.	Discon.	Current Market Value		
						U.K. £	U.S. $	Can. $
D6924	Mid	Doulton	5"	1992	Current	32.50	—	—

MAORI

The Maori people of Polynesian descent were the first inhabitants of present-day New Zealand. Beginning as hunters and fishermen, the Maori later turned to agriculture and woodworking.

STYLE ONE: BLUE-GREY HAIR, FRIENDLY EXPRESSION

Designer: Unknown
Handle: Plain with plaque of Maori
Colourway: Brown and grey

Backstamp: Doulton

Doulton Number	Size	Backstamp	Height	Intro.	Discon.	Current Market Value U.K. £	U.S. $	Can. $
D6080	Large	Doulton	7"	1939	1939		Extremely rare	

MAORI

STYLE TWO: DARK HAIR, TWO WHITE-TIPPED FEATHERS IN HAIR, SERIOUS EXPRESSION

Designer: Unknown
Handle: Plain with plaque of Maori
Colourway: Brown and grey

Backstamp: Doulton

Doulton Number	Size	Backstamp	Height	Intro.	Discon.	Current Market Value		
						U.K. £	U.S. $	Can. $
D6080	Large	Doulton	7"	1939	1939		Extremely rare	

THE MARCH HARE

ALICE IN WONDERLAND,
ONE OF SIX

At the March Hare's home in Wonderland it is always six o'clock and time for tea. Not having a moment to tidy up, he and his friends, the Mad Hatter and the dormouse, sit at a table laid for a great number and change seats as they dirty the dishes. Alice makes herself unpopular by asking what they do when they arrive back at the beginning.

Royal Doulton®

THE MARCH HARE

D 6776

Modelled by

William K. Harper

© 1988 ROYAL DOULTON

Designer: William K. Harper
Handle: One of the hare's ears
Colourway: Green hat; yellow bow tie
with blue spots

Backstamp: Doulton

Doulton Number	Size	Backstamp	Height	Intro.	Discon.	Current Market Value U.K. £	U.S. $	Can. $
D6776	Large	Doulton	6"	1989	1991	100.00	275.00	295.00

MARILYN MONROE

THE CELEBRITY COLLECTION

PROTOTYPE

Norma Jean Baker (1926-1962) made her screen debut in 1948, and as Marilyn Monroe, her beauty and charisma established her as an international sex symbol. She died at the age of 36.

There are only two of these jugs known to exist. One is in the Doulton Museum, Stoke-on-Trent. The other came to auction in 1992 in Toronto and fetched $17,500.00. It was not issued due to copyright problems.

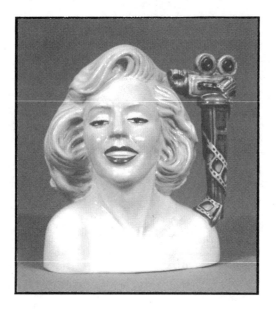

Designer: Eric Griffiths   **Backstamp:** Doulton
Handle: A cine-camera encircled by a roll of film
Colourway: Yellow, white and grey

Doulton Number	Size	Variation	Height	Intro.	Discon.	Current Market Value U.K. £	U.S. $	Can. $
D6719	Large	Prototype	7 1/4"	1983	1983	Sold at auction, Toronto, 1992 — $17,500. Can.		

MARK TWAIN

Born Samuel Langhorne Clemens (1835-1910), Mark Twain was an American writer and humourist. He was best loved for his classic adventure stories, *Tom Sawyer* (1876) and *The Adventures of Huckleberry Finn* (1884), which told of life in his native Mississippi.

The small jug was modelled for "The Queen's Table," Royal Doulton's exhibit at the United Kingdom Showcase at Walt Disney's Epcot Center in Orlando, Florida. The jug was sold exclusively to Epcot tourists visiting the exhibition during 1982.

Designer: Eric Griffiths
Handle: Quill and ink pot
Colourway: Black coat and bow tie; grey hair

Royal Doulton
MARK TWAIN
D 6654
Modelled by

© ROYAL DOULTON TABLEWARE
LIMITED 1979

Backstamp: Doulton

Doulton Number	Size	Backstamp	Height	Intro.	Discon.	Current Market Value U.K. £	U.S. $	Can. $
D6654	Large	Doulton	7 1/2"	1980	1990	75.00	225.00	240.00
D6694	Small	Doulton	4"	1983	1990	50.00	140.00	150.00
D6758	Miniature	Doulton	2 1/2"	1986	1990	50.00	165.00	175.00

THE MASTER / EQUESTRIAN

This piece was released in the U.K. as The Master, and in North America as The Equestrian.

Royal Doulton®
THE MASTER
D 6898
Modelled by

Stanley James Taylor

© 1991 ROYAL DOULTON

Designer: Stanley J. Taylor
Handle: Horse head
Colourway: Dark blue, red and white

Backstamp: Doulton

Doulton Number	Size	Backstamp	Height	Intro.	Discon.	Current Market Value U.K. £	U.S. $	Can. $
D6898	Small	Doulton	4"	1991	Current	29.95	69.50	120.00

McCALLUM

PROTOTYPE

This jug carries the Burslem lion and crown backstamp with the number "—0—" signifying 1927. The jug is controversial, but the backstamp date might lead one to believe that it was a trial piece for the 1930 issues.

Backstamp: Doulton

Designer: McCallum
Handle: Plain
Colourway: White hair with pale green and pink highlights; black with red and green glengarry; green base

Doulton Number	Size	Variation	Height	Intro.	Discon.	Current Market Value U.K. £	U.S. $	Can. $
D ---	Large	Prototype	7"	1927			Unique	

McCALLUM

Produced as a promotional item for the D & J McCallum Distillery, Scotland, this jug exists in three different colour varieties, all in very limited quantities. This jug was also produced by other manufacturers from an almost identical design. The colourways and size are extremely close to the jug produced by Doulton. The backstamp is the best way to tell the difference.

VARIATION No. 1:   Kingsware
                            Colourway — Light and dark browns
                            Approximately 1,000 to 1,500 pieces are thought to have been made

Designer: McCallum
Handle: Plain
Colourway: Light and dark browns

Backstamp: Doulton

Doulton Number	Size	Variation	Height	Intro.	Discon.	Current Market Value U.K. £	U.S. $	Can. $
D —	Large	Kingsware glaze	7"	1930	Unknown	1,250.00	3,300.00	3,300.00

VARIATION No. 2:   Colourway — Ivory glaze
Approximately 1,000 pieces were produced

Doulton Number	Size	Variation	Height	Intro.	Discon.	Current Market Value		
						U.K. £	U.S. $	Can. $
D ---	Large	Ivory glaze	7"	1930	Unknown	750.00	2,850.00	2,500.00

VARIATION No. 3:   Colourway — Treacle body; green hat, collar and handle

Doulton Number	Size	Variation	Height	Intro.	Discon.	Current Market Value		
						U.K. £	U.S. $	Can. $
D ---	Large	Treacle glaze	7"	1930	Unknown		Extremely rare	

MEPHISTOPHELES

First found in 16th-century German legend, Mephistopheles became best known in Johann von Goethe's drama, *Faust* (1808). In it he is portrayed as an evil spirit or devil to whom Faust sells his soul in return for services.

When the devil was sick
the devil a' Saint would be
when the devil got well
devil a Saint was he

BACKSTAMP A

Designer: Charles Noke
Harry Fenton
Handle: Plain
Colourway: Red and brown
Backstamps: A. Doulton — With verse
B. Doulton — Without verse

Doulton Number	Size	Backstamp	Height	Intro.	Discon.	Current Market Value U.K. £	U.S. $	Can. $
D5757	Large	With verse	7"	1937	1948	850.00	2,750.00	2,750.00
D5757	Large	Without verse	7"	1937	1948	750.00	2,500.00	2,500.00
D5758	Small	With verse	3 3/4"	1937	1948	450.00	1,500.00	1,500.00
D5758	Small	Without verse	3 3/4"	1937	1948	400.00	1,300.00	1,300.00

MERLIN

CHARACTERS FROM LITERATURE,
ONE OF 11

In the legend of King Arthur of Camelot, Merlin appears as wizard and aide to the King. He is credited with the creation of the famous Round Table.

Designer: Garry Sharpe
Handle: An owl
Colourway: Black, grey and brown

Merlin
D 6543
COPR 1959
DOULTON & CO LIMITED
Rd No 893842
Rd No 39650
Rd No 8314
Rd No 41/959

Backstamp: Doulton

Doulton Number	Size	Backstamp	Height	Intro.	Discon.	Current Market Value		
						U.K. £	U.S. $	Can. $
D6529	Large	Doulton	7 1/4"	1960	Current	55.00	125.00	175.00
D6536	Small	Doulton	3 3/4"	1960	Current	27.00	69.50	100.00
D6543	Miniature	Doulton	2 3/4"	1960	1991	40.00	70.00	80.00

MICHAEL DOULTON

This jug was manufactured in an edition of 9,500 pieces. It was only available for sale at retail locations where and when Michael Doulton was present.

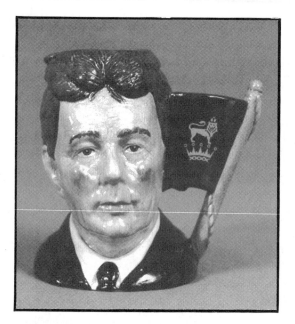

Royal Doulton®
D 6808
MICHAEL DOULTON
Modelled by

William K. Harper

© 1988 ROYAL DOULTON

Designer: William K. Harper
Handle: Flag bearing the Royal Doulton logo
Colourway: Black, brown and blue

Backstamp: Doulton

Doulton Number	Size	Backstamp	Height	Intro.	Discon.	Current Market Value U.K. £	U.S. $	Can. $
D6808	Small	Doulton	4 1/4"	1988	1989	40.00	140.00	125.00

THE MIKADO

"Mikado" is the ancient title for the emperor of Japan, beginning with the reign of the Mikado Jimmu in 660 B.C. Believed by many to have descended from the all-powerful Sun Goddess, the same family line has been traced through 124 reigns. The mikado is popularly known through the Gilbert and Sullivan operetta (1885) of the same name.

The Mikado.
D.6501
COPR 1958
DOULTON & CO LIMITED
Rd No 889572
Rd No 38228
Rd No 8038
Rd No 421,58

Designer: Max Henk
Handle: A fan
Colourway: Black and turquoise hat;
green and white robes

Backstamp: Doulton

Doulton Number	Size	Backstamp	Height	Intro.	Discon.	Current Market Value U.K. £	U.S. $	Can. $
D6501	Large	Doulton	6 1/2"	1959	1969	325.00	850.00	875.00
D6507	Small	Doulton	3 3/4"	1959	1969	250.00	475.00	500.00
D6525	Miniature	Doulton	2 1/2"	1960	1969	225.00	525.00	550.00

MINE HOST

The forerunner of today's English publican, this cheerful man would hang a pine bough on the door of his home to let travellers know that refreshments were available. As the handle shows, these often ran to a good pint of strong ale!

Mine Host
D.6513
COPR 1957
DOULTON & CO LIMITED
Rd No 886230
Rd No 37212
Rd No 7854
Rd No 389/57

Designer: Max Henk
Handle: Evergreen bough and barrel
Colourway: Black tricorn; red coat; white bow tie with gold spots

Backstamp: Doulton

Doulton Number	Size	Backstamp	Height	Intro.	Discon.	Current Market Value U.K. £	U.S. $	Can. $
D6468	Large	Doulton	7"	1958	1982	85.00	175.00	195.00
D6470	Small	Doulton	3 1/2"	1958	1982	50.00	100.00	115.00
D6513	Miniature	Doulton	2 1/2"	1960	1982	60.00	140.00	150.00

MONTY

Bernard Law Montgomery (1887-1976), first Viscount Montgomery of Alamein, was referred to familiarly as Monty. The highlights of his long and distinguished military career include the first Allied victory of World War II in North Africa in 1942 and the acceptance of the German surrender at Luneburg Heath in 1945. He was Deputy Supreme Commander of the Allied Powers in Europe from 1951 to 1958.

In 1954 a minor colourway change occurred when the yellow highlighting on the cap badge was dropped.

Monty
D 6202

Designer: Harry Fenton
Handle: Plain
Colourway: Brown beret; khaki uniform

Backstamp: Doulton

Doulton Number	Size	Backstamp	Height	Intro.	Discon.	Current Market Value U.K. £	U.S. $	Can. $
D6202	Large	Doulton	5 3/4"	1946	1954	100.00	175.00	195.00
D6202	Large	Doulton	5 3/4"	1954	1991	75.00	140.00	160.00

Note: For Field Marshall Montgomery, see page 222. For Viscount Montgomery of Alamein, see page 464.

MR. BUMBLE

CHARLES DICKENS COMMEMORATIVE SET,
DICKENS TINIES, ONE OF 12

Mr. Bumble ran a local parish workhouse for orphans in Dickens's *Oliver Twist*. It was from here that Oliver escaped and ran away to London.

The Mr. Bumble jug was issued to commemorate the 170th anniversary of the birth of Charles Dickens. There are 12 jugs in this set, each issued with a certificate of authenticity. A mahogany display shelf completes the set. The set was first sold by Lawleys By Post in the U.K. from 1982 to 1988, and from 1985 in North America and Australia.

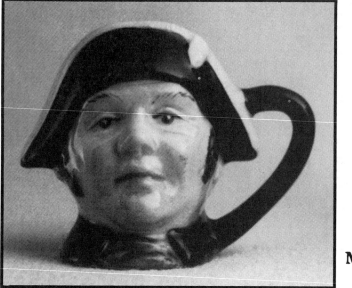

Mr Bumble
D 6686

Designer: Robert Tabbenor
Handle: Plain
Colourway: Yellow, dark blue and green

Backstamp: Doulton

Doulton Number	Size	Backstamp	Height	Intro.	Discon.	Current Market Value		
						U.K. £	U.S. $	Can. $
D6686	Tiny	Doulton 1 1/2"		1982	1989	40.00	65.00	75.00
		Display stand for 12 tinies				65.00	45.00	50.00

MR. MICAWBER

In Charles Dickens's classic, *David Copperfield*, Wilkins Micawber is Copperfield's landlord and friend. A sanguine idler, Micawber unmasks Uriah Heep as a villain and is rewarded with passage to Australia, where he settles happily in a prominent neighbourhood.

Micawber.
RᵈNᵒ822825.
REGᵈ IN AUSTRALIA

Designer:	Leslie Harradine / Harry Fenton	**Backstamp:** Doulton
Handle:	Plain	
Colourway:	Black hat; green coat; blue polka-dot bow tie	

Doulton Number	Size	Backstamp	Height	Intro.	Discon.	Current Market Value U.K. £	U.S. $	Can. $
D5843	Mid	Doulton	5 1/2"	1938	1948	140.00	265.00	280.00
D5843	Small	Doulton	3 1/4"	1948	1960	65.00	150.00	165.00
D6138	Miniature	Doulton	2 1/4"	1940	1960	50.00	100.00	115.00
D6143	Tiny	Doulton	1 1/4"	1940	1960	70.00	150.00	165.00

Mr. Micawber Derivatives

Doulton Number	Item	Height	Intro.	Discon.	Current Market Value U.K. £	U.S. $	Can. $
D5843	Table lighter	3 1/2"	1958	1959	175.00	350.00	365.00
D6050	Bust	2 1/4"	1939	1960	65.00	140.00	150.00
HN1615	Bookend	4"	1934	c. 1939	1,000.00	2,500.00	2,500.00
M58	Napkin ring	3 1/2"	c. 1935	1939	295.00	750.00	750.00

MR. PICKWICK

Founder and chairman of the Pickwick Club, this gentleman is the elegant and genial hero of Charles Dickens's *The Posthumous Papers of the Pickwick Club,* first published in 1837.

STYLE ONE: HANDLE — PLAIN

Designer: Leslie Harradine/Harry Fenton
Handle: Plain
Colourway: Green hat; brown coat; red bow tie

Backstamp: Doulton

Doulton Number	Size	Backstamp	Height	Intro.	Discon.	Current Market Value U.K. £	U.S. $	Can. $
D6060	Large	Doulton	7"	1940	1960	120.00	250.00	275.00
D5839	Mid	Doulton	4 1/4"	1938	1948	130.00	250.00	275.00
D5839	Small	Doulton	3 1/2"	1948	1960	70.00	140.00	160.00
D6254	Miniature	Doulton	2 1/4"	1947	1960	50.00	100.00	115.00
D6260	Tiny	Doulton	1 1/4"	1947	1960	125.00	350.00	365.00

Mr. Pickwick Derivatives

Doulton Number	Item	Height	Intro.	Discon.	Current Market Value U.K. £	U.S. $	Can. $
D5839	Table lighter	3 1/2"	1958	1961	175.00	375.00	395.00
D6049	Bust	3 1/2"	1939	1960	75.00	140.00	150.00
HN1623	Bookend	4"	1934	c. 1939	950.00	2,500.00	2,500.00
M57	Napkin ring	3 1/2"	c. 1935	c. 1939	275.00	750.00	750.00

MR. PICKWICK

Sold by Lawleys By Post in a limited edition of 2,500 pieces, Mr. Pickwick was issued with metal spectacles, like the Glenn Miller jug.

STYLE TWO: HANDLE — FIGURE OF SAM WELLER

Designer: William K. Harper
Handle: The figure of Sam Weller
Colourway: Blue, black, green and cream

Backstamp: Doulton

Doulton Number	Size	Backstamp	Height	Intro.	Discon.	Current Market Value U.K. £	U.S. $	Can. $
D6959	Large	Doulton	7"	1994	Ltd. ed.	99.00	—	—

MR. QUAKER

These jugs were made as an advertising piece for the internal use of Quaker Oats Limited, and a few were sold to members of the Royal Doulton International Collectors Club. They were issued with a certificate signed by Sir Richard Bailey and Michael Doulton.

Mr. Quaker was commissioned by Quaker Oats Limited and issued in 1985 in a limited edition of 3,500 pieces.

D.6738
MR QUAKER ®
Specially Commissioned from
Royal Doulton ®
by
© QUAKER OATS LIMITED 1984
in celebration of the Company's 85th year
Hand modelled & Hand Painted
Designed by *Harry Sales*
Modelled by *John Tongue*
A LIMITED EDITION OF 3,500
of which this is no 1811

Designer: Harry Sales
Modeller: Graham Tongue
Handle: A sheaf of wheat
Colourway: Black, white and yellow

Backstamp: Doulton/Quaker Oats Ltd

Doulton Number	Size	Backstamp	Height	Intro.	Discon.	Current Market Value		
						U.K. £	U.S. $	Can. $
D6738	Large	Doulton/Quaker	7 1/2"	1985	Ltd. ed.	275.00	850.00	750.00

MRS BARDELL

CHARLES DICKENS COMMEMORATIVE SET,
DICKENS TINIES, ONE OF 12

In Dickens's *The Pickwick Papers*, Mrs. Bardell sues Mr. Pickwick for breach of promise.

Mrs Bardell was issued to commemorate the 170th anniversary of the birth of Charles Dickens. There are 12 jugs in this set, each issued with a certificate of authenticity. A mahogany display shelf completes the set. The set was first sold by Lawleys By Post in the U.K. from 1982 to 1988, and from 1985 in North America and Australia.

Mrs Bardell
D 6687

Designer: Robert Tabbenor
Handle: Plain
Colourway: Yellow and green

Backstamp: Doulton

Doulton Number	Size	Backstamp	Height	Intro.	Discon.	Current Market Value U.K. £	U.S. $	Can. $
D6687	Tiny	Doulton	1 1/2"	1982	1989	40.00	65.00	75.00
		Display stand for 12 tinies				65.00	45.00	50.00

MRS. CLAUS

CHRISTMAS MINIATURES SERIES,
ONE OF FIVE

Commissioned for the North American market, Mrs. Claus has her handle to the left so she can be paired with her husband Santa Claus (D6900), whose handle points in the opposite direction.

Royal Doulton ®

MRS. CLAUS

D 6922

© 1992 ROYAL DOULTON

Designer: Stanley J. Taylor
Handle: Holly wreath
Colourway: Red, cream and green

Backstamp: Doulton

Doulton Number	Size	Backstamp	Height	Intro.	Discon.	Current Market Value		
						U.K. £	U.S. $	Can. $
D6922	Miniature	Doulton	2 3/8"	1992	Sp. ed.	50.00	115.00	125.00

NAPOLEON

Issued in a limited edition of 2,000 pieces, the Napoleon jug bears a special backstamp and comes with a certificate of authenticity.

STYLE ONE: HANDLE — AN EAGLE

Royal Doulton®
NAPOLEON
D 6941
Modelled by
Stanley James Taylor
© 1993 ROYAL DOULTON
ISSUED IN A LIMITED EDITION
OF 2,000
THIS IS No. **457**

Designer: Stanley J. Taylor
Handle: An eagle
Colourway: Black and gold

Backstamp: Doulton

Doulton Number	Size	Backstamp	Height	Intro.	Discon.	Current Market Value U.K. £	U.S. $	Can. $
D6941	Large	Doulton	7"	1993	Ltd. ed. (1994)	110.00	340.00	365.00

NAPOLEON

WATERLOO SERIES
ONE OF TWO

This jug, and its matching pair, Wellington D7002, was issued to commemorate the 180th anniversary of the Battle of Waterloo. The jugs were commissioned by Lawleys By Post and issued in a limited edition of 2,500 pieces.

STYLE TWO: HANDLE — CROWN AND SCROLLS

Designer: William K. Harper
Handle: Gold emblazoned crown atop scrolls
showing the names of famous battles
Colourway:

Backstamp: Doulton

Doulton Number	Size	Backstamp	Height	Intro.	Discon.	Current Market Value U.K. £	U.S. $	Can. $
D7001	Small	Doulton	4"	1995	Ltd. ed.	125.00 (set of two jugs)		

NAPOLEON AND JOSEPHINE

STAR-CROSSED LOVERS (TWO-FACED JUG),
ONE OF FOUR

Napoleon (1769-1821) stood only 5 feet 2 inches tall, but he was a military genius who amassed an empire that covered most of western and central Europe. Josephine (1763-1814) married him in 1796, after her first husband, the Vicomte de Beauharnais, was killed during the French Revolution. Unable to produce an heir, Napoleon divorced Josephine in 1809 to marry a younger woman.

This jug was issued in 1986 in a limited edition of 9,500 pieces.

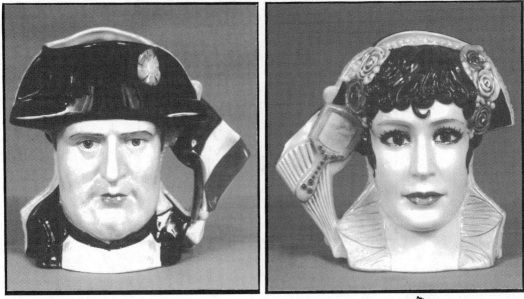

Designer: Michael Abberley
Handle: Napoleon: French Flag
Josephine: A fan and mirror
Colourway: Black, white, yellow and brown
Backstamp: Doulton

Royal Doulton®
THE
S*TAR-CROSSED* L*OVERS*
COLLECTION

Napoleon & Josephine
D 6750

Modelled by Michael Abberley .

Michael Abberley

Worldwide Limited Edition of 9.500
This is Number *1976*
© 1985 Royal Doulton (UK)

Doulton Number	Size	Backstamp	Height	Intro.	Discon.	Current Market Value		
						U.K. £	U.S. $	Can. $
D6750	Large	Doulton	7"	1986	Ltd. ed. (1991)	100.00	250.00	265.00

NELSON

ROYAL DOULTON INTERNATIONAL COLLECTORS CLUB SERIES

Issued by the Royal Doulton International Collectors Club, the Nelson jug was available only to their members from 1994 to March 1995.

Designer: Warren Platt
Handle: The naval ensign
Colourway: Black, white, red and gold

Backstamp: Doulton

Doulton Number	Size	Backstamp	Height	Intro.	Discon.	Current Market Value		
						U.K. £	U.S. $	Can. $
D	Small	Doulton	4 1/2"	1994	1995	49.95	120.00	125.00

Note: For Lord Nelson see page 310. For Vice-Admiral Lord Nelson see page 461.

NEPTUNE

In Roman mythology, Neptune is the god of the sea. According to legend Neptune married the sea nymph Amphitrite and together they had a son named Triton, who was half man and half fish.

Neptune
D 6552
COPR 1960
DOULTON & CO LIMITED
Rd No 897937
Rd No 40887
Rd No 8596
Rd No 547/60

Designer: Max Henk
Handle: Trident and fish
Colourway: Blue, grey and green

Backstamp: Doulton

Doulton Number	Size	Backstamp	Height	Intro.	Discon.	Current Market Value		
						U.K. £	U.S. $	Can. $
D6548	Large	Doulton	6 1/2"	1961	1991	75.00	175.00	195.00
D6552	Small	Doulton	3 3/4"	1961	1991	50.00	90.00	110.00
D6555	Miniature	Doulton	2 1/2"	1961	1991	45.00	80.00	95.00

NIGHT WATCHMAN

CHARACTER JUGS FROM WILLIAMSBURG,
ONE OF EIGHT

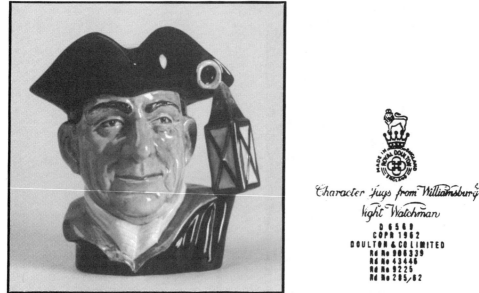

Designer: Max Henk
Handle: Lantern
Colourway: Black-purple tricorn and cloak

Backstamp: Doulton

Doulton Number	Size	Backstamp	Height	Intro.	Discon.	Current Market Value		
						U.K. £	U.S. $	Can. $
D6569	Large	Doulton	7"	1963	1983	85.00	200.00	225.00
D6576	Small	Doulton	3 1/2"	1963	1983	60.00	140.00	160.00
D6583	Miniature	Doulton	2 1/2"	1963	1983	50.00	140.00	160.00

NORTH AMERICAN INDIAN

VARIATION No. 1: Colourway — Red, white and black feathers; yellow and white band; green robes

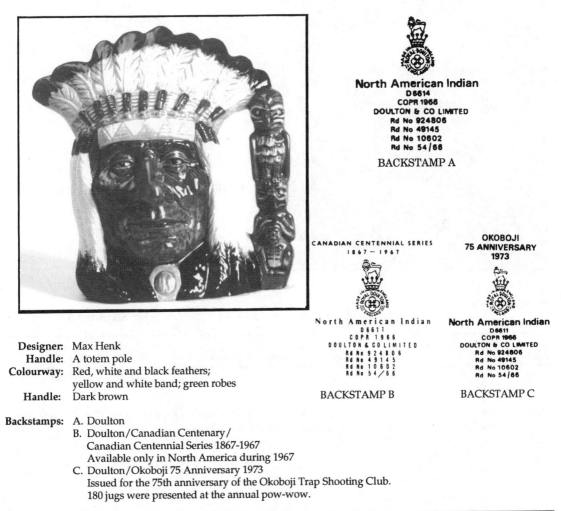

North American Indian
D6614
COPR 1966
DOULTON & CO LIMITED
Rd No 924806
Rd No 49145
Rd No 10602
Rd No 54/66

BACKSTAMP A

Designer:	Max Henk	
Handle:	A totem pole	
Colourway:	Red, white and black feathers; yellow and white band; green robes	
Handle:	Dark brown	

CANADIAN CENTENNIAL SERIES
1867 — 1967

North American Indian
D6611
COPR 1966
DOULTON & CO LIMITED
Rd No 924806
Rd No 49145
Rd No 10602
Rd No 54/66

BACKSTAMP B

OKOBOJI
75 ANNIVERSARY
1973

North American Indian
D6611
COPR 1966
DOULTON & CO LIMITED
Rd No 924806
Rd No 49145
Rd No 10602
Rd No 54/66

BACKSTAMP C

Backstamps: A. Doulton
B. Doulton/Canadian Centenary/
Canadian Centennial Series 1867-1967
Available only in North America during 1967
C. Doulton/Okoboji 75 Anniversary 1973
Issued for the 75th anniversary of the Okoboji Trap Shooting Club.
180 jugs were presented at the annual pow-wow.

Doulton Number	Size	Backstamp	Height	Intro.	Discon.	Current Market Value U.K. £	U.S. $	Can. $
D6611	Large	A	7 3/4"	1967	1991	75.00	160.00	175.00
D6611	Large	B	7 3/4"	1967	1967	125.00	400.00	425.00
D6611	Large	C	7 3/4"	1973	1973	425.00	3,000.00	3,000.00
D6614	Small	A	4 1/4"	1967	1991	50.00	95.00	110.00
D6665	Miniature	A	2 3/4"	1981	1991	40.00	70.00	80.00

VARIATION No. 2: Colourway —Yellow, blue, white and black feathers; green and white band; orange robes
Handle — Light brown

Royal Doulton®
NORTH AMERICAN INDIAN
D 6786
Modelled by

© 1966 ROYAL DOULTON
NEW COLOURWAY 1987
SPECIAL EDITION OF 1000
FOR JOHN SINCLAIR SHEFFIELD

Backstamp: Doulton / John Sinclair
Commissioned by John Sinclair, Sheffield, England. Issued in 1987 in a special edition of 1,000 pieces

Doulton Number	Size	Backstamp	Height	Intro.	Discon.	Current Market Value U.K. £	U.S. $	Can. $
D6786	Large	Doulton/Sinclair	7 1/2"	1987	Sp. ed.	75.00	275.00	295.00

Note: The North American Indian is one of three jugs which received a special backstamp in 1967. The other two, the Lumberjack and the Trapper form a three-jug Canadian Centennial Series.

OLD CHARLEY

"Ten o'clock and all's well" was the familiar call of the Charlies, watchmen who originated during the reign of Charles II and were named after him. They enjoyed a history of almost two hundred years, before being replaced in the early 1800s by a version of the present-day policeman.

VARIATION No. 1:   Colourway — Brown hat; dark green coat; blue polka-dot bow tie

Old Charley
D5420
DOULTON & CO LIMITED
BACKSTAMP A

BACKSTAMP B   BACKSTAMP C

Designer: Charles Noke
Handle: Plain
Colourway: Brown hat; dark green coat;
blue polka-dot bow tie

Backstamps: A.   Doulton
B.   Doulton/Bentalls/
Souvenir from Bentalls. Jubilee Year, 1935.
Bentalls Ltd. is a London department store.
C.   Doulton/Bentalls/
Souvenir from Bentalls. 1936.

Doulton Number	Size	Backstamp	Height	Intro.	Discon.	Current Market Value U.K. £	U.S. $	Can. $
D5420	Large	Doulton	5 1/2"	1934	1983	75.00	140.00	160.00
D5527	Small	Doulton	3 1/4"	1935	1983	40.00	100.00	110.00
D5527	Small	Bentalls B	3 1/4"	1935	1935	400.00	1,000.00	1,000.00
D5527	Small	Bentalls C	3 1/4"	1936	1936	400.00	1,000.00	1,000.00
D6046	Miniature	Doulton	2 1/4"	1939	1983	35.00	75.00	85.00
D6144	Tiny	Doulton	1 1/4"	1940	1960	75.00	140.00	160.00

VARIATION No. 2: Colourway — Black hat; maroon coat; black polka-dot bow tie

BACKSTAMP B

Backstamps: A. Doulton/Higbee/
Specially Commissioned from Royal Doulton by The Higbee Company
To Commemorate the First Anniversary of the Opening of the First Royal Doulton Room
Higbee's, Cleveland, Ohio, U.S.A.
Commissioned by the Higbee Department Store in 1985. Issued in 1986 in a limited edition of 250
pieces.

B. Doulton/Higbee/
Specially Commissioned from Royal Doulton by The Higbee Company
To Commemorate the Second Anniversary of the Opening of the First Royal Doulton Room
Higbee's, Cleveland, Ohio, U.S.A.
Commissioned by the Higbee Department Store and issued in a limited edition of 500 pieces.

Doulton Number	Size	Backstamp	Height	Intro.	Discon.	Current Market Value U.K. £	U.S. $	Can. $
D6761	Large	A. Higbee	5 1/2"	1986	1986	325.00	450.00	475.00
D6791	Small	B. Higbee	3 1/4"	1987	1987	145.00	250.00	275.00

Old Charley Derivatives

Doulton Number	Item	Height	Intro.	Discon.	Current Market Value U.K. £	U.S. $	Can. $
D5227	Table lighter	3 1/2"	1959	1973	150.00	250.00	275.00
D5844	Tobacco jar	5 1/2"	1937	1960	650.00	2,250.00	2,250.00
D5858	Musical jug	5 1/2"	1938	1939	375.00	1,200.00	1,200.00
D5599	Ashtray	2 3/4	1936	1960	100.00	200.00	225.00
D5925	Ash bowl	3"	1939	1960	100.00	200.00	225.00
D6012	Sugar bowl	2 1/2"	1939	1960	425.00	950.00	975.00
D6017	Teapot	7"	1939	1960	750.00	2,000.00	2,000.00
D6110	Wall pocket	7 1/4"	1940	1960	950.00	2,500.00	2,500.00
D6152	Toothpick holder	2 1/4"	1940	1960	400.00	2,000.00	2,000.00

Note: The tune played on the musical jug is "Here's a Health Unto His Majesty."

OLD KING COLE

"Old King Cole was a merry old soul" are the words of the nursery rhyme that inspired the design of this jug. The collar frill was remodelled around 1939 and variation two can be found with both deep and shallow white ruff modellings.

VARIATION No. 1: Colourway — Yellow crown; frills in the white ruff are deep and pronounced

Designer: Harry Fenton
Handle: Plain
Colourway: Yellow crown; frills in the white ruff are deep and pronounced

Backstamp: Doulton

Doulton Number	Size	Variation	Height	Intro.	Discon.	Current Market Value U.K. £	U.S. $	Can. $
D6036	Large	Var. 1	5 3/4"	1938	1939	1,450.00	4,500.00	4,500.00
D6037	Small	Var. 1	3 1/2"	1938	1939	900.00	3,000.00	3,000.00

VARIATION No. 2:   Colourway — Brown crown

Backstamps: A. Doulton
B. Doulton/Royal Doulton International Collectors Club

Doulton Number	Size	Backstamp	Height	Intro.	Discon.	Current Market Value U.K. £	U.S. $	Can. $
D6036	Large	A	5 3/4"	1939	1960	150.00	400.00	425.00
D6037	Small	A	3 1/2"	1939	1960	110.00	200.00	225.00
D6871	Tiny	B	1 1/2"	1990	1990	75.00	225.00	175.00

Old King Cole Derivatives, Musical Jugs

Doulton Number	Variation	Height	Intro.	Discon.	Current Market Value U.K. £	U.S. $	Can. $
D —	Yellow crown	7 1/2"	1939	1939	1,500.00	4,500.00	4,500.00
D6014	Brown crown	7 1/2"	1939	1939	750.00	2,250.00	2,500.00

Note: The tune played on the musical jugs is "Old King Cole was a Merry Old Soul."

OLD SALT

When the miniature Old Salt jug was launched in 1984, it had a hollow crook in the mermaid's arm. Later that year, because of production problems, the arm was moulded to the body. The first version of this miniature has attained near pilot status and commands a large premium over the general issue.

VARIATION No. 1: Colourway — Dark blue fisherman's jersey
Handle — Mermaid has blue tail

Old Salt
D 6551
COPR 1960
DOULTON & CO LIMITED
Rd No 898030
Rd No 40938
Rd No 8616
Rd No 572/60

Designer: Gary Sharpe — Large and small
Peter Gee — Miniature
Handle: A mermaid
Colourway: Dark blue fisherman's jersey

Backstamp: Doulton

Doulton Number	Size	Variation	Height	Intro.	Discon.	Current Market Value U.K. £	U.S. $	Can. $
D6551	Large	Var. 1	7 1/2"	1961	Current	55.00	150.00	175.00
D6554	Small	Var. 1	4"	1961	Current	29.95	82.50	100.00
D6557	Miniature	Open arm	2 1/2"	1984	1984	600.00	1,500.00	1,500.00
D6557	Miniature	Closed arm	2 1/2"	1984	1991	40.00	75.00	85.00

VARIATION No. 2: Colourway — Light and dark blue fisherman's jersey
Handle — Mermaid has yellow and black tail

Royal Doulton®
OLD SALT
D 6782
Modelled by

Gary Sharpe

© 1960 ROYAL DOULTON
NEW COLOURWAY 1987

Doulton Number	Size	Variation	Height	Intro.	Discon.	Current Market Value U.K. £	U.S. $	Can. $
D6782	Large	Var. 2	8"	1987	1990	85.00	275.00	295.00

Old Salt Derivative

INTERNATIONAL COLLECTORS CLUB
ROYAL DOULTON

OLD SALT
EXCLUSIVELY FOR
COLLECTORS CLUB
© 1989 ROYAL DOULTON
MODELLED BY

Doulton Number	Item	Height	Intro.	Discon.	Current Market Value U.K. £	U.S. $	Can. $
D6818	Teapot	6 1/4"	1989	1989	120.00	325.00	350.00

OLIVER CROMWELL

This is a two-handled jug, with Colonel Fairfax and Charles I forming the handles. It was issued in a limited edition of 2,500.

STYLE ONE: LARGE-SIZE, TWO-HANDLED JUG

Designer: William K. Harper
Handle: Colonel Fairfax and Charles I
Colourways: Brown, cream, blue and black

Backstamp: Doulton

Doulton Number	Size	Backstamp	Height	Intro.	Discon.	Current Market Value U.K. £	U.S. $	Can. $
D6968	Large	Doulton	7"	1994	Ltd. ed.	200.00	475.00	660.00

OLIVER CROMWELL

ENGLISH CIVIL WAR SERIES,
ONE OF TWO

Commissioned by Lawleys By Post, Oliver Cromwell (1599-1659) and the companion jug, Charles I, form a pair issued in a limited edition of 2,500. See page 169 for the Charles I jug.

STYLE TWO: HANDLE — SILVER MACE AND SASH

Designer: William K. Harper
Handle: Silver mace and sash
Colourway: Grey and white with silver details

Backstamp: Doulton

Doulton Number	Size	Backstamp	Height	Intro.	Discon.	Current Market Value U.K. £	U.S. $	Can. $
D6986	Small	Doulton	4 1/2"	1995	Ltd. ed.	50.00	—	—

OLIVER TWIST

CHARLES DICKENS COMMEMORATIVE SET,
DICKENS TINIES, ONE OF 12

The hero of Dickens's novel of Victorian London, Oliver Twist is an orphan who runs away from a workhouse to the city, only to be forced into thieving for the wicked Fagin.

The 12 jugs in this set were issued to commemorate the 170th anniversary of the birth of Charles Dickens, and each one came with a certificate of authenticity. A mahogany display shelf completed the set. The set was first sold by Lawleys By Post in the U.K. from 1982 to 1988, and from 1985 in North America and Australia.

Oliver Twist
D. 6677

Designer: Robert Tabbenor
Handle: Plain
Colourway: Dark and light blue

Backstamp: Doulton

Doulton Number	Size	Backstamp	Height	Intro.	Discon.	Current Market Value U.K. £	U.S. $	Can. $
D6677	Tiny	Doulton	1 1/2"	1982	1989	40.00	60.00	75.00
		Display stand for 12 tinies				65.00	45.00	50.00

OTHELLO

THE SHAKESPEAREAN COLLECTION,
ONE OF SIX

In Shakespeare's tragic play of 1604, Othello is a successful Venetian soldier who marries the attractive Desdemona. Out of spite and jealousy, his subordinate Iago convinces Othello that Desdemona has been unfaithful. Outraged, Othello kills her then commits suicide.

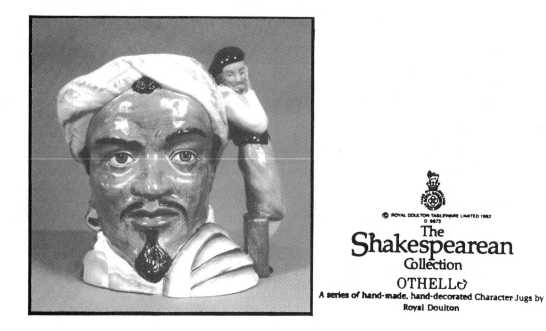

© ROYAL DOULTON TABLEWARE LIMITED 1982
D 6673

The
Shakespearean
Collection
OTHELLO
A series of hand-made, hand-decorated Character Jugs by
Royal Doulton

Designer: Michael Abberley
Handle: A figure of Iago
Colourway: Yellow turban; green, yellow and white robes

Backstamp: Doulton

Doulton Number	Size	Backstamp	Height	Intro.	Discon.	Current Market Value U.K. £	U.S. $	Can. $
D6673	Large	Doulton	7 1/4"	1982	1989	95.00	200.00	225.00

PADDY

Paddy, a colloquial term for an Irishman, is derived from St. Patrick, the country's patron saint. This gent is dressed in traditional green for St. Patrick's Day.

"Paddy."

Designer:	Harry Fenton	
Handle:	Plain	
Colourway:	Brown hat; green coat; yellow and red scarf	

Backstamp: Doulton

Doulton Number	Size	Backstamp	Height	Intro.	Discon.	Current Market Value U.K. £	U.S. $	Can. $
D5753	Large	Doulton	6"	1937	1960	95.00	225.00	240.00
D5768	Small	Doulton	3 1/4"	1937	1960	50.00	120.00	135.00
D6042	Miniature	Doulton	2 1/4"	1939	1960	45.00	90.00	100.00
D6145	Tiny	Doulton	1 1/4"	1940	1960	70.00	150.00	165.00

Paddy Derivatives

Doulton Number	Item	Backstamp	Height	Intro.	Discon.	Current Market Value U.K. £	U.S. $	Can. $
D5845	Tobacco jar	Doulton	5 1/2"	1939	1942	650.00	2,250.00	2,250.00
D5845	Tobacco jar	Salt River	5 1/2"	1939	1942	1,500.00	3,500.00	3,500.00
D5845	Tobacco jar	Coleman's	5 1/2"	1939	1942	1,000.00	2,750.00	2,750.00
D5887	Musical jug	Doulton	7"	1938	c.1939	375.00	1,200.00	1,200.00
D5926	Ash bowl	Doulton	3"	1938	1960	95.00	200.00	225.00
D6151	Toothpick holder	Doulton	2 1/4"	1940	1941	350.00	1,000.00	1,000.00

Note: The tune played on the musical jug is an Irish jig.

PARSON BROWN

A Parson Brown jug with a silver rim was made in 1937. The tiny version of Parson Brown was one of a set of six tinies issued in 1994, in a limited edition of 2,500, to celebrate the diamond anniversary of the first character jug.

BACKSTAMP C

SHEFFIELD &
ROTHERHAM

BACKSTAMP D

Designer: Charles Noke — Large and small
William K. Harper — Tiny
Handle: Plain
Colourway: Dark grey

Backstamps: A. Doulton/Commissioned by Bentalls to celebrate Bentalls Jubilee Year 1935
B. Doulton/Bentalls/Souvenir from the silver jubilee of King George VI
C. Doulton/Bentalls/Souvenir from Bentalls. 1936.
D. Doulton/Darley/Souvenir from Darley & Son Sheffield & Rotherham

Doulton Number	Size	Backstamp	Height	Intro.	Discon.	Current Market Value U.K. £	U.S. $	Can. $
D5486	Large	Doulton	6 1/2"	1935	1960	95.00	225.00	240.00
D5529	Small	Doulton	3 1/4"	1935	1960	55.00	120.00	135.00
D5529	Small	Bentalls / '35	3 1/2"	1935	1935	350.00	1,200.00	1,200.00
D5529	Small	Bentalls / '36	3 1/4"	1936	1936	350.00	1,000.00	1,000.00
D5529	Small	Doulton/Darley	3 1/4"	1936	1936	350.00	1,100.00	1,100.00
D6955	Tiny	Doulton	1 1/4"	1994	Ltd. ed (1994)	45.00	90.00	100.00

Parson Brown Derivatives

Doulton Number	Size	Backstamp	Height	Intro.	Discon.	Current Market Value U.K. £	U.S. $	Can. $
D5600	Ashtray	Doulton	3 1/2"	1936	1960	95.00	200.00	225.00
D6008	Ash bowl	Doulton	3"	1939	1960	95.00	200.00	225.00

PAUL McCARTNEY

THE BEATLES
ONE OF FOUR

Paul McCartney (b. 1942) was a singer, songwriter and the bass player with the Beatles, until they disbanded in 1970. He then performed with his own band, Wings, until 1981, and since then has remained active in the music field. This jug was issued only in Great Britain, due to copyright reasons.

Royal Doulton
THE BEATLES
Paul McCartney
D 6724
Modelled by
Stanley James Taylor.
© ROYAL DOULTON TABLEWARE
LIMITED 1984

Designer: Stanley J. Taylor
Handle: Plain
Colourway: Yellow tunic; blue collar and epaulettes

Backstamp: Doulton

Doulton Number	Size	Backstamp	Height	Intro.	Discon.	Current Market Value		
						U.K. £	U.S. $	Can. $
D6724	Mid	Doulton	5 1/2"	1984	1991	85.00	175.00	195.00

PEARLY BOY

The Pearly Boy is a coster or costermonger, one who sells fruits and vegetables from a barrow in the streets of London. His finest attire consists of clothes covered in pearl buttons. 'Arry (page 119) is a costermonger without his buttons.

VARIATION No. 1: Colourway — Brown hat with blue peak; blue coat; pearl buttons

" 'arry. "

COPR. 1946.
DOULTON & CO LIMITED.
RdNo 847679
RdNo 23908.
RdNo 133/46
RdNo 5194.

Designer: Harry Fenton
Handle: Plain
Colourway: Brown hat with blue peak; blue coat; white buttons.

Backstamp: Doulton

Doulton Number	Size	Variation	Height	Intro.	Discon.	Current Market Value U.K. £	Current Market Value U.S. $	Current Market Value Can. $
D —	Large	Var. 1	6 1/2"	1947	Unknown	3,000.00	12,000.00	7,000.00
D —	Small	Var. 1	3 1/2"	1947	Unknown	1,750.00	5,000.00	4,000.00
D —	Miniature	Var. 1	2 1/2"	1947	Unknown	Extremely rare		

VARIATION No. 2: Colourway — Brown hat and coat; pearl buttons

Doulton Number	Size	Variation	Height	Intro.	Discon.	Current Market Value U.K. £	Current Market Value U.S. $	Current Market Value Can. $
D —	Large	Var. 2	6 1/2"	1947	Unknown	Extremely rare		
D —	Small	Var. 2	3 1/2"	1947	Unknown	2,500.00	4,500.00	4,500.00
D —	Miniature	Var. 2	2 1/2"	1947	Unknown	2,500.00	4,000.00	4,500.00

VARIATION No. 3: Colourway — Brown hat and coat; brown buttons

Doulton Number	Size	Variation	Height	Intro.	Discon.	Current Market Value		
						U.K. £	U.S. $	Can. $
D —	Large	Var. 3	6 1/2"	1947	1947	950.00	2,400.00	2,400.00
D —	Small	Var. 3	3 1/2"	1947	1947	475.00	1,000.00	1,000.00
D —	Miniature	Var. 3	2 1/2"	1947	1947	375.00	850.00	850.00

VARIATION No. 4: Colourway — Beige hat; brown coat; pearl buttons

Doulton Number	Size	Variation	Height	Intro.	Discon.	Current Market Value		
						U.K. £	**U.S. $**	**Can. $**
D —	Large	Var. 4	6 1/2"	1947	Unknown	Extremely rare		
D —	Small	Var. 4	3 1/2"	1947	Unknown	1,750.00	4,500.00	4,000.00
D —	Miniature	Var. 4	2 1/2"	1947	Unknown	1,250.00	4,000.00	3,000.00

PEARLY GIRL

Pearly Girl is the female counterpart of Pearly Boy. She was a costermonger who sold her produce in the streets of London. Pearly Girl is 'Arriet (page 118) dressed in her finest.

VARIATION No. 1: Colourway — Blue jacket; lime-green feather; maroon hat and button

'arriet.'

COPR. 1946.
DOULTON & CO LIMITE.
R.N: 847682.
R.N: 23909.
R.N: 132/46.
R.N: 5195.

Designer:	Harry Fenton
Handle:	Hat feather
Colourway:	Blue jacket; lime-green feather; maroon hat and button

Backstamp: Doulton

Doulton						Current Market Value		
Number	Size	Variation	Height	Intro.	Discon.	U.K. £	U.S. $	Can. $
D —	Large	Var. 1	6 1/2"	1946	Unknown	3,000.00	10,000.00	7,000.00
D —	Small	Var. 1	3 1/4"	1946	Unknown	1,750.00	4,750.00	4,000.00
D----	Miniature	Var. 1	2 1/2"	1946	Unknown		Extremely rare	

VARIATION No. 2: Colourway — Dark brown jacket; lime-green feather; pink hat and button

Doulton						Current Market Value		
Number	Size	Variation	Height	Intro.	Discon.	U.K. £	U.S. $	Can. $
D —	Large	Var. 2	6 1/2"	1946	Unknown		Extremely rare	
D —	Small	Var. 2	3 1/4"	1946	Unknown		Extremely rare	

PEARLY KING

THE LONDON COLLECTION,
ONE OF TEN

The Pearly King is the head spokesman for the street-market costers of London. Over a hundred years ago, his chief mandate was as a go-between for the costers and the London police. Today the Pearlies have turned their energy to raising money for charity.

Designer: Stanley J. Taylor
Handle: The Bow Bells; pearl buttons
Colourway: Black cap and jacket with silver buttons; yellow scarf with red polka dots

Royal Doulton®
PEARLY KING
D 6760
Modelled by
Stanley James Taylor.
© 1986 ROYAL DOULTON

Backstamp: Doulton

Doulton Number	Size	Backstamp	Height	Intro.	Discon.	Current Market Value U.K. £	U.S. $	Can. $
D6760	Large	Doulton	6 3/4"	1987	1991	80.00	225.00	240.00
D6844	Small	Doulton	3 1/2"	1987	1991	45.00	120.00	130.00

PEARLY QUEEN

THE LONDON COLLECTION,
ONE OF TEN

The Pearly Queen, like the Pearly King, is the chief spokesperson for the street-market costers of London. The office is both hereditary and elected.

Designer: Stanley J. Taylor
Handle: The Bow Bells and pink and blue feathers
Colourway: Black coat with silver buttons; black hat with white, pink and blue feathers

Royal Doulton®
PEARLY QUEEN
D 6759
Modelled by
Stanley James Taylor.
© 1986 ROYAL DOULTON

Backstamp: Doulton

Doulton Number	Size	Backstamp	Height	Intro.	Discon.	Current Market Value		
						U.K. £	U.S. $	Can. $
D6759	Large	Doulton	7"	1987	1991	80.00	225.00	240.00
D6843	Small	Doulton	3 1/2"	1987	1991	45.00	120.00	130.00

THE PENDLE WITCH

This jug was the first and only jug issued in the proposed series, Myths, Fantasies and Legends. It was commissioned and distributed by Kevin Francis Ceramics (KFC) in 1989 in a special edition of 5,000 pieces.

Original Design and Concept by Alison Faulds of My Fair Lady

Hand made and hand decorated

Royal Doulton®

THE PENDLE WITCH

D 6826

Modelled by

Stanley James Taylor

A Special Edition of 5000
Produced by Royal Doulton
for Kevin Francis Ceramics

© 1988 ROYAL DOULTON
AND KEVIN FRANCIS CERAMICS

Designer: Stanley J. Taylor
Handle: A Hound
Colourway: Grey hair; black dress

Backstamp: Doulton/
Kevin Francis Ceramics

Doulton Number	Size	Backstamp	Height	Intro.	Discon.	Current Market Value		
						U.K. £	U.S. $	Can. $
D6826	Large	Doulton/KFC	7 1/4"	1989	Sp. ed.	125.00	350.00	375.00

PIED PIPER

PROTOTYPE

STYLE ONE: HANDLE — ONE WHITE RAT, FLUTE

Designer: Geoff Blower
Handle: White rat at the top of a dark brown flute
Colourway: Light brown hat; blond hair

Backstamp: Doulton

Doulton Number	Size	Variation	Height	Intro.	Discon.	Current Market Value U.K. £	U.S. $	Can. $
D6403	Large	Prototype	7"	Unknown			Unique	

PIED PIPER

In German legend, a stranger came to the town of Hamelin and told the mayor he would rid the village of rats for a sum of money. The Pied Piper walked through town playing a flute, and the rats followed him to the Weser River, where they drowned. When the mayor refused to pay him, the Pied Piper played his flute again, and this time the village children followed him into a cave, never to be seen again.

STYLE TWO: HANDLE — THREE BROWN RATS, FLUTE

Pied Piper
D 6403
COPR 1953
DOULTON & CO LIMITED

Designer: Geoff Blower
Handle: Three brown rats atop a flute
Colourway: Green cap; maroon and yellow tunic

Backstamp: Doulton

Doulton Number	Size	Backstamp	Height	Intro.	Discon.	Current Market Value		
						U.K. £	U.S. $	Can. $
D6403	Large	Doulton	7"	1954	1981	90.00	225.00	250.00
D6462	Small	Doulton	3 3/4"	1957	1981	50.00	130.00	150.00
D6514	Miniature	Doulton	2 5/8"	1960	1981	45.00	125.00	150.00

PIERRE ELLIOT TRUDEAU

PROTOTYPE

Joseph Philippe Pierre Yves Elliott Trudeau (b. 1919) became Canada's Minister of Justice and Attorney General in 1967. He was elected Prime Minister from 1968 to 1979 and from 1980 to 1984.

Doulton was unable to obtain permission to issue this jug.

Designer: William K. Harper
Handle: The Canadian flag
Colourway: Black and grey

Backstamp: Doulton

Doulton Number	Size	Variation	Height	Intro.	Discon.	U.K. £	U.S. $	Can. $
						Current Market Value		
D —	Large	Prototype	7"	Unknown			Unique	

PILGRIM FATHER

PROTOTYPE

Designer: David Biggs
Handle: The *Mayflower*
Colourway: Black suit; white collar; brown and white ship

Backstamp: Doulton

Doulton Number	Size	Variation	Height	Intro.	Discon.	Current Market Value		
						U.K. £	U.S. $	Can. $
D —	Large	Prototype	8 1/4"	1969	1969		Unique	

THE PIPER

The Piper jug was issued in a limited edition of 2,500 pieces.

Royal Doulton®
THE PIPER
D 6918
Modelled by
Stanley James Taylor
© 1992 ROYAL DOULTON
LIMITED EDITION OF 2,500
THIS IS NO. 425

Designer: Stanley J. Taylor
Handle: Bagpipes
Colourway: Black, red, white and yellow

Backstamp: Doulton

Doulton Number	Size	Backstamp	Height	Intro.	Discon.	Current Market Value		
						U.K. £	U.S. $	Can. $
D6918	Large	Doulton	8 1/4""	1992	Ltd. ed.	175.00	400.00	425.00

THE POACHER

VARIATION No. 1: Colourway — Green coat; red scarf; light brown hat

"The Poacher"
D 6429
COPR 1954
DOULTON & CO LIMITED
Rd No 875201
Rd No 33325
Rd No 7095
Rd No 321/54

Designer: Max Henk
Handle: A salmon
Colourway: Green coat; red scarf; light brown hat

Backstamp: Doulton

Doulton Number	Size	Variation	Height	Intro.	Discon.	Current Market Value U.K. £	U.S. $	Can. $
D6429	Large	Var. 1	7"	1955	Current	49.95	150.00	175.00
D6464	Small	Var. 1	4"	1957	Current	25.00	82.50	100.00
D6515	Miniature	Var. 1	2 1/2"	1960	1991	40.00	70.00	85.00

VARIATION No 2: Colourway — Maroon coat; yellow striped scarf; black hat

Royal Doulton®

THE POACHER
D 6781
Modelled by

© 1954 ROYAL DOULTON
NEW COLOURWAY 1987

Doulton Number	Size	Variation	Height	Intro.	Discon.	Current Market Value U.K. £	U.S. $	Can. $
D6781	Large	Var. 2	7"	1987	1989	75.00	225.00	250.00

The Poacher Derivative

Doulton Number	Item	Height	Intro.	Discon.	Current Market Value U.K. £	U.S. $	Can. $
D6464	Table lighter	4 3/4"	c. 1960	1973	135.00	225.00	250.00

THE POLICEMAN

JOURNEY THROUGH BRITAIN,
ONE OF FOUR

The Policeman was commissioned by Lawleys By Post and issued in 1989 in a limited edition of 5,000 pieces. The Doulton backstamp is set within the design of a policeman's badge.

Designer: Stanley J. Taylor
Handle: Handcuffs and truncheon
Colourway: Black and white

Backstamp: Doulton

Doulton Number	Size	Backstamp	Height	Intro.	Discon.	Current Market Value U.K. £	U.S. $	Can. $
D6852	Small	Doulton	4"	1989	Ltd. ed. (1991)	60.00	225.00	250.00

PORTHOS

THE THREE MUSKETEERS, ONE OF FOUR,
NOW PART OF THE CHARACTERS FROM LITERATURE, ONE OF 11

One of the much-loved three musketeers in the 1844 novel by Alexandre Dumas, Porthos roamed Europe with his merry band in search of adventure. "One of the Three Musketeers" was included in the early backstamp to indicate that Porthos was one of the famous Musketeers.

VARIATION No. 1:   Colourway — Black hat; red cloak; black hair and moustache

Porthos
D 6440
COPR 1955
DOULTON & CO LIMITED
BACKSTAMP A

Porthos
(One of the "Three Musketeers")
D 6453
COPR 1955
DOULTON & CO LIMITED
Rd No 877526
Rd No 34107
Rd No 7246
Rd No 291/55

BACKSTAMP B

Designer: Max Henk
Handle: A sword
Colourway: Black hat; red cloak; black hair and moustache

Backstamps: A. Doulton
B. Doulton/(One of the "Three Musketeers")

Doulton Number	Size	Backstamp	Height	Intro.	Discon.	Current Market Value U.K. £	U.S. $	Can. $
D6440	Large	Doulton	7 1/4"	1956	1991	70.00	150.00	165.00
D6440	Large	Doulton/One...	7 1/4"	1956	1970	70.00	150.00	165.00
D6453	Small	Doulton	4"	1956	1991	40.00	90.00	100.00
D6453	Small	Doulton/One...	4"	1956	1970	40.00	90.00	100.00
D6516	Miniature	Doulton	2 3/4"	1960	1991	45.00	90.00	100.00
D6516	Miniature	Doulton/One...	2 1/2"	1960	1970	45.00	90.00	100.00

VARIATION No. 2: Colourway — Maroon hat; blue cloak; ginger hair and moustache

Royal Doulton®
PORTHOS
D 6828
Modelled by

© 1955 ROYAL DOULTON
NEW COLOURWAY 1988
SPECIAL COMMISSION 1000
PETER JONES CHINA
LEEDS AND WAKEFIELD

Backstamp: Doulton / Peter Jones China Ltd.
Commissioned by Peter Jones China Ltd., Sheffield, England.
Issued in 1988 in a limited edition of 1,000 pieces.

Doulton Number	Size	Backstamp	Height	Intro.	Discon.	Current Market Value		
						U.K. £	U.S. $	Can. $
D6828	Large	Doulton/Jones	7 1/4"	1988	1988	85.00	225.00	250.00

Porthos Derivative

Doulton Number	Item	Height	Intro.	Discon.	Current Market Value		
					U.K. £	U.S. $	Can. $
D6453	Table lighter	3 1/2"	1958	Unknown	300.00	750.00	750.00

THE POSTMAN

JOURNEY THROUGH BRITAIN,
ONE OF FOUR

The Postman was commissioned by Lawleys By Post and issued in 1988 in a limited edition of 5,000 pieces. The Doulton backstamp is set within the design of a postage stamp.

Designer: Stanley J. Taylor
Handle: A pillar box
Colourway: Black jacket and cap; white shirt; red pillar box

Backstamp: Doulton

Doulton Number	Size	Backstamp	Height	Intro.	Discon.	Current Market Value U.K. £	U.S. $	Can. $
D6801	Small	Doulton	4"	1988	Ltd. ed.	150.00	400.00	425.00

PUNCH AND JUDY

ROYAL DOULTON INTERNATIONAL COLLECTORS CLUB SERIES

This two-faced jug was created exclusively for the Royal Doulton International Collectors Club, in a limited edition of 2,500.

PUNCH AND JUDY
D 6946
Modelled by

Stanley James Taylor.

EXCLUSIVELY FOR
COLLECTORS CLUB
© 1993 ROYAL DOULTON
LIMITED EDITION OF 2,500
THIS IS No. *103*

Designer: Stanley J. Taylor
Handle: Punch — dog; Judy — crocodile
Colourway: Red, yellow, blue, white and green

Backstamp: Doulton/RDICC

Doulton Number	Size	Backstamp	Height	Intro.	Discon.	Current Market Value		
						U.K. £	U.S. $	Can. $
D6946	Large	Doulton/RDICC	7"	1994	Ltd. ed. (1994)	199.95	400.00	495.00

PUNCH AND JUDY MAN

Coming to England in the 17th century by way of Italy and France, the Punch and Judy puppet show features Punch, the hunchbacked boastful husband, who beats his shrew-like wife Judy.

The colours on Punch's bat are occasionally reversed with no effect on the market value.

Designer: David Biggs
Handle: Punch
Colourway: Brown hat; green coat; yellow scarf

Backstamp: Doulton

Doulton Number	Size	Backstamp	Height	Intro.	Discon.	Current Market Value U.K. £	U.S. $	Can. $
D6590	Large	Doulton	7"	1964	1969	325.00	950.00	950.00
D6593	Small	Doulton	3 1/2"	1964	1969	245.00	575.00	575.00
D6596	Miniature	Doulton	2 1/2"	1964	1969	225.00	575.00	575.00

QUEEN ELIZABETH I

Daughter of Anne Boleyn, the second wife of Henry VIII, Elizabeth (1533-1603) enjoyed a 45 year reign. With the leadership of Sir Francis Drake, her Royal Navy defeated the Spanish Armada and Philip's attempted invasion of England. Issued by Lawleys By Post in 1988, this jug was one of a pair (with King Philip of Spain) that was produced to celebrate the 400th anniversary of the defeat of the Spanish Armada in 1588. Both jugs were issued in limited editions of 9,500 pieces.

Designer: William K. Harper
Handle: Warship sailing on the right
Colourway: Grey, dark red and white

Backstamp: Doulton

Doulton Number	Size	Backstamp	Height	Intro.	Discon.	Current Market Value U.K. £	U.S. $	Can. $
D6821	Small	Doulton	4"	1988	Ltd. ed.	95.00	225.00	250.00

Note: For Elizabeth I see page 295.

QUEEN VICTORIA

Alexandrina Victoria (1819-1901) succeeded her uncle William IV to the throne on her eighteenth birthday in 1837. Reigning until her death in 1901, she had a longer rule than any other British monarch, and her reign became known as one of the most peaceful in English history.

VARIATION No. 1: Colourway — Dark blue and yellow crown; beige and pink veils

BACKSTAMP A

Designer: Stanley J. Taylor
Handle: Yellow sceptre
Colourway: Dark blue and yellow crown; beige and pink veils; yellow jewel in sceptre

Backstamps: A. Doulton
B. Special Limited Edition of 1500
The small size jug was commissioned by Pascoe & Co. in a special edition of 1,500.

BACKSTAMP B

Doulton Number	Size	Backstamp	Height	Intro.	Discon.	Current Market Value		
						U.K. £	U.S. $	Can. $
D6816	Large	Doulton	7 1/4"	1989	1991	75.00	275.00	295.00
D6913	Small	Doulton	3 1/2"	1992	Sp. ed.	60.00	165.00	180.00

Note: For Victoria see page 295.

VARIATION No. 2:   Colourway — Purple and yellow crown; grey veil with
white frills; red jewel in sceptre

Backstamp: The Guild of Specialist China & Glass Retailers
Commissioned by the Guild of Specialist China & Glass Retailers
in 1988 and issued in a special edition of 3,000 pieces.

Doulton Number	Size	Backstamp	Height	Intro.	Discon.	Current Market Value		
						U.K. £	U.S. $	Can. $
D6788	Large	Doulton / Guild	7 1/4"	1988	Sp. ed.	75.00	375.00	395.00

RANGERS (FOOTBALL CLUB)

THE FOOTBALL SUPPORTERS,
ONE OF NINE

Royal Doulton®
FOOTBALL SUPPORTER'S
CHARACTER JUG.
D 6929
Modelled by
Stanley James Taylor
© 1992 ROYAL DOULTON
"RANGERS"

Designer: Stanley J. Taylor
Handle: Team coloured scarf
Colourway: Blue, white and red uniform

Backstamp: Doulton

Doulton Number	Size	Backstamp	Height	Intro.	Discon.	Current Market Value U.K. £	U.S. $	Can. $
D6929	Mid	Doulton	5"	1992	Current	32.50	—	—

THE RED QUEEN

ALICE IN WONDERLAND,
ONE OF SIX

A character from Lewis Carroll's *Alice's Adventures in Wonderland,* the Queen of Hearts shows her suit on the blade of an axe and cries, "Off with his head." Issued in 1987, it was the first in the Alice in Wonderland series.

Designer: William K. Harper
Handle: An axe
Colourway: Yellow, red and blue

Royal Doulton®

THE RED QUEEN
D 6777
Modelled by

William K. Harper

© 1987 ROYAL DOULTON

Backstamp: Doulton

Doulton Number	Size	Backstamp	Height	Intro.	Discon.	Current Market Value U.K. £	U.S. $	Can. $
D6777	Large	Doulton	7 1/4"	1987	1991	75.00	225.00	240.00
D6859	Small	Doulton	3"	1990	1991	50.00	165.00	180.00
D6860	Miniature	Doulton	2"	1990	1991	55.00	200.00	215.00

REGENCY BEAU

The regency of the Prince of Wales lasted from 1811 to 1820, when the Prince became George IV. The Regency Period, however, is a term loosely applied to the years from 1805 to 1830, when classical mythology and Greek and Roman authors were popular.

Regency Beau
D 6 5 5 9
COPR 1961
DOULTON & CO LIMITED
Rd No 902090
Rd No 42142
Rd No 8925
Rd No R 84/6 '

Designer: David Biggs
Handle: Cane and handkerchief
Colourway: Green coat; green and yellow hat

Backstamp: Doulton

Doulton Number	Size	Backstamp	Height	Intro.	Discon.	Current Market Value		
						U.K. £	U.S. $	Can. $
D6559	Large	Doulton	7 1/4"	1962	1967	550.00	1,500.00	1,500.00
D6562	Small	Doulton	4 1/4"	1962	1967	350.00	950.00	950.00
D6565	Miniature	Doulton	2 3/4"	1962	1967	450.00	1,300.00	1,300.00

RICK PARFITT

STATUS QUO,
ONE OF TWO

Produced in a limited edition of 2,500, the Rick Parfitt jug was issued in conjunction with the Francis Rossi jug, commemorating the U.K. band, Status Quo. The Parfitt jug handle is on the left, and the Rossi handle is on the right, so they can be displayed as a pair.

Designer: Martyn C. R. Alcock
Handle: Cream and brown guitar
Colourway: Blue and brown

Backstamp: Doulton:
Signed "Rick Parfitt" and
Phantom Music Ltd.

Doulton Number	Size	Backstamp	Height	Intro.	Discon.	Current Market Value U.K. £	U.S. $	Can. $
D6962	Small	Doulton	5"	1993	Ltd. ed.	50.00	75.00	100.00

THE RINGMASTER

THE CIRCUS,
ONE OF FOUR

Royal Doulton®
THE RING MASTER
D 6863
Modelled by

Stanley James Taylor

© 1990 ROYAL DOULTON

BACKSTAMP A

The International Royal Doulton Collectors Weekend 1990

Royal Doulton®
THE RING MASTER
D 6863
Modelled by
Stanley James Taylor
© 1990 ROYAL DOULTON

Toronto, Ontario, Canada

The Maple Leaf Edition

BACKSTAMP B

Designer: Stanley J. Taylor
Handle: Horse's head and plume
Colourway: Black top hat with a light blue ribbon; red jacket;
black lapel; green plume atop horses head

Backstamps: A. Doulton
For general release, 1991.
B. Doulton/The Maple Leaf Edition/
The International Royal Doulton Collectors Weekend 1990 Toronto, Ontario, Canada/
The Maple Leaf Edition
Commissioned to commemorate the International Royal Doulton Collectors Weekend,
September 14, 15 and 16, 1990. The design incorporates a red maple leaf in honour of the
25th anniversary of Canada's flag. Issued with a certificate of authenticity.
Pre-released in 1990 in a special edition of 750 pieces.

Doulton Number	Size	Backstamp	Height	Intro.	Discon.	Current Market Value U.K. £	U.S. $	Can. $
D6863	Large	Doulton	7 1/2"	1991	1993	85.00	225.00	250.00
D6863	Large	Doulton/Maple	7 1/2"	1990	Sp. ed.	160.00	275.00	300.00

RINGO STARR

THE BEATLES,
ONE OF FOUR

Richard Starkey (b. 1940) was the drummer for the Beatles until they disbanded in 1970.

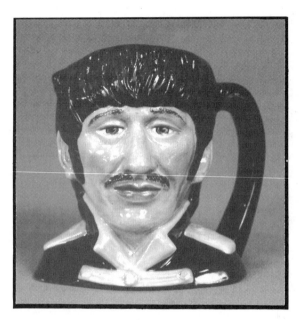

Royal Doulton
THE BEATLES
Ringo Starr
D 6726
Modelled by

Stanley James Taylor.

© ROYAL DOULTON TABLEWARE
LIMITED 1984

Designer: Stanley J. Taylor
Handle: Plain
Colourway: Black tunic; yellow collar and epaulettes

Backstamp: Doulton

Doulton Number	Size	Backstamp	Height	Intro.	Discon.	Current Market Value		
						U.K. £	U.S. $	Can. $
D6726	Mid	Doulton	5 1/2"	1984	1991	85.00	165.00	180.00

RIP VAN WINKLE

CHARACTERS FROM LITERATURE,
ONE OF 11

In 1820, the American writer Washington Irving wrote the story of Rip Van Winkle, based on legends he had heard from Dutch settlers. While walking in the Catskill Mountains of New York, Rip drinks a fairy potion and falls asleep for 20 years. He wakes to find an unrecognizable world.

VARIATION No. 1: Colourway — Grey-blue cap; brown robes; figure dressed in blue resting against tree

"Rip Van Winkle"
D.6438.
COPR.1954.
DOULTON & CO.LIMITED.
R⁰N° 874255.
R⁰N° 32854.
R⁰N° 7022.
R⁰N° 193/54.

Backstamp: Doulton

Designer: Geoff Blower
Handle: A man resting against the trunk of a tree, with a blackbird sitting atop it
Colourway: Grey-blue cap; brown robes; figure dressed in blue resting against tree

Doulton Number	Size	Backstamp	Height	Intro.	Discon.	Current Market Value U.K. £	U.S. $	Can. $
D6438	Large	Doulton	6 1/2"	1955	Current	49.95	125.00	175.00
D6463	Small	Doulton	4"	1957	Current	25.00	69.50	100.00
D6517	Miniature	Doulton	2 1/2"	1960	1991	35.00	65.00	75.00

VARIATION No. 2: Colourway — Black cap; green robes; figure dressed in black resting against tree

Royal Doulton®
RIP VAN WINKLE
D 6785
Modelled by

© 1954 ROYAL DOULTON
NEW COLOURWAY 1987
SPECIAL EDITION OF 1000
FOR JOHN SINCLAIR SHEFFIELD

Backstamp: **Doulton/John Sinclair**
Commissioned by John Sinclair, Sheffield, England. Issued in 1987 in a special edition of 1,000 pieces.

Doulton Number	Size	Backstamp	Height	Intro.	Discon.	Current Market Value U.K. £	U.S. $	Can. $
D6785	Large	Doulton/Sinclair	7"	1987	Sp. ed.	85.00	225.00	250.00

Rip Van Winkle Derivative

Doulton Number	Item	Height	Intro.	Discon.	Current Market Value U.K. £	U.S. $	Can. $
D6463	Table lighter	3 1/2"	1958	Unknown	400.00	750.00	750.00

ROBIN HOOD

PROTOTYPE

*Photograph
Not Available
At Press Time*

Designer: Eric Griffiths   **Backstamp:** Doulton
Handle: Plain
Colourway: Black, brown and green

Doulton Number	Size	Variation	Height	Intro.	Discon.	U.K. £	Current Market Value U.S. $	Can. $
D —	Large	Prototype	6 1/2"	1987	1987		Unique	

ROBIN HOOD

A legendary figure from the reign of Richard I in 12th-century England, Robin Hood and his group of benevolent bandits had many adventures while robbing the rich to help the poor.

STYLE ONE: HAT WITH NO FEATHER
HANDLE — PLAIN

Robin Hood

COPR.1946.
DOULTON & CO LIMITED.
RdNo 847681.
RdNo 23906.
RdNo 134/46.
RdNo 5192.

Designer: Harry Fenton
Handle: Two feathers
Colourway: Brown hat; green robes

Backstamp: Doulton

Doulton Number	Size	Backstamp	Height	Intro.	Discon.	Current Market Value		
						U.K. £	U.S. $	Can. $
D6205	Large	Doulton	6 1/4"	1947	1960	95.00	225.00	250.00
D6234	Small	Doulton	3 1/4"	1947	1960	55.00	120.00	135.00
D6252	Miniature	Doulton	2 1/4"	1947	1960	45.00	100.00	115.00

ROBIN HOOD

CHARACTERS FROM LITERATURE,
ONE OF 11

STYLE TWO: HAT WITH FEATHER
HANDLE — BOW, QUIVER AND ARROWS

Robin Hood
D 6527
COPR 1959
DOULTON & CO LIMITED
Rd No 893840
Rd No 39648
Rd No 8312
Rd No 421/59

Royal Doulton
ROBIN HOOD
D 6541
© ROYAL DOULTON
TABLEWARE LTD 1959

Designer: Max Henk
Handle: Bow and quiver of arrows
Colourway: Brown hat with white feather on one side
and oak leaves and acorns on the other;
green robes

Backstamp: Doulton

Doulton Number	Size	Backstamp	Height	Intro.	Discon.	Current Market Value		
						U.K. £	U.S. $	Can. $
D6527	Large	Doulton	7 1/2"	1960	1992	75.00	160.00	175.00
D6534	Small	Doulton	4"	1960	1992	45.00	95.00	110.00
D6541	Miniature	Doulton	2 3/4"	1960	1991	40.00	85.00	95.00

ROBIN HOOD

Style three was issued in a limited edition of 2,500.

STYLE THREE: HANDLE — FIGURES OF MAID MARION, FRIAR TUCK,
LITTLE JOHN AND THE SHERIFF OF NOTTINGHAM

Designer: William K. Harper
Handle: Figures of Maid Marion, Friar Tuck
Little John and the Sheriff of Nottingham
Colourway: Green hat and tunic collar with brown

Backstamp: Doulton

Doulton Number	Size	Backstamp	Height	Intro.	Discon.	Current Market Value U.K. £	U.S. $	Can. $
D6998	Large	Doulton	7"	1995	Ltd. ed.	250.00	500.00	725.00

ROBINSON CRUSOE

In 1719, Daniel Defoe wrote *Robinson Crusoe*, based on the experiences of Alexander Selkirk, who was marooned on a deserted Pacific island for five years.

Robinson Crusoe
D 6532
COPR 1959
DOULTON & CO LIMITED
Rd No 893845
Rd No 39653
Rd No 8317
Rd No 416/59

Backstamp: Doulton

Designer: Max Henk
Handle: The man Friday peers from behind a palm tree
Colourway: Brown and green

Doulton						Current Market Value		
Number	Size	Backstamp	Height	Intro.	Discon.	U.K. £	U.S. $	Can. $
D6532	Large	Doulton	7 1/2"	1960	1982	75.00	180.00	195.00
D6539	Small	Doulton	4"	1960	1982	45.00	95.00	110.00
D6546	Miniature	Doulton	2 3/4"	1960	1982	40.00	90.00	110.00

ROMEO

PROTOTYPE

STYLE ONE: HANDLE — A VIAL OF POISON SPILLS OVER A DAGGER BELOW

Designer: David Biggs
Handle: A vial of poison spills over a dagger below
Colourway: Brown and white

Backstamp: Doulton

Doulton Number	Size	Variation	Height	Intro.	Discon.	Current Market Value		
						U.K. £	U.S. $	Can. $
D6670	Large	Prototype	7"	1981	1981		Extremely rare	

ROMEO

THE SHAKESPEAREAN COLLECTION,
ONE OF SIX

The hero of Shakespeare's 1596 romantic play, Romeo falls in love with Juliet, the daughter of a Verona family feuding with his own. The lives of these two clandestine lovers end tragically and, with bitter irony, cause the reconciliation of the two families.

STYLE TWO: HANDLE — A DAGGER SUPERIMPOSED ON THE COLUMN SUPPORTING A BALCONY

© ROYAL DOULTON TABLEWARE LIMITED 1982
D 6670

The
Shakespearean
Collection
ROMEO
A series of hand-made, hand-decorated Character Jugs by Royal Doulton

Designer: David Biggs
Handle: A dagger superimposed on the column supporting a balcony
Colourway: Brown and white

Backstamp: Doulton

Doulton Number	Size	Backstamp	Height	Intro.	Discon.	Current Market Value		
						U.K. £	U.S. $	Can. $
D6670	Large	Doulton	7 1/2"	1983	1989	85.00	185.00	200.00

RONALD REAGAN

PROTOTYPE

STYLE ONE: THE U.S. FLAG WITH GREEN CORD AND NO CAP

*Photograph
Not Available
At Press Time*

Designer: Eric Griffiths
Handle: The U.S. flag with green cord, no cap
Colourway: Blue grey suit; dark blue tie

Backstamp: Doulton

Doulton Number	Size	Variation	Height	Intro.	Discon.	Current Market Value		
						U.K. £	U.S. $	Can. $
D6718	Large	Prototype	7 3/4"	1984	1984		Unique	

RONALD REAGAN

Ronald Wilson Reagan (b. 1911) began as an Iowa sports announcer, then worked as a movie actor for 30 years. In 1966 Reagan was elected governor of California, then he became President of the United States in 1980 and served two terms until 1988.

This jug was commissioned for the Republican National Committee. Originally planned as a limited edition of 5,000 pieces, the jug did not sell well and only 2,000 pieces were said to have been produced. It was issued with a certificate and photograph of President Reagan in a decorative folio.

STYLE TWO: THE U.S. FLAG WITH YELLOW CORD AND GOLD CAP

Designer: Eric Griffiths
Handle: The U.S. flag with yellow cord, gold cap
Colourway: Dark blue suit; white shirt; purple striped tie

Backstamp: Doulton/Reagan

Doulton Number	Size	Backstamp	Height	Intro.	Discon.	Current Market Value U.K. £	U.S. $	Can. $
D6718	Large	Doulton/Reagan	7 3/4"	1984	Ltd. ed.	265.00	650.00	650.00

THE SAILOR

THE ARMED FORCES,
ONE OF THREE

STYLE ONE: WITHOUT "R.C.N." ON BINOCULARS

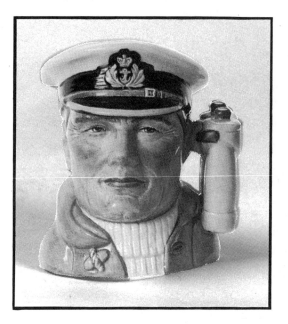

Designer: William K. Harper
Handle: Binoculars
Colourway: White Royal Navy cap; light brown coat; white sweater

Backstamp: Doulton

Doulton Number	Size	Backstamp	Height	Intro.	Discon.	Current Market Value		
						U.K. £	U.S. $	Can. $
D6875	Small	Doulton	4 1/2"	1991	1991	35.00	69.50	110.00

THE SAILOR

THE CANADIANS,
ONE OF THREE

The Sailor was commissioned by The British Toby in a limited edition of 250 pieces. The set sold originally for $465.00 Canadian.

STYLE TWO: WITH "R.C.N." ON BINOCULARS

Designer: William K. Harper
Handle: R.C.N. binoculars
Colourway: White Royal Canadian Navy cap; dark brown coat; white sweater

Backstamp: Doulton/The British Toby

Doulton Number	Size	Backstamp	Height	Intro.	Discon.	U.K. £	U.S. $	Can. $
						Current Market Value		
D6904	Small	Doulton/British	4 1/2"	1991	Ltd. ed.	140.00	275.00	295.00

THE SAILOR

NATIONAL SERVICE SERIES, ONE OF THREE

Commissioned by Lawleys By Post, it was possible to have a National Service number incorporated within the accompanying certificate.

STYLE THREE: HANDLE — AN ANCHOR

Designer: William K. Harper
Handle: Anchor
Colourway: White, black, brown and gold

Backstamp: Doulton

Doulton Number	Size	Backstamp	Height	Intro.	Discon.	Current Market Value U.K. £	U.S. $	Can. $
D6984	Small	Doulton	4 1/2"	1994	Sp. ed.	49.50	—	—

SAIREY GAMP

In Charles Dickens's 1843 novel, *Martin Chuzzlewit*, Sairey Gamp is a gossiping, gin-drinking midwife and nurse.
Misnumbered large-size jugs exist with the number D5528, which is the number allocated to the small-size jug. This does not add any premium to the price.

VARIATION No. 1: Colourway — Black hair; light green band; dark green coat; yellow and burgundy bow
Handle — green umbrella

BACKSTAMP B

SHEFFIELD &
ROTHERHAM

BACKSTAMP C

Designer: Leslie Harradine / Harry Fenton
Handle: A green umbrella with brown handle
Colourway: Black hair; light green band; dark
green coat; yellow and burgundy bow
Backstamp: A. Doulton
B. Doulton/Bentalls/
Souvenir From Bentalls. Jubilee Year, 1935.
Commissioned by Bentalls to commemorate the silver jubilee in 1935 of King George V.
C. Doulton/Darley/
Souvenir from Darley & Son Sheffield & Rotherham

Doulton Number	Size	Backstamp	Height	Intro.	Discon.	Current Market Value U.K. £	Current Market Value U.S. $	Current Market Value Can. $
D5451	Large	Doulton	6 1/4"	1935	1986	70.00	140.00	150.00
D5528	Small	Doulton	3 1/8"	1935	1986	40.00	85.00	95.00
D5528	Small	Doulton/Bentalls	3 1/8"	1935	1935	350.00	1,000.00	1,000.00
D5528	Small	Doulton/Darley	3 1/8"	1936	1936	350.00	1,200.00	1,200.00
D6045	Miniature	Doulton	2 1/8"	1939	1986	35.00	75.00	90.00
D6146	Tiny	Doulton	1 1/4"	1940	1960	75.00	140.00	150.00

VARIATION No. 2:   Colourway —Yellow band on hat; yellow bow; maroon umbrella

"SAIREY GAMP"
D.6770
Specially Commissioned
from
Royal Doulton®
by
STRAWBRIDGE & CLOTHIER
Celebrating the opening of
The Royal Doulton Room
Strawbridge & Clothier, Philadelphia, U.S.
HAND MODELLED AND HAND DECORATED
A LIMITED EDITION OF 250
THIS IS NO. 39
© 1986 ROYAL DOULTON

Backstamps: A. Strawbridge and Clothier/
Celebrating the opening of The Royal Doulton Room at Strawbridge and Clothier,
Philadelphia, U.S.A.
Commissioned by Strawbridge and Clothier, Philadelphia.
Issued in 1986 in a limited edition of 250 pieces.

B. Strawbridge and Clothier/
Made for the First Anniversary of the Royal Doulton Room at Strawbridge and Clothier
Commissioned by Strawbridge and Clothier in 1987 and issued in a limited edition of 500 pieces.

Doulton Number	Size	Variation	Height	Intro.	Discon.	Current Market Value U.K. £	U.S. $	Can. $
D6770	Large	Var. 2A	6 1/4"	1986	Ltd. ed.	225.00	350.00	375.00
D6789	Small	Var. 2B	3"	1987	Ltd. ed.	145.00	225.00	250.00

Sairey Gamp Derivatives

Doulton Number	Item	Height	Intro.	Discon.	Current Market Value U.K. £	U.S. $	Can. $
D6009	Ash bowl	3"	1939	1960	95.00	250.00	275.00
D6011	Sugar bowl	2 1/2"	1939	1942	375.00	850.00	850.00
D6015	Teapot	7"	1939	1942	750.00	2,000.00	2,000.00
D6047	Bust	2 1/4"	1939	1960	75.00	160.00	175.00
D6150	Toothpick holder	2 3/4"	1940	1942	225.00	600.00	600.00
HN1625	Bookend	3 1/2"	1934	1939	1,000.00	2,500.00	2,500.00
M62	Napkin ring	3 1/2"	c.1935	1939	245.00	800.00	800.00

SAM JOHNSON

A celebrated poet, essayist and lexicographer, Dr. Johnson (1709-1784) published his *Dictionary* in 1755, which was the first systematic study of the English language. His literary club met regularly at a London pub and included such famous figures as David Garrick, Oliver Goldsmith and Edmund Burke.

"Sam Johnson."

COPR. 1949.
DOULTON & CO. LIMITED.
R⁴N⁰ 857579
R⁴N⁰ 5906.
R⁴N⁰ 77/49

Designer: Harry Fenton
Handle: Plain
Colourway: Dark brown hat; light brown, maroon and white robes

Backstamp: Doulton

Doulton Number	Size	Backstamp	Height	Intro.	Discon.	Current Market Value		
						U.K. £	U.S. $	Can. $
D6289	Large	Doulton	6 1/4"	1950	1960	200.00	525.00	550.00
D6296	Small	Doulton	3 1/4"	1950	1960	140.00	300.00	325.00

SAM WELLER

In the 1837 Charles Dickens's novel, *The Pickwick Papers*, Sam Weller was a boots employed at the White Hart Inn. He became a faithful aide and valet to Mr. Pickwick and eventually married Napkins's housemaid.

This character jug is unusual in that its modelling changes dramatically between the large and smaller versions.

"Sam Weller"
Rᵈ Nº 822824
REGᵈ IN AUSTRALIA

Designer: Leslie Harradine / Harry Fenton
Handle: Plain
Colourway: Dark brown hat; light brown coat; red kerchief with white spots

Backstamp: Doulton

Doulton Number	Size	Backstamp	Height	Intro.	Discon.	Current Market Value U.K. £	U.S. $	Can. $
D6064	Large	Doulton	6 1/2"	1940	1960	95.00	225.00	250.00
D5841	Mid	Doulton	4 1/2"	1938	1948	140.00	265.00	280.00
D5841	Small	Doulton	3 1/4"	1948	1960	60.00	150.00	165.00
D6140	Miniature	Doulton	2 1/4"	1940	1960	45.00	100.00	115.00
D6147	Tiny	Doulton	1 1/4"	1940	1960	65.00	140.00	160.00

Sam Weller Derivatives

Doulton Number	Item	Height	Intro.	Discon.	Current Market Value U.K. £	U.S. $	Can. $
D6052	Bust	2 1/2"	1939	1960	75.00	140.00	160.00
M61	Napkin ring	3 1/2"	c. 1939	1939	225.00	750.00	750.00

SAMSON AND DELILAH

THE STAR-CROSSED LOVERS COLLECTION (TWO-FACED JUG),
ONE OF FOUR

Samson was an Israelite judge from Biblical times, famous for his strength. Delilah, a Philistine, was paid to find the secret of Samson's strength, so that her people could overthrow their Israelite enemies. Samson fell in love with Delilah and told her that his strength lay in his hair. She shaved his head while he slept and the Philistines captured and blinded him. When his hair grew back, Samson avenged himself by pulling down a Philistine temple, killing himself and many of his enemies.

This jug was issued in 1988 in a limited edition of 9,500 pieces.

Designer: Stanley J. Taylor
Handle: Samson — Jawbone of an ass
Delilah — A broken column
Colourway: Brown, black and cream

Royal Doulton®
THE
STAR-CROSSED **L**OVERS
COLLECTION
Samson & Delilah
D 6787
Modelled by Stanley James Taylor
Stanley James Taylor.
Worldwide Limited Edition of 9,500
This is Number 1053
© 1987 Royal Doulton

Backstamp: Doulton

Doulton Number	Size	Backstamp	Height	Intro.	Discon.	Current Market Value		
						U.K. £	U.S. $	Can. $
D6787	Large	Doulton	7"	1988	Ltd. ed. (1991)	85.00	225.00	250.00

SANCHO PANÇA

This amiable peasant was employed as the squire to Don Quixote in Cervantes's 17th-century novel. Accompanying Quixote on many adventures, his down-to-earth common sense acted as a foil to his master's romantic musing.

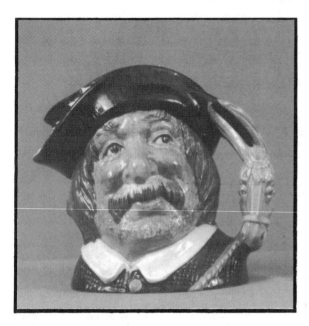

Sancho Panca
(A Servant to Don Quixote)
D 6461
COPR 1956
DOULTON & CO LIMITED
Rd No 881510
Rd No 35706
Rd No 7561
Rd No 332/56

BACKSTAMP B

Designer: Geoff Blower
Handle: Light brown donkey
Colourway: Black hat with a white feather; black coat with a white collar

Backstamps: A. Doulton
  B. Doulton/Sancho Panca/(A Servant to Don Quixote)
  Produced from 1957 to the early 1970s, with no cedilla.
  C. Doulton/Sancho Pança
  The spelling of the name Pança with the cedilla gives a soft "s" sound in pronunciation.
  Early versions of the backstamp included the cedilla, but it was dropped in the late fifties.
  The incised name shows that the cedilla was included in the modelling.

Doulton Number	Size	Backstamp	Height	Intro.	Discon.	Current Market Value U.K. £	U.S. $	Can. $
D6456	Large	Doulton	6 1/2"	1957	1983	85.00	225.00	250.00
D6456	Large	A Servant ...	6 1/2"	1957	1970	85.00	250.00	275.00
D6456	Large	Cedilla	6 1/2	1957	1959	85.00	275.00	300.00
D6461	Small	Doulton	3 1/4"	1957	1983	50.00	120.00	135.00
D6461	Small	A Servant ...	3 1/4"	1957	1970	50.00	140.00	160.00
D6461	Small	Cedilla	3 1/4"	1957	1959	50.00	140.00	160.00
D6518	Miniature	Doulton	2 1/2"	1960	1983	50.00	120.00	135.00
D6518	Miniature	A Servant ...	2 1/2"	1960	1970	50.00	140.00	160.00

Note: The dates for the discontinuance of the backstamp varieties are only approximate.

SANTA CLAUS

The Santa Claus jug was introduced in 1981 and was the first to undergo annual design changes. Featuring different well-known Christmas themes, the handle has changed several times since 1981.

STYLE ONE: HANDLE — A DOLL AND DRUM

Designer: Michael Abberley
Handle: A doll stands on a drum
Colourway: Red, white and light brown

Backstamp: Doulton

Doulton Number	Size	Backstamp	Height	Intro.	Discon.	Current Market Value U.K. £	U.S. $	Can. $
D6668	Large	Doulton	7 1/2"	1981	1981	85.00	250.00	275.00

SANTA CLAUS

STYLE TWO: HANDLE — THE HEAD OF A REINDEER

© ROYAL DOULTON
TABLEWARE LTD 1982

Santa Claus
D.6675

Designer: Michael Abberley
Handle: The head of a reindeer
Colourway: Red, white and brown

Backstamp: Doulton

Doulton Number	Size	Backstamp	Height	Intro.	Discon.	Current Market Value		
						U.K. £	U.S. $	Can. $
D6675	Large	Doulton	7 1/4"	1982	1982	100.00	300.00	325.00

SANTA CLAUS

STYLE THREE: HANDLE — A SACK OF TOYS

© ROYAL DOULTON
TABLEWARE LTD. 1983

Santa Claus
D 6690

Designer: Michael Abberley
Handle: A sack of toys
Colourway: Red, white and light brown

Backstamp: Doulton

Doulton Number	Size	Backstamp	Height	Intro.	Discon.	Current Market Value		
						U.K. £	U.S. $	Can. $
D6690	Large	Doulton	7 1/2"	1983	1983	125.00	450.00	475.00

SANTA CLAUS

STYLE FOUR: HANDLE — PLAIN RED

Royal Doulton
SANTA CLAUS
D6704
Modelled by

© ROYAL DOULTON TABLEWARE
LIMITED 1983

BACKSTAMP A

BACKSTAMP B

Designer: Michael Abberley
Handle: Plain
Colourway: Red and white

Backstamps: A. Doulton
B. Doulton/Seaway China
Commissioned by Seaway China
Marine City MI, U.S.A.
Issued in a special edition of 2,500.

Doulton Number	Size	Backstamp	Height	Intro.	Discon.	Current Market Value U.K. £	U.S. $	Can. $
D6704	Large	Doulton	7 1/2"	1984	Current	59.95	125.00	175.00
D6705	Small	Doulton	3 1/4"	1984	Current	27.00	69.50	100.00
D6706	Miniature	Doulton	2 1/2"	1984	1991	40.00	120.00	135.00
D6950	Tiny	Doulton/Seaway	1 1/4"	1993	Sp. ed.	50.00	100.00	110.00

SANTA CLAUS

CHRISTMAS MINIATURE SERIES,
ONE OF FIVE

STYLE FIVE: HANDLE — A HOLLY WREATH

Royal Doulton®
SANTA CLAUS
D 6900
© 1987 ROYAL DOULTON

Designer: Michael Abberley
Handle: A holly wreath
Colourway: Red, white and green

Backstamps: A.   Doulton
Issued in a limited edition
of 5,000 for Christmas 1991.
B.   Doulton/Home Shopping
Commissioned by the Home Shopping
Network, Florida.
Issued in a special edition of 5,000.

Doulton Number	Size	Backstamp	Height	Intro.	Discon.	Current Market Value U.K. £	U.S. $	Can. $
D6794	Large	Doulton/Home	7"	1988	Sp. ed.	200.00	550.00	575.00
D6900	Miniature	Doulton	2 1/2"	1991	Ltd. ed. (1991)	50.00	120.00	135.00

SANTA CLAUS

STYLE SIX: HANDLE — A CANDY CANE

VARIATION No. 1: Handle — Candy cane with red and white stripes

Designer:	Michael Abberley
Handle:	Candy cane with red and white stripes
Colourway:	Red and white

Backstamp: A. Doulton/Cable Value
Commissioned by the Cable Value
Network.
Issued in a special edition of 1,000.
B. Doulton/Seaway China
Commissioned by Seaway China
Marine City MI U.S.A.
Issued in a special edition of 2,500.

Doulton Number	Size	Backstamp	Height	Intro.	Discon.	Current Market Value U.K. £	U.S. $	Can. $
D6793	Large	Doulton/Cable	7 1/2"	1988	Sp. ed.	300.00	1,000.00	1,000.00
D6980	Tiny	Doulton/Seaway	1 1/4"	1994	Sp. ed.	50.00	—	—

VARIATION No. 2: Handle — Candy cane with red, white and green stripes

Royal Doulton®
SANTA CLAUS
D 6840
Modelled by

Michael Alcock

SPECIAL EDITION SIZE OF 1,000

© 1989 ROYAL DOULTON

American Collectors Society

Backstamp: Doulton/American Collectors Society
Commissioned by the American Collectors Society. Issued in 1989 in a special edition of 1,000 pieces.

Doulton Number	Size	Backstamp	Height	Intro.	Discon.	Current Market Value		
						U.K. £	U.S. $	Can. $
D6840	Large	Doulton/ American	7 1/2"	1989	Sp. ed.	175.00	550.00	575.00

SANTA CLAUS

STYLE SEVEN: HANDLE — CHRISTMAS PARCELS

Designer:
Handle: Blue and green Christmas parcels
Colourway: Red and white

Backstamp: Doulton/Seaway China
Commissioned by Seaway China
Marine City MI U.S.A.
Issued in a special edition of 2,500.

Doulton Number	Size	Backstamp	Height	Intro.	Discon.	Current Market Value U.K. £	U.S. $	Can. $
D7020	Tiny	Doulton/Seaway	1 1/4"	1995	Sp. ed.	35.00	55.00	75.00

SCARAMOUCHE

In the 17th-century comedy, written by Edward Ravenscroft, Scaramouche appears as a boastful, foolish character, dressed in the old Spanish style.

STYLE ONE   HANDLE — A GUITAR WITH THE TWO
MASKS OF COMEDY AND TRAGEDY

Scaramouche
D 6558
COPR 1961
DOULTON & CO LIMITED
Rd No 902089
Rd No 42141
Rd No 8924
Rd No R83/61

Designer: Max Henk
Handle: A guitar
Colourway: Blue-black, brown and green

Backstamp: Doulton

Doulton Number	Size	Backstamp	Height	Intro.	Discon.	Current Market Value U.K. £	U.S. $	Can. $
D6558	Large	Doulton	7"	1962	1967	550.00	1,100.00	1,150.00
D6561	Small	Doulton	3 1/4"	1962	1967	350.00	725.00	750.00
D6564	Miniature	Doulton	2 1/2"	1962	1967	350.00	675.00	700.00

SCARAMOUCHE

CHARACTERS FROM LITERATURE,
ONE OF 11

STYLE TWO: HANDLE —A CURTAIN WITH THE TWO MASKS
OF COMEDY AND TRAGEDY

VARIATION No. 1: Colourway —Yellow hat; turquoise tunic; white ruff; light brown hair
Handle — Lavender

Royal Doulton®
SCARAMOUCHE
D 6814
Modelled by

Stanley James Taylor.

© 1987 ROYAL DOULTON
NEW COLOURWAY 1988

Designer: Stanley J. Taylor

Handle: The masks of tragedy and comedy
rest against a curtain

Colourway: Yellow hat; turquoise tunic; white ruff;
light brown hair; lavender handle

Backstamp: Doulton

Doulton Number	Size	Variation	Height	Intro.	Discon.	Current Market Value		
						U.K. £	U.S. $	Can. $
D6814	Large	Var. 1	6 3/4"	1988	1991	75.00	225.00	250.00

VARIATION No. 2:   Colourway — Black hat; green tunic; white ruff; dark brown hair; yellow handle

Royal Doulton®
SCARAMOUCHE
D 6774
Modelled by
Stanley James Taylor
SPECIAL EDITION OF 1500

THE
GUILD OF
SPECIALIST
CHINA & GLASS
RETAILERS

© 1987 ROYAL DOULTON

1093

Designer:	Stanley J. Taylor	
Handle:	The masks of tragedy and comedy rest against a curtain	
Colourway:	Black hat; green tunic; white ruff; dark brown hair; yellow handle	

Backstamp: Doulton/Guild
Commissioned by the Guild of Specialist China & Glass Retailers in 1987 and issued in a special edition of 1,500 pieces.

Doulton Number	Size	Variation	Height	Intro.	Discon.	Current Market Value		
						U.K. £	**U.S. $**	**Can. $**
D6774	Large	Var. 2	6 3/4"	1987	Sp. ed.	125.00	425.00	450.00

SCARLET PIMPERNEL

PROTOTYPE

In the 1905 novel by the Hungarian Baroness Orczy, the Scarlet Pimpernel was a group of Englishmen dedicated to the rescue of victims of the Reign of Terror in Paris. Sir Percy Blakeney, the group's leader, bested his opponents by clever wit and courage while disguising his identity from his friends back in England.

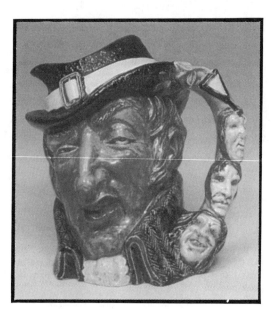

Designer: Geoff Blower
Handle: Characters in assorted disguises
Colourway: Black, white and blue

Backstamp: Doulton

Doulton Number	Size	Variation	Height	Intro.	Discon.	Current Market Value U.K. £	U.S. $	Can. $
D —	Large	Prototype	7"	Unknown			Unique	

SCROOGE

CHARLES DICKENS COMMEMORATIVE SET,
DICKENS TINIES, ONE OF 12

In Dickens's famous novel, *A Christmas Carol*, Scrooge is a loveless, miserly businessman, who changes his ways after being visited by three ghosts on Christmas Eve.

The 12 jugs in this set were issued to commemorate the 170th anniversary of the birth of Charles Dickens and each one came with a certificate of authenticity. A mahogany display shelf completes the set. The set was first sold by Lawleys By Post in the U.K. from 1982 to 1988, and from 1985 in North America and Australia.

Scrooge
D. 6683

Designer: Michael Abberley
Handle: Plain
Colourway: Yellow and brown

Backstamp: Doulton

Doulton Number	Size	Backstamp	Height	Intro.	Discon.	Current Market Value U.K. £	U.S. $	Can. $
D6683	Tiny	Doulton	1 1/2"	1982	1989	40.00	60.00	75.00
		Display stand for 12 tinies				65.00	45.00	50.00

SHAKESPEARE

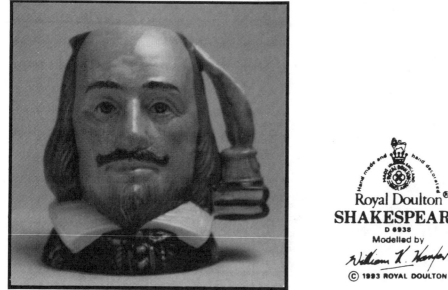

Royal Doulton®
SHAKESPEARE
D 6938
Modelled by

William K. Harper

© 1993 ROYAL DOULTON

Designer: William K. Harper
Handle: Inkwell and books
Colourway: Black coat; yellow collar; light brown hair and beard; burgundy books; grey inkwell and quill

Backstamp: Doulton

Doulton Number	Size	Backstamp	Height	Intro.	Discon.	Current Market Value U.K. £	U.S. $	Can. $
D6938	Small	Doulton	3 1/2"	1993	Current	35.00	99.00	120.00

Note: For William Shakespeare see page 470.

SHEFFIELD WEDNESDAY (FOOTBALL CLUB)

THE FOOTBALL SUPPORTERS,
ONE OF NINE

This jug is sold exclusively through John Sinclair of Sheffield, England.

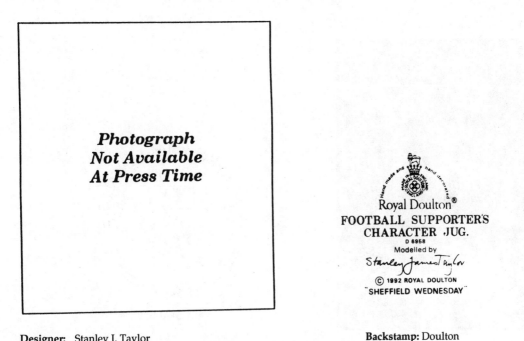

Designer: Stanley J. Taylor
Handle: Team coloured scarf
Colourway: Blue and cream striped uniform

Backstamp: Doulton

Doulton Number	Size	Backstamp	Height	Intro.	Discon.	Current Market Value		
						U.K. £	U.S. $	Can. $
D6958	Mid	Doulton	5"	1993	Current	32.50	—	—

SIMON THE CELLARER

Simon was the subject of a 19th-century English folksong. The keys on the handle are those to his cellar, full of great wines and ales. He was always good for standing a drink for his friends.

The tiny version of Simon the Cellarer was one of a set of six tinies issued in 1994, in a limited edition of 2,500, to commemorate the diamond anniversary of the first character jug. The set, modelled by William K. Harper, was sold out within the first year. Other tinies in this series are Dick Turpin, Granny, the Jester, John Barleycorn and Parson Brown. The issue price was £150.00.

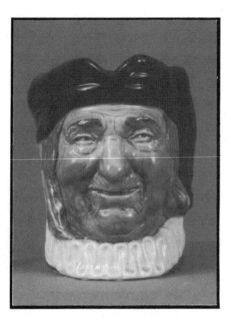

BACKSTAMP B

Designer: Charles Noke / Harry Fenton
Handle: A bunch of keys
Colourway: Maroon hat; white ruff

Backstamps: A. Doulton
B. Doulton/Bentalls/ Souvenir from Bentalls. 1936.

Doulton Number	Size	Backstamp	Height	Intro.	Discon.	Current Market Value U.K. £	U.S. $	Can. $
D5504	Large	Doulton	6 1/2"	1935	1960	100.00	225.00	250.00
D5616	Small	Doulton	3 1/2"	1936	1960	50.00	130.00	150.00
D5616	Small	Doulton/Bentalls	3 1/2"	1936	1936	350.00	1,000.00	1,000.00
D6956	Tiny	Doulton	1 1/4"	1994	Ltd. ed. (1994)	45.00	90.00	100.00

SIMPLE SIMON

The subject of this jug dates back to a 17th-century nursery rhyme of Simon meeting a pieman.

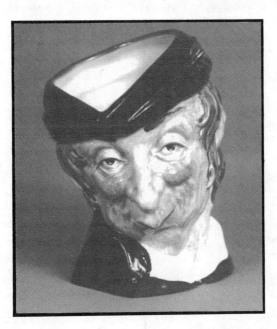

Designer: Geoff Blower
Handle: Plain
Colourway: Green, brown and white

Backstamp: Doulton

Doulton Number	Size	Backstamp	Height	Intro.	Discon.	Current Market Value U.K. £	Current Market Value U.S. $	Current Market Value Can. $
D6374	Large	Doulton	7"	1953	1960	250.00	750.00	800.00

SIR FRANCIS DRAKE

This version of the Drake jug was produced to celebrate the 400th anniversary of the defeat of the Spanish Armada in 1588. Commissioned by the Guild of Specialist China & Glass Retailers, this jug was issued in 1988 in a special edition of 6,000 pieces.

Designer: Peter Gee
Handle: The *Golden Hind*'s bow and sails
Colourway: Black and white

Backstamp: Doulton/Guild

Doulton Number	Size	Backstamp	Height	Intro.	Discon.	Current Market Value U.K. £	U.S. $	Can. $
D6805	Large	Doulton/Guild	7"	1988	Sp. ed.	75.00	275.00	300.00

SIR HENRY DOULTON

ROYAL DOULTON INTERNATIONAL COLLECTORS CLUB SERIES

In the mid 1830s, Henry Doulton (1820-1897) joined his father's firm just in time to capitalize on the expanding market that was developing in London for modern sanitation products. The manufacture of stoneware sewer and water pipes led Doulton and Company, as they were known after 1854, to become a large and flourishing concern. John Doulton retired around this time leaving Doulton and Company in the hands of his son Henry. In the 1860s, with decorative wares expanding, Henry Doulton was persuaded to hire students from the Lambeth School of Art as designers and decorators of the new ornamental wares his company was introducing. Their outstanding creations heralded the beginning of the studio-art pottery movement.

D 6703
SIR HENRY DOULTON
1820 · 1897
EXCLUSIVELY FOR
COLLECTORS CLUB
© ROYAL DOULTON
TABLEWARE LTD 1983
MODELLED BY

Designer: Eric Griffiths
Handle: A Doulton art pottery vase
Colourway: Black coat; yellow cravat; grey hair; brown and blue vase

Backstamp: Doulton / RDICC

Doulton Number	Size	Backstamp	Height	Intro.	Discon.	Current Market Value U.K. £	U.S. $	Can. $
D6703	Small	RDICC	4 1/2"	1984	1984	100.00	225.00	250.00

SIR HENRY DOULTON AND MICHAEL DOULTON

This two-faced jug was a special edition jug issued to mark Michael Doulton's personal appearances at retail locations. This piece is one of the few two-faced jugs made in the small size.

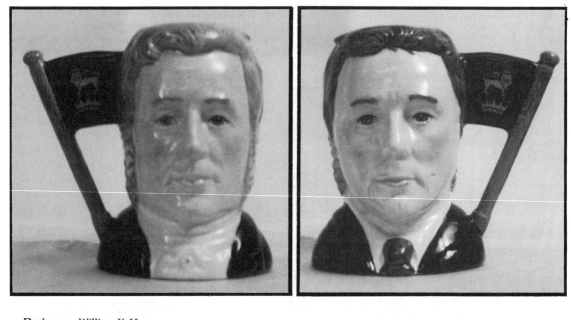

Designer: William K. Harper
Handle: Flag bearing the lion and crown backstamp of Royal Doulton
Colourway: Henry — Grey hair; yellow cravat
Michael — Brown hair; dark blue suit; white shirt; light blue tie
Backstamp: Doulton

Royal Doulton®
Sir Henry Doulton
◆
Michael Doulton
D 6921
This small-size Character Jug, modelled by William K. Harper, is a special edition issued to mark personal appearances by Michael Doulton.

© 1992 ROYAL DOULTON

Doulton Number	Size	Backstamp	Height	Intro.	Discon.	Current Market Value		
						U.K. £	U.S. $	Can. $
D6921	Small	Doulton	4 1/2"	1992	Sp. ed.	60.00	140.00	150.00

SIR THOMAS MORE

HENRY AND HIS SIX WIVES, ONE OF EIGHT

Thomas More (1478-1535) entered the service of King Henry VIII in 1518 as royal councillor. He was knighted and became Lord Chancellor after the dismissal of Cardinal Wolsey in 1529. At this time Henry was embroiled in a battle with Rome over his decision to divorce Catherine of Aragon. Unable to support his King, More resigned.

In 1534 More was arrested for high treason when he refused to swear an oath of supremacy, stating that Henry VIII ranked above all foreign leaders, including the Pope. He was beheaded in 1535 and canonized by the Catholic Church 400 years later, in 1935.

Royal Doulton®
SIR THOMAS MORE
D 6792
Modelled by
Stanley James Taylor
© 1987 ROYAL DOULTON

Designer: Stanley J. Taylor
Handle: A window arch and a bible
Colourway: Dark green hat; brown fur-trimmed collar; gold chain of office

Backstamp: Doulton

Doulton Number	Size	Backstamp	Height	Intro.	Discon.	Current Market Value U.K. £	U.S. $	Can. $
D6792	Large	Doulton	6 3/4"	1988	1991	85.00	250.00	275.00

SIR WINSTON CHURCHILL

HEROIC LEADERS
ONE OF THREE

This Churchill jug was a new design, commissioned by Lawleys By Post. It was issued in 1989 as part of a set of three, and limited to 9,500 pieces.

Royal Doulton®
SIR WINSTON CHURCHILL
1874-1965
D 6849
Modelled by
Stanley James Taylor
© 1989 ROYAL DOULTON
A LIMITED EDITION OF 9500
THIS IS NO. *1609*

Designer: Stanley J. Taylor
Handle: The Union Jack flag
Colourway: Black, grey and white

Backstamp: Doulton

Doulton Number	Size	Backstamp	Height	Intro.	Discon.	Current Market Value U.K. £	U.S. $	Can. $
D6849	Small	Doulton	3 1/4"	1989	Ltd. ed.	90.00	225.00	250.00

Note: For Churchill see page 180. For Winston Churchill see page 472.

THE SLEUTH

Arthur Conan Doyle (1859-1930), an unsuccessful doctor, published the first of his widely popular detective stories in 1887. The amateur sleuth Sherlock Holmes shared rooms on Baker Street , as well as many adventures, with his friend and foil, Dr. Watson.

VARIATION No. 1:   Colourway — Black deerstalker hat, brown cloak

The Sleuth
D 6631
© **DOULTON & CO LIMITED 1972**
REGISTRATION APPLIED FOR

Designer: Alan Moore
Handle: A pipe and magnifying glass
Colourway: Dark green deerstalker hat; brown cloak

Backstamp: Doulton

Doulton Number	Size	Backstamp	Height	Intro.	Discon.	Current Market Value U.K. £	U.S. $	Can. $
D6631	Large	Doulton	7"	1973	Current	55.00	125.00	175.00
D6635	Small	Doulton	3 1/4"	1973	Current	29.95	69.50	100.00
D6639	Miniature	Doulton	2 3/4"	1973	1991	40.00	100.00	115.00

VARIATION No. 2:   Colourway — Brown deerstalker hat; red cloak

Backstamp: Doulton/Lawleys/
This Limited Edition of 5,000 Commemorates The Centenary of the Publication
of the First Sherlock Holmes story "A Study In Scarlet"
Commissioned by Lawleys By Post and issued in 1987 in a limited edition of 5,000 pieces.

Doulton Number	Size	Backstamp	Height	Intro.	Discon.	Current Market Value U.K. £	U.S. $	Can. $
D6773	Small	Lawleys	3 1/4"	1987	Ltd. ed.	75.00	250.00	275.00

SMUGGLER

The detailing on the barrel of the small-size jug is often less distinguishable than that on the large jug.

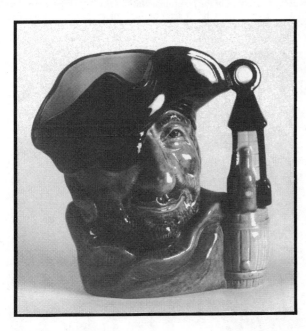

Smuggler
D6616
COPR. 1967
DOULTON & CO. LIMITED
Rd No 932060
Rd No 61328
Rd No 11138
Rd No 630/67

Designer: David Biggs
Handle: Lantern above a barrel
Colourway: Green hat; red scarf

Backstamp: Doulton

Doulton Number	Size	Backstamp	Height	Intro.	Discon.	Current Market Value		
						U.K. £	U.S. $	Can. $
D6616	Large	Doulton	7 1/4"	1968	1981	90.00	225.00	250.00
D6619	Small	Doulton	3 1/4"	1968	1981	50.00	120.00	135.00

SMUTS

A South African attorney, militaryman and politician, Jan Christiaan Smuts (1870-1950) served as a member of the British War Cabinet in World War I and was one of the authors of the Covenant of the League of Nations. In 1945, after again serving the Allies in World War II, Smuts is credited with writing the preamble to the Charter of the United Nations. He became the Prime Minister of South Africa in 1919 and again in 1939.

Designer: Harry Fenton
Handle: Springbok
Colourway: Light brown

Backstamp: Doulton

Doulton Number	Size	Backstamp	Height	Intro.	Discon.	Current Market Value U.K. £	U.S. $	Can. $
D6198	Large	Doulton	6 1/2"	1946	1948	850.00	2,000.00	2,000.00

THE SNAKE CHARMER

This jug was issued in a limited edition of 2,500 pieces.

Royal Doulton®
THE SNAKE CHARMER
D 6912
Modelled by
Stanley James Taylor.
© 1991 ROYAL DOULTON
A SPECIALLY COMMISSIONED
LIMITED EDITION OF 2,500
THIS IS Nº *833*

Designer: Stanley J. Taylor
Handle: Cobra, basket and pipe
Colourway: Yellow turban with blue and pink jewel;
burgundy and yellow robes

Backstamp: Doulton

Doulton Number	Size	Backstamp	Height	Intro.	Discon.	Current Market Value		
						U.K. £	U.S. $	Can. $
D6912	Large	Doulton	7"	1992	Ltd. ed.	150.00	350.00	375.00

THE SNOOKER PLAYER

CHARACTERS FROM LIFE,
ONE OF SEVEN

Royal Doulton®

THE SNOOKER PLAYER

D 6879

Modelled by

Stanley James Taylor.

© 1990 ROYAL DOULTON

Designer: Stanley J. Taylor
Handle: Cue with chalk and red and black cue balls
Colourway: Black hair; white shirt; black
bow tie and vest

Backstamp: Doulton

Doulton Number	Size	Backstamp	Height	Intro.	Discon.	Current Market Value		
						U.K. £	U.S. $	Can. $
D6879	Small	Doulton	4"	1991	Current	29.95	69.50	110.00

SNOWMAN

CHRISTMAS MINIATURES SERIES,
ONE OF FIVE

This jug was commissioned by Royal Doulton (U.S.A.) Limited. It is also listed in the *Charlton Standard Catalogue of Royal Doulton Beswick Storybook Figurines*, under the Snowman series.

Royal Doulton®
SNOWMAN
D 6972
© 1994 ROYAL DOULTON

Backstamp: Doulton

Designer:	Martyn C.R. Alcock and Graham Tongue
Handle:	Scarf
Colourway:	White, green and black

Doulton Number	Size	Backstamp	Height	Intro.	Discon.	U.K. £	Current Market Value U.S. $	Can. $
D6972	Miniature	Doulton	2 3/4"	1994	Current	—	62.00	—

THE SOLDIER

THE ARMED FORCES,
ONE OF THREE

STYLE ONE: DESERT RAT PATCH ON CANTEEN

Royal Doulton®
THE SOLDIER
D 6876
Modelled by

William K. Harper

© 1990 ROYAL DOULTON

Designer: William K. Harper
Handle: Bayonet and water canteen
Colourway: Army steel helmet with netting; khaki tunic

Backstamp: Doulton

Doulton Number	Size	Backstamp	Height	Intro.	Discon.	Current Market Value U.K. £	U.S. $	Can. $
D6876	Small	Doulton	4 1/2"	1991	Current	35.00	69.50	110.00

THE SOLDIER

THE CANADIANS,
ONE OF THREE

Commissioned by The British Toby in a limited edition of 250 pieces, the Soldier originally sold in a set for $465.00 Canadian.

STYLE TWO: RED PATCH ON CANTEEN

Designer: William K. Harper
Handle: Bayonet and water canteen with red patch
Colourway: Army steel helmet with netting; khaki tunic

Backstamp: Doulton/The British Toby

Doulton Number	Size	Backstamp	Height	Intro.	Discon.	Current Market Value		
						U.K. £	U.S. $	Can. $
D6905	Small	Doulton/ British Toby	4 1/2"	1991	Ltd. ed.	150.00	275.00	300.00

THE SOLDIER

NATIONAL SERVICE SERIES,
ONE OF THREE

The Soldier (style three) was a special edition for Lawleys By Post and paid tribute to all those who were called up for national service in the U.K.

STYLE THREE: HANDLE — JERRY CAN AND HAVERSACK

Designer: William K. Harper
Handle: A jerry can and haversack
Colourways: Black and brown

Backstamp: Doulton

Doulton Number	Size	Backstamp	Height	Intro.	Discon.	Current Market Value U.K. £	U.S. $	Can. $
D6983	Small	Doulton	4 1/2"	1994	Sp. ed.	49.50	—	—

ST. GEORGE

The patron saint of England since the 13th century, George is the hero of a legend which describes him as a chivalrous knight who single-handedly slayed a huge dragon, saving the princess Melisande.

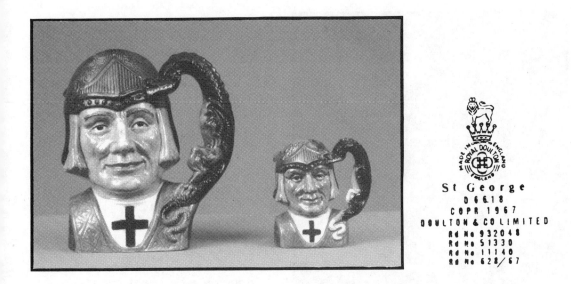

St George
D 6618
COPR 1967
DOULTON & CO LIMITED
Rd No 932048
Rd No 51330
Rd No 11140
Rd No 628/67

Designer: Max Henk

Handle: A dragon

Colourway: Grey helmet; turquoise armour

Backstamp: Doulton

Doulton Number	Size	Backstamp	Height	Intro.	Discon.	Current Market Value U.K. £	U.S. $	Can. $
D6618	Large	Doulton	7 1/2"	1968	1975	175.00	400.00	450.00
D6621	Small	Doulton	3 3/4"	1968	1975	110.00	275.00	300.00

TAM O'SHANTER

In a poem written by Robert Burns in 1791, Tam O'Shanter is a drunken farmer who happens upon witches who pursue him and his horse. He escapes, but his horse doesn't quite make it—one witch pulls its tail off. The Scottish woollen cap is reputedly named after this poem's hero.

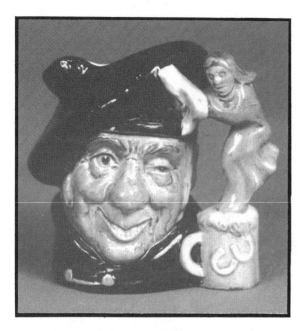

Tam o'Shanter
D 6632
ⓒ DOULTON & CO LIMITED 1972
REGISTRATION APPLIED FOR

Designer: Max Henk
Handle: Witch holding horse's tail above a mug of ale
Colourway: Dark blue tam; green cloak

Backstamp: Doulton

Doulton Number	Size	Backstamp	Height	Intro.	Discon.	Current Market Value U.K. £	U.S. $	Can. $
D6632	Large	Doulton	7"	1973	1980	95.00	225.00	250.00
D6636	Small	Doulton	3 1/4"	1973	1980	60.00	120.00	140.00
D6640	Miniature	Doulton	2 1/2"	1973	1980	50.00	140.00	160.00

TERRY FOX

Canadian Terrance Stanley Fox (1958-1981) was a student and athlete until diagnosed with a rare form of bone cancer. While recovering from the amputation of most of one leg, Fox conceived the idea of a "Marathon of Hope," a run across Canada to raise money for cancer research. He began on April 12, 1980, but had to abort his run on September 1, after being diagnosed with lung cancer. He raised over $24 million and became a source of inspiration for millions of people. Only three jugs were produced. One was given to his family, one resides in the Sir Henry Doulton Gallery and one was put up for auction at the International Royal Doulton Collectors Weekend, September 14 to 16, 1990, which realized $21,000 for charity.

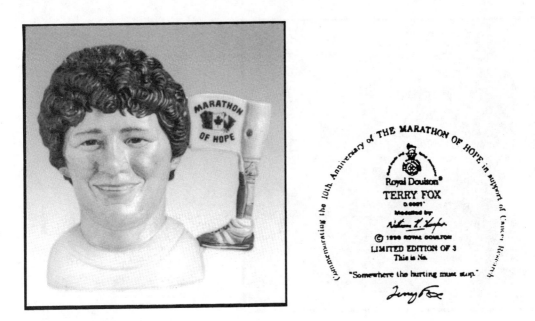

Designer: William K. Harper
Handle: Fox's artificial leg
Colourway: Brown and white

Backstamp: Doulton

Doulton Number	Size	Backstamp	Height	Intro.	Discon.	Current Market Value		
						U.K. £	U.S. $	Can. $
D6881	Large	Doulton	7"	1990	Ltd. ed.	Extremely rare. Only 3 known. Sold at auction, Toronto, 1990— $21,000.00 Can.		

THOMAS JEFFERSON

PRESIDENTIAL SERIES,
ONE OF THREE

This jug was issued in a limited edition of 2,500 to commemorate the 250th anniversary of Thomas Jefferson's birth in 1743. It was available only within the U.S.A., with an allocation of jugs for overseas members of the Royal Doulton International Collectors Club.

Royal Doulton®
PRESIDENTIAL SERIES
THOMAS JEFFERSON
D 6943
Modelled by
Stanley James Taylor.
© 1993 ROYAL DOULTON
A SPECIALLY COMMISSIONED
LIMITED EDITION OF 2,500
THIS IS N° 736

Designer: Stanley J. Tayler
Handle: "Life, Liberty and the pursuit of happiness" on scroll, feather quill and ink pot
Colourway: Grey hair; dark blue coat; grey cravat

Backstamp: Doulton

Doulton Number	Size	Backstamp	Height	Intro.	Discon.	Current Market Value U.K. £	U.S. $	Can. $
D6943	Large	Doulton	6 3/4"	1994	Ltd. ed.	—	200.00	—

TOBY GILLETTE

Jimmy Saville's British television show, "Jim'll Fix It," invites public requests and it received one from Toby Gillette to have a character jug created in his likeness.

In 1984 three were produced: one was given to Toby Gillette, one remains in the Sir Henry Doulton Gallery, and the third was auctioned by Sotheby's, with the proceeds ($30,000) going to one of the charities Jimmy Saville supported. In 1986 Toby Gillette sold his own jug at a Sotheby's auction.

Royal Doulton

TOBY GILLETTE

D6717

Modelled by

Eric Griffiths

© ROYAL DOULTON TABLEWARE
LIMITED 1983
WORLDWIDE
LIMITED EDITION OF 3
This is No. 1

Designer: Eric Griffiths
Handle: Plain
Colourway: Brown

Backstamp: Doulton

Doulton Number	Size	Backstamp	Height	Intro.	Discon.	U.K. £	U.S. $	Can. $
						Current Market Value		
D6717	Large	Doulton	7"	1984	Ltd. ed.	Extremely rare. Only 3 known.		

TOBY PHILPOTS

A "thirsty old soul" in an 18th-century drinking song, Toby is thought by some to be the source of the traditional British toby jug, in which a character sits astride a barrel of ale. Popular opinion suggests his name is a derivation of the French *topé*, to toast.

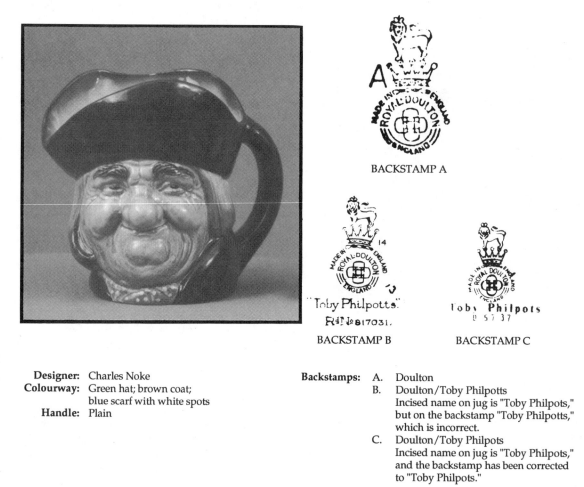

BACKSTAMP A

BACKSTAMP B

BACKSTAMP C

Designer: Charles Noke
Colourway: Green hat; brown coat; blue scarf with white spots
Handle: Plain

Backstamps: A. Doulton
B. Doulton/Toby Philpotts
Incised name on jug is "Toby Philpots," but on the backstamp "Toby Philpotts," which is incorrect.
C. Doulton/Toby Philpots
Incised name on jug is "Toby Philpots," and the backstamp has been corrected to "Toby Philpots."

Doulton Number	Size	Backstamp	Height	Intro.	Discon.	Current Market Value U.K. £	U.S. $	Can. $
D5736	Large	A. Doulton	6 1/4"	1937	1951	95.00	225.00	250.00
D5736	Large	B. Philpotts	6 1/4"	1937	1951	95.00	225.00	250.00
D5736	Large	C. Philpots	6 1/4"	1952	1969	95.00	225.00	250.00
D5737	Small	A. Doulton	3 1/4"	1937	1951	55.00	100.00	125.00
D5737	Small	B. Philpotts	3 1/4"	1937	1951	55.00	100.00	125.00
D5737	Small	C. Philpots	3 1/4"	1952	1969	55.00	100.00	125.00
D6043	Miniature	A. Doulton	2 1/4"	1939	1951	50.00	80.00	100.00
D6043	Miniature	B. Philpotts	2 1/4"	1939	1951	50.00	80.00	100.00
D6043	Miniature	C. Philpots	2 1/4"	1952	1969	50.00	80.00	100.00

TONY WELLER

In Charles Dickens's *The Pickwick Papers* (1837), Tony is a coachman who inherits a pub from his wife. He is the father of Sam Weller, who works for him at the inn.

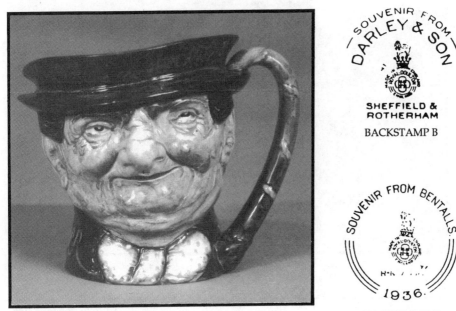

SOUVENIR FROM
DARLEY & SON

SHEFFIELD &
ROTHERHAM

BACKSTAMP B

SOUVENIR FROM BENTALLS

1936.

BACKSTAMP D

Designer: Leslie Harradine / Harry Fenton
Handle: Plain
Colourway: Grey hat; maroon coat; white bow with yellow spots

Backstamps: A. Doulton
B. Doulton/Darley & Son/Souvenir From Darley & Son/Sheffield & Rotherham
  Commissioned by Darley & Son, Sheffield and Rotherham.
C. Doulton/Bentalls/Souvenir From Bentalls Jubilee Year 1935
  Commissioned by Bentalls to commemorate the silver jubilee in 1935 of King George V.
D. Doulton/Bentalls/Souvenir from Bentalls. 1936.

Doulton Number	Size	Backstamp	Height	Intro.	Discon.	Current Market Value U.K. £	U.S. $	Can. $
D5531	Ext. Large	Doulton	8 1/2"	1936	1942	175.00	425.00	450.00
D5531	Large	Doulton	6 1/2"	1936	1960	95.00	250.00	275.00
D5530	Small	Doulton	3 1/4"	1936	1960	55.00	120.00	135.00
D5530	Small	Doulton/Darley	3 1/4"	1936	1936	375.00	1,200.00	1,200.00
D5530	Small	Doulton/Bentalls	3 1/4"	1935	1935	375.00	1,100.00	1,100.00
D5530	Small	Doulton/Bentalls	3 1/4"	1936	1936	375.00	1,000.00	1,000.00
D6044	Miniature	Doulton	2 1/4"	1939	1960	45.00	75.00	95.00

Tony Weller Derivatives

TONY WELLER TEAPOT

Doulton Number	Item	Height	Intro.	Discon.	Current Market Value		
					U.K. £	U.S. $	Can. $
D5888	Musical jug	6 1/2"	1937	1939	350.00	1,200.00	1,200.00
D6013	Sugar bowl	2 1/2"	1939	1960	400.00	850.00	850.00
D6016	Teapot	7"	1939	1960	1,100.00	2,500.00	2,500.00
D6051	Bust	4"	1939	1960	85.00	140.00	160.00
HN1616	Bookend	4"	1934	1939	1,100.00	3,500.00	3,500.00
M60	Napkin ring	3 1/2"	1935	1939	250.00	750.00	750.00

TOUCHSTONE

In Shakespeare's comedy, *As You Like It*, Touchstone is a jester to the court of the exiled Duke of Frederick. The Duke accompanies Rosalind and Celia into the Forest of Arden.

Designer: Charles Noke
Handle: Head of a clown
Colourway: Maroon, green and light brown

Backstamp: Doulton

Doulton Number	Size	Backstamp	Height	Intro.	Discon.	Current Market Value		
						U.K. £	U.S. $	Can. $
D5613	Large	Doulton	7"	1936	1960	150.00	375.00	400.00

TOWN CRIER

STYLE ONE: HANDLE — BELL ON SCROLL

Designer: David Biggs	**Backstamp:** Doulton
Handle: Bell on scroll	
Colourway: Black hat trimmed with gold; scarlet coat trimmed with gold	

Doulton Number	Size	Backstamp	Height	Intro.	Discon.	Current Market Value		
						U.K. £	U.S. $	Can. $
D6530	Large	Doulton	7"	1960	1973	150.00	350.00	375.00
D6537	Small	Doulton	3 1/4"	1960	1973	120.00	200.00	225.00
D6544	Miniature	Doulton	2 1/2"	1960	1973	130.00	250.00	275.00

TOWN CRIER

STYLE TWO: HANDLE — SCROLL WRAPPED AROUND BELL

Royal Doulton®
TOWN CRIER
D 6895
Modelled by

Stanley James Taylor

© 1991 ROYAL DOULTON

Designer: Stanley J. Taylor
Handle: Scroll wrapped around bell
Colourway: Black, maroon and white

Backstamp: Doulton

Doulton Number	Size	Backstamp	Height	Intro.	Discon.	Current Market Value		
						U.K. £	U.S. $	Can. $
D6895	Large	Doulton	7"	1991	1994	85.00	200.00	250.00

THE TRAPPER

CANADIAN CENTENNIAL SERIES, 1867-1967, ONE OF THREE

An integral part of Canadian history, the early trappers, or voyageurs, were largely responsible for the early exploration of the country. In search of animal pelts for export to the European market, these rugged men spent the winter travelling by canoe, snowshoe and foot through the wild Canadian north.

The miniature version of the Trapper character jug was put into production briefly in 1983; however, before any quantity was produced, the decision was made to withdraw the character. Several dozen have appeared on the market.

The Trapper is one of three jugs that received a special backstamp in 1967. The other two, the Lumberjack and the North American Indian, complete the three-jug Canadian Centennial Series.

The Trapper
D 6612
COPR 1966
DOULTON & CO LIMITED
Rd No 924808
Rd No 49144
Rd No 10600
Rd No 52/66

BACKSTAMP A

CANADIAN CENTENNIAL SERIES
1867 – 1967

The Trapper
D6600
COPR 1966
DOULTON & CO LIMITED
Rd No 924808
Rd No 10600
Rd No 52/66

BACKSTAMP B

Designer: Max Henk / David Biggs
Handle: A horn and a pair of snowshoes
Colourway: Dark green and white hat; brown and green clothing

Backstamps: A. Doulton
B. Doulton/Canadian Centennial Series 1867-1967

Doulton Number	Size	Backstamp	Height	Intro.	Discon.	Current Market Value		
						U.K. £	U.S. $	Can. $
D6609	Large	Doulton	7 1/4"	1967	1983	85.00	175.00	200.00
D6609	Large	Doul/Cent	7 1/4"	1967	1967	125.00	450.00	475.00
D6612	Small	Doulton	3 3/4"	1967	1983	60.00	100.00	120.00
D —	Miniature	Doulton	2 1/2"	1983	1983	Extremely rare		

UGLY DUCHESS

ALICE IN WONDERLAND,
ONE OF SIX

The ugly Duchess lives in Wonderland and plays croquet with the Queen. Alice found the game a curious one, with live hedgehogs for balls, flamingos for mallets and playing-cards soldiers, who doubled over to serve as the arches.

Backstamp: Doulton

Designer: Max Henk
Handle: A flamingo
Colourway: Green, purple and pink

Doulton Number	Size	Backstamp	Height	Intro.	Discon.	Current Market Value U.K. £	U.S. $	Can. $
D6599	Large	Doulton	6 3/4"	1965	1973	350.00	900.00	950.00
D6603	Small	Doulton	3 1/2"	1965	1973	250.00	500.00	525.00
D6607	Miniature	Doulton	2 1/2"	1965	1973	250.00	500.00	525.00

ULYSSES S. GRANT AND ROBERT E. LEE

THE ANTAGONISTS' COLLECTION (TWO-FACED JUG),
ONE OF FOUR

Ulysses Samuel Grant (1822-1885), an native of Ohio, was made Lieutenant General by President Lincoln and put in command of the Union Army in the American Civil War. His successes led to his election as president in 1868.

Robert E. Lee (1807-1870) was the general in command of the Confederate Army. He was ruthlessly pursued by General Grant, who forced him to retreat from his defence of Richmond, Virginia, in 1865. Lee's troops were surrounded at the great battle of Appomattox, where he and the Confederate Army surrendered.

This jug was issued in 1983 in a limited edition of 9,500 pieces.

Designer: Michael Abberley
Handle: Grant — Flag of the Union
Lee — Flag of the Confederacy
Colourway: Black, grey, brown and red

Backstamp: Doulton

Doulton Number	Size	Backstamp	Height	Intro.	Discon.	Current Market Value U.K. £	U.S. $	Can. $
D6698	Large	Doulton	7"	1983	Ltd. ed. (1986)	175.00	425.00	450.00

UNCLE TOM COBBLEIGH

In the popular 18th-century Devonshire song, Tom Cobbleigh and six friends borrow Tom Pearse's old mare to ride to the fair. Unable to support so many, the mare becomes sick and dies and still haunts the night-time moors to this day.

"Uncle Tom Cobbleigh"
D.6337
COPR 1951
DOULTON & CO.LIMITED.
R⁴N° 864845.
R⁴N° 29158
R⁴N° 6408
R⁴N° 114/51

Designer: Max Henk
Handle: Horseshoe
Colourway: Dark brown hat; green coat; dark grey horseshoe

Backstamp: Doulton

Doulton Number	Size	Backstamp	Height	Intro.	Discon.	Current Market Value		
						U.K. £	U.S. $	Can. $
D6337	Large	Doulton	7"	1952	1960	250.00	675.00	725.00

URIAH HEEP

CHARLES DICKENS COMMEMORATIVE SET,
DICKENS TINIES, ONE OF 12

The Uriah Heep jug was issued to commemorate the 170th anniversary of the birth of Charles Dickens. There are 12 jugs in this set, each issued with a certificate of authenticity. A mahogany display shelf completes the set. The set was first sold by Lawleys By Post in the U.K. from 1982 to 1988, and from 1985 in North America and Australia.

Uriah Heep
D 6682

Designer: Robert Tabbenor
Handle: Plain
Colourway: Grey and green

Backstamp: Doulton

Doulton Number	Size	Backstamp	Height	Intro.	Discon.	Current Market Value U.K. £	U.S. $	Can. $
D6682	Tiny	Doulton	1 1/2"	1982	1989	40.00	60.00	75.00
		Display stand for 12 tinies				65.00	45.00	50.00

VETERAN MOTORIST

Veteran Motorist
D.6637
© DOULTON & CO. LIMITED.1972
REGISTRATION APPLIED FOR.

Designer: David Biggs
Handle: A horn
Colourway: Yellow hat; green coat; white scarf

Backstamp: Doulton

Doulton Number	Size	Backstamp	Height	Intro.	Discon.	Current Market Value U.K. £	U.S. $	Can. $
D6633	Large	Doulton	7 1/2"	1973	1983	95.00	225.00	250.00
D6637	Small	Doulton	3 1/4"	1973	1983	60.00	140.00	160.00
D6641	Miniature	Doulton	2 1/2"	1973	1983	65.00	175.00	200.00

VICAR OF BRAY

In a popular song of the 18th century, this very adaptable parson boasted that he was able to accommodate himself to the religious views of Charles, James, William, Anne and George, and that "whosoever King may reign, he would always be the Vicar of Bray."

Prior to 1940 these jugs had a distinctive yellow rim.

"Vicar of Bray."
R.N.807475.

Designer: Charles Noke/Harry Fenton
Handle: Plain
Colourway: Brown hat; green coat

Backstamp: Doulton

Doulton Number	Size	Backstamp	Height	Intro.	Discon.	Current Market Value		
						U.K. £	U.S. $	Can. $
D5615	Large	Doulton	6 3/4"	1936	1960	135.00	350.00	375.00

VICE-ADMIRAL LORD NELSON

This was the character jug of the year for 1993. It was issued to commemorate the Battle of Trafalgar, on October 21, 1805.

Royal Doulton®
CHARACTER JUG OF THE YEAR
VICE-ADMIRAL
LORD NELSON
D 6932
October 21st 1805
Battle of Trafalgar edition
"England expects that every man will do his duty"
Modelled by

Stanley James Taylor

This special edition will only
be available during the year
1993
© 1992 ROYAL DOULTON

Designer: Stanley Taylor
Handle: The *Victory*
Colourway: Black, gold and cream

Backstamp: Doulton/Character Jug of the Year

Doulton Number	Size	Backstamp	Height	Intro.	Discon.	Current Market Value U.K. £	U.S. $	Can. $
D6932	Large	Doulton	8"	1993	1993	110.00	300.00	325.00

Note: For Napoleon see page 341.

VIKING

The large-size Viking character jug is reported to also carry the Stoke-on-Trent backstamp.

Viking
D.6496
COPR 1958
DOULTON & CO LIMITED
Rd No 889567
Rd No 38223
Rd No 1033
Rd No 426/58

Backstamp: Doulton

Designer: Max Henk
Handle: The prow of a Viking long ship
Colourway: Black, green and brown

Doulton Number	Size	Backstamp	Height	Intro.	Discon.	Current Market Value U.K. £	U.S. $	Can. $
D6496	Large	Doulton	7 1/4"	1959	1975	150.00	365.00	390.00
D6502	Small	Doulton	4"	1959	1975	95.00	175.00	200.00
D6526	Miniature	Doulton	2 1/2"	1960	1975	120.00	250.00	275.00

THE VILLAGE BLACKSMITH

PROTOTYPE

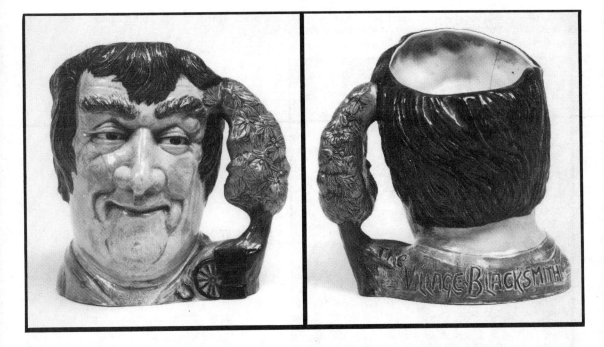

Designer: Max Henk
Handle: Tree above anvil, wheel and horseshoe
Colourway: Blue, brown, black and green

Backstamp: None shown

Doulton Number	Size	Backstamp	Height	Intro.	Discon.	Current Market Value U.K. £	U.S. $	Can. $
D6549	Large	None	7 1/2"	1961	1961	Unique Sold at auction, London, England, May 1993 — £6,000.00.		

VISCOUNT MONTGOMERY OF ALAMEIN

HEROIC LEADERS,
ONE OF THREE

This new design was specially commissioned by Lawleys By Post and was produced in a limited edition of 9,500 pieces. It was sold in a set of three: Montgomery, Mountbatten and Churchill.

Royal Doulton®
VISCOUNT MONTGOMERY OF ALAMEIN
1887-1976
D 6850
Modelled by
Stanley James Taylor
© 1989 ROYAL DOULTON
A LIMITED EDITION OF 9500
THIS IS NO. 1609

Designer: Stanley J. Taylor
Handle: Imperial Army flag
Colourway: Black beret, khaki uniform, red flag

Backstamp: Doulton

Doulton Number	Size	Backstamp	Height	Intro.	Discon.	U.K. £	U.S. $	Can. $
						Current Market Value		
D6850	Small	Doulton	3 1/4"	1990	Ltd. ed.	95.00	200.00	225.00

Note: For Field Marshall Montgomery see page 222. For Monty see page 333.

W. C. FIELDS

THE CELEBRITY COLLECTION,
ONE OF SIX

Born Claude William Dukenfield (1880-1946), W.C. Fields began his entertainment career at the age of 11 as a juggler. Much later he appeared in the Ziegfeld Follies and then in 1925 began his work in film. With his rasping voice and bulbous nose, he became a very successful satiric comedian.

The following quote appears on the base of the jug: "I was in love with a beautiful blonde once. She drove me to drink — 'tis the one thing I'm indebted to her for."

BACKSTAMP B

Designer: David Biggs
Handle: A walking cane
Colourway: Black, grey and yellow

Backstamps: A. Doulton
B. Doulton/American Express/ Premier Edition for American Express Introduced in the U.S.A. as a promotional jug for American Express. Approximately 1,500 jugs bore the special backstamp.

Doulton Number	Size	Backstamp	Height	Intro.	Discon.	Current Market Value U.K. £	U.S. $	Can. $
D6674	Large	Doulton	7"	1983	1986	95.00	225.00	250.00
D6674	Large	Doulton/Amex	7 1/2"	1983	Sp. ed.	165.00	350.00	375.00

W. G. GRACE

William Gilbert Grace (1848-1915) began playing professional cricket at the age of 16 and rose quickly to the status of England's best batsman, earning the title of "The Champion." Throughout his long career, he set many records, retiring at the age of 60 after 44 seasons.

This jug was commissioned by Lawleys By Post and issued in 1989 in a limited edition of 9,500 pieces.

Designer: Stanley J. Taylor
Handle: Cricket bat and ball
Colourway: Yellow and orange striped cap; black beard

Backstamp: Doulton

Doulton Number	Size	Backstamp	Height	Intro.	Discon.	Current Market Value U.K. £	U.S. $	Can. $
D6845	Small	Doulton	3 1/4"	1989	Ltd. ed.	60.00	165.00	180.00

THE WALRUS & CARPENTER

ALICE IN WONDERLAND,
ONE OF SIX

On a beach in Wonderland, the walrus and carpenter invited a number of oysters for evening conversation, which the walrus promptly ate.

Designer: Max Henk
Handle: A walrus
Colourway: Black, green and red

The Walrus & Carpenter
D 6600
COPR 1964
DOULTON & CO LIMITED
Rd No 917233
Rd No 46579
Rd No 10002
Rd No 591/64

Backstamp: Doulton

Doulton Number	Size	Backstamp	Height	Intro.	Discon.	Current Market Value		
						U.K. £	U.S. $	Can. $
D6600	Large	Doulton	7 1/4"	1965	1980	95.00	275.00	300.00
D6604	Small	Doulton	3 1/4"	1965	1980	65.00	175.00	200.00
D6608	Miniature	Doulton	2 1/2"	1965	1980	75.00	200.00	225.00

WELLINGTON

WATERLOO SERIES,
ONE OF TWO

This jug, and its matching pair, Napoleon D7001, was issued to commemorate the 180th anniversary of the Battle of Waterloo. The jugs were commissioned by Lawleys By Post in 1995 in a limited edition of 2,500 pieces.

Designer: William K. Harper
Handle: Gold emblazoned crown atop scrolls
showing the names of famous battles
Colourway:

Backstamp: Doulton

Doulton Number	Size	Backstamp	Height	Intro.	Discon.	Current Market Value U.K. £	U.S. $	Can. $
D7002	Small	Doulton	4"	1995	Ltd. ed.	125.00 (set of two jugs)		

WILD BILL HICKOCK

THE WILD WEST COLLECTION,
ONE OF SIX

After serving as a Union scout in the American Civil War, James Butler Hickock (1837-1876) became a marshall and then sheriff of several western frontier towns. An excellent gunman, he earned his nickname from his trigger-happy method of upholding the law at the many shootouts that erupted from poker games. He toured briefly with Buffalo Bill's Wild West Show (1872-1873) and was later murdered at Deadwood.

Royal Doulton

THE WILD WEST
Collection

WILD BILL HICKOCK
D6736
Modelled by

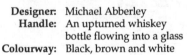

© ROYAL DOULTON (UK) 1984

Backstamp: Doulton

Designer: Michael Abberley
Handle: An upturned whiskey bottle flowing into a glass
Colourway: Black, brown and white

Doulton Number	Size	Backstamp	Height	Intro.	Discon.	Current Market Value		
						U.K. £	U.S. $	Can. $
D6736	Mid	Doulton	5 1/2"	1985	1989	60.00	140.00	160.00

WILLIAM SHAKESPEARE

THE SHAKESPEAREAN COLLECTION,
ONE OF SIX

Shakespeare (1564-1616) was born in Stratford-upon-Avon. Apparently he moved to London in 1585 and by 1592 had emerged as a promising actor and playwright. He was a part of the theatre company, the King's Men of James I, throughout his London career, and in 1599, he became the new owner of the Globe Theatre. Immensely successful as a playwright, director, poet and actor, Shakespeare was said to have been quite wealthy by the time he returned to Stratford in 1613.

STYLE ONE: HANDLE — INK WELL WITH THE APPEARANCE
OF THE GLOBE THEATRE

Royal Doulton
The
Shakespearean
Collection
WILLIAM SHAKESPEARE
D 6689
Modelled by

© ROYAL DOULTON TABLEWARE LIMITED 1982

Designer: Michael Abberley
Handle: A feather quill with an inkwell of
the appearance of the Globe Theatre
Colourway: White, grey and yellow

Backstamp: Doulton

Doulton Number	Size	Backstamp	Height	Intro.	Discon.	Current Market Value U.K. £	U.S. $	Can. $
D6689	Large	Doulton	7 3/4"	1983	1991	85.00	225.00	250.00

Note: For Shakespeare see page 424.

WILLIAM SHAKESPEARE

STYLE TWO: HANDLE — CHARACTERS FROM DIFFERENT PLAYS

This jug was issued in a limited edition of 2,500 pieces.

Royal Doulton®
WILLIAM SHAKESPEARE
D 6933
Modelled by

William K. Harper

© 1992 ROYAL DOULTON
LIMITED EDITION OF 2,500
THIS IS N⁰ 224

Designer: William K. Harper
Handle: Two handles, characters from different plays
Colourway: Brown

Backstamp: Doulton

Doulton Number	Size	Backstamp	Height	Intro.	Discon.	Current Market Value		
						U.K. £	U.S. $	Can. $
D6933	Large	Doulton	7"	1992	Ltd. ed. (1993)	250.00	625.00	750.00

Note: For Shakespeare see page 424.

WINSTON CHURCHILL

STYLE ONE: HANDLE — UNION JACK AND BULLDOG

This Winston Churchill jug was the character jug of the year for 1992.

Royal Doulton®
CHARACTER JUG OF THE YEAR
WINSTON CHURCHILL
D 6907
Modelled by

Stanley James Taylor

This special edition will only
be available during the year
1992
© 1991 ROYAL DOULTON

Designer: Stanley J. Taylor
Handle: Union Jack and bulldog
Colourway: Black, brown and white

Backstamp: Doulton/Character Jug of the Year, 1992

Doulton Number	Size	Backstamp	Height	Intro.	Discon.	Current Market Value		
						U.K. £	**U.S. $**	**Can. $**
D6907	Large	Doulton	7"	1992	1992	125.00	365.00	395.00

Note: For Churchill see page 180. For Sir Winston Churchill see page 432.

WINSTON CHURCHILL

STYLE TWO: HANDLE — *NEWS CHRONICLE* VICTORY ISSUE

Royal Doulton
WINSTON CHURCHILL
D 6934
Modelled by

Stanley James Taylor

© 1991 ROYAL DOULTON

Designer: Stanley J. Taylor
Handle: *News Chronicle* victory issue
Colourway: Black, grey, white and cream

Backstamp: Doulton

Doulton Number	Size	Backstamp	Height	Intro.	Discon.	Current Market Value		
						U.K. £	U.S. $	Can. $
D6934	Small	Doulton	4"	1992	Current	35.00	99.00	120.00

Note: For Churchill see page 180. For Sir Winston Churchill see page 432.

THE WITCH

MYSTICAL SERIES,
ONE OF THREE

Royal Doulton®
THE WITCH
D 6893
Modelled by

Stanley James Taylor

© 1991 ROYAL DOULTON

Designer: Stanley J. Taylor
Handle: Part of the witch's hat
Colourway: Black and greys

Backstamp: Doulton

Doulton Number	Size	Backstamp	Height	Intro.	Discon.	Current Market Value		
						U.K. £	U.S. $	Can. $
D6893	Large	Doulton	7"	1991	1991	150.00	340.00	375.00

THE WIZARD

MYSTICAL SERIES,
ONE OF THREE

Royal Doulton®
THE WIZARD
D 6862
Modelled by

Stanley James Taylor

© 1990 ROYAL DOULTON

Designer: Stanley J. Taylor
Handle: Black cat and a magic wand
Colourway: Blue-grey cap; black coat; red collar

Backstamp: Doulton

Doulton Number	Size	Backstamp	Height	Intro.	Discon.	Current Market Value U.K. £	U.S. $	Can. $
D6862	Large	Doulton	6 3/4"	1990	Current	67.00	175.00	275.00
D6909	Small	Doulton	3 3/4"	1992	Current	31.00	69.50	110.00

WYATT EARP

THE WILD WEST COLLECTION,
ONE OF SIX

Wyatt Berry Stapp Earp (1848-1929) was an expert gunfighter. He worked as a police officer and armed guard and, in 1881, was involved in the famous shootout at the O.K. Corral. Later Earp travelled around the West, operating a number of saloons.

Designer: Stanley J. Taylor
Handle: A gun and sheriff's badge
Colourway: Brown coat; light brown hat with red band

Backstamp: Doulton

Doulton Number	Size	Backstamp	Height	Intro.	Discon.	Current Market Value		
						U.K. £	U.S. $	Can. $
D6711	Mid	Doulton	5 1/2"	1985	1989	65.00	140.00	160.00

YACHTSMAN

The small and miniature jugs of the Yachtsman were piloted, but never put into production.

STYLE ONE: YACHTSMAN WITH LIFE JACKET

Designer: David Biggs
Handle: A yacht sailing from the front to back
Colourway: Blue cap and jersey; yellow lifejacket

Backstamp: Doulton

Doulton Number	Size	Backstamp	Height	Intro.	Discon.	U.K. £	U.S. $	Can. $
						Current Market Value		
D6626	Large	Doulton	8"	1971	1980	95.00	225.00	250.00
D –	Small	Doulton	3"	Unknown			Extremely rare	

YACHTSMAN

STYLE TWO: YACHTSMAN WITH PEAK CAP AND SCARF

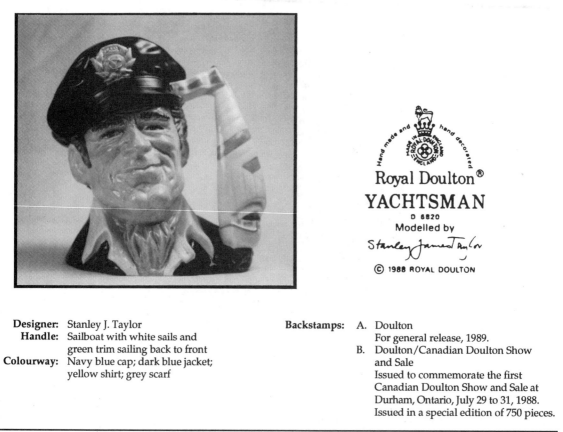

Royal Doulton®
YACHTSMAN
D 6820
Modelled by

Stanley James Taylor

© 1988 ROYAL DOULTON

Designer: Stanley J. Taylor
Handle: Sailboat with white sails and green trim sailing back to front
Colourway: Navy blue cap; dark blue jacket; yellow shirt; grey scarf

Backstamps: A. Doulton
For general release, 1989.
B. Doulton/Canadian Doulton Show and Sale
Issued to commemorate the first Canadian Doulton Show and Sale at Durham, Ontario, July 29 to 31, 1988. Issued in a special edition of 750 pieces.

Doulton Number	Size	Backstamp	Height	Intro.	Discon.	Current Market Value U.K. £	U.S. $	Can. $
D6820	Large	Doulton	6 1/2"	1989	1991	75.00	175.00	200.00
D6820	Large	Doulton/Durham	6 1/2"	1988	Sp. ed.	140.00	200.00	225.00

THE YEOMAN OF THE GUARD

THE LONDON COLLECTION,
ONE OF TEN

In 1485 Henry VIII organized the Yeomen of the Guard, bodyguards to the monarch of England. Today the Yeomen, or Beefeaters as they are more commonly known, serve only as ceremonial guards.

Royal Doulton®
THE YEOMAN OF THE GUARD
D 6873
Modelled by

Stanley James Taylor

© 1990 ROYAL DOULTON

BACKSTAMP A

Designer: Stanley J. Taylor
Handle: Raven and tree trunk
Colourway: Black hat; white frills; red jacket

Royal Doulton®

THE YEOMAN OF THE GUARD
D 6883
Modelled by
Stanley James Taylor

Specially Commissioned from
Royal Doulton

To commemorate the third anniversary of
the opening of the Royal Doulton Room
Dillards New Orleans Louisiana U S A
©1990 ROYAL DOULTON
A LIMITED EDITION OF 50
THIS IS N° 37

BACKSTAMP B

Royal Doulton®

THE YEOMAN OF THE GUARD
D 6885
Modelled by
Stanley James Taylor

Specially Commissioned from
Royal Doulton

To commemorate the fourth anniversary of
the opening of the Royal Doulton Room
Strawbridge and Clothier Philadelphia. Pennsylvania U.S A
©1990 ROYAL DOULTON
A LIMITED EDITION OF 75
THIS IS N° 29

BACKSTAMP D

Backstamps: A. Doulton

The jugs bearing backstamps B, C, D and E were released in the U.S.A. to commemorate the anniversaries of the opening of the four Royal Doulton Rooms in the U.S.A. They were issued in a limited edition of 450 pieces total and bore a special backstamp.

B. Doulton/Dillards/
To Commemorate the third anniversary of the opening of the Royal Doulton Room Dillards, New Orleans, Louisiana, U.S.A.
Issued in a limited edition of 50 pieces.

C. Doulton/Joseph Horne/
To Commemorate the third anniversary of the opening of the Royal Doulton Room Joseph Horne, Pittsburgh, Pennsylvania, U.S.A.
Issued in a limited edition of 75 pieces.

D. Doulton/Strawbridge and Clothier/
To Commemorate the fourth anniversary of the opening of the Royal Doulton Room Strawbridge and Clothier, Philadelphia, Pennsylvania, U.S.A.
Issued in a limited edition of 75 pieces.

E. Doulton/Higbee/
To Commemorate the fifth anniversary of the opening of the Royal Doulton Room Higbee Cleveland, Ohio, U.S.A.
Issued in a limited edition of 250 pieces.

Doulton Number	Size	Backstamp	Height	Intro.	Discon.	Current Market Value		
						U.K. £	U.S. $	Can. $
D6873	Large	Doulton	7"	1991	Current	65.00	125.00	220.00
D6883	Large	Dillards	7"	1990	Ltd. ed.	200.00	350.00	375.00
D6882	Large	Horne	7"	1990	Ltd. ed.	165.00	350.00	375.00
D6885	Large	Strawbridge	7"	1990	Ltd. ed.	165.00	350.00	375.00
D6884	Large	Higbee	7"	1990	Ltd. ed.	150.00	350.00	375.00

LIQUOR
CONTAINERS
AND JUGS

CAPTAIN COOK

THE INTERNATIONAL COLLECTION, ONE OF FOUR

LIQUOR CONTAINER

This Captain Cook liquor container was commissioned by Pick-Kwik Wines and Spirits in a limited edition of 2,000 pieces.

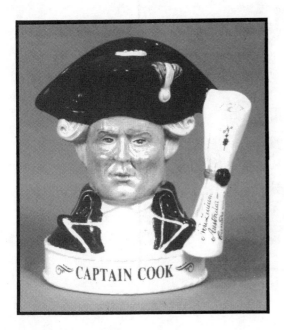

THIRD OF A SERIES
THE INTERNATIONAL COLLECTION
Specially Commissioned from
Royal Doulton®

200ml.   JIM BEAM BOURBON WHISKEY   40% Vol.
PICK-KWIK WINES & SPIRITS
MICKLEOVER, DERBY, ENGLAND
with special permission from
JAMES B. BEAM DISTILLING INTERNATIONAL CO.

Designer: Harry Sales
Modeller: Graham Tongue
Handle: Scroll
Colourway: Black hat; black and yellow uniform
Inscription around Base: "Captain Cook"

Backstamp: Doulton/Pick-Kwik

Doulton Number	Size	Backstamp	Height	Intro.	Discon.	Current Market Value U.K. £	U.S. $	Can. $
D —	Small	Doulton	4 3/4"	1985	Ltd. ed.	65.00	100.00	120.00

FALSTAFF

LIQUEUR CONTAINER

The Falstaff, Poacher and Rip Van Winkle character jugs were adapted by Royal Doulton as liqueur containers for Bols liqueur for the bottling firm of W. Walklate Ltd. The small-size jugs were commissioned about 1960 by W. Walklate Ltd.

Designer: Harry Fenton
Handle: Plain
Colourway: Rose tunic; black hat trimmed with rose plumes; grey beard

Backstamp: Doulton

Doulton Number	Size	Backstamp	Height	Intro.	Discon.	Current Market Value U.K. £	U.S. $	Can. $
D6385	Small	Falstaff	4"	c. 1960	c. 1960	55.00	165.00	175.00

IRISHMAN

WHISKEY DECANTER

Two whisky flasks, one depicting an Irishman and the other a Scotsman (page 499), were made in the 1920s for Asprey and Co., New Bond Street, London, England. Each was set within a wooden tantalus, and the head of the flask was detachable. The Irishman contained Irish whiskey, and the Scotsman, Scottish whisky. These two flasks are usually traded as a set.

ASPREY & C? LTD
LONDON
R⁴ N? 675852

Designer: Harry Fenton
Colourway: Black hat and coat; green
cravat; maroon vest

Backstamp: Doulton

Doulton Number	Size	Backstamp	Height	Intro.	Discon.	Current Market Value U.K. £	U.S. $	Can. $
D6873	Large	Doulton	9 1/2"	1920	1930	800.00	2,000.00	2,000.00

JOHN BULL

THE INTERNATIONAL COLLECTION,
ONE OF FOUR

LIQUOR CONTAINER

The John Bull liquor container was commissioned by Pick-Kwik Wines and Spirits in a limited edition of 2,000 pieces.

SECOND OF A SERIES
THE INTERNATIONAL COLLECTION
Specially Commissioned
from
Royal Doulton®

200ml.　JIM BEAM BOURBON WHISKEY　40% Vol.
PICK-KWIK WINES & SPIRITS
MICKLEOVER, DERBY, ENGLAND
with special permission from
JAMES B. BEAM DISTILLING INTERNATIONAL CO

Designer: Harry Sales
Modeller: Graham Tongue
Handle: Cane with bull dog head
Colourway: Black hat with yellow band, red coat
Inscription around Base: "John Bull"

Backstamp: Doulton/Pick-Kwik

Doulton Number	Size	Backstamp	Height	Intro.	Discon.	Current Market Value		
						U.K. £	U.S. $	Can. $
D —	Small	Doulton	5"	1985	Ltd. ed.	65.00	120.00	130.00

MR. MICAWBER

STYLE ONE: LIQUOR CONTAINER

This liquor container was commissioned by Pick-Kwik Wines and Spirits.

VARIATION No. 1: Colourway — Brown hat; dark blue blazer; maroon cravat
Handle — Dewar's
Inscription on Base —"Dewar's"
Issued — 2,000 pieces

Designer: Harry Sales
Modeller: Graham Tongue
Handle: Dewar's
Colourway: Brown hat; dark blue blazer; maroon cravat
Inscription around Base: "Dewar's"

Backstamp: Doulton/Pick-Kwik

Doulton Number	Size	Variation	Height	Intro.	Discon.	Current Market Value		
						U.K. £	U.S. $	Can. $
D —	Small	Var. 1	5"	1983	Ltd. ed.	65.00	120.00	130.00

VARIATION No. 2:   Colourway — Grey hat; green blazer; light blue cravat
Handle — Pickwick Deluxe
Inscription around Base — "Pickwick Deluxe Whiskey"
Issued — 2,000 pieces

Doulton Number	Size	Variation	Height	Intro.	Discon.	Current Market Value U.K. £	U.S. $	Can. $
D —	Small	Var. 2	5"	1983	Ltd. ed.	65.00	120.00	130.00

VARIATION No. 3:   Colourway — White
Handle — Pickwick Deluxe
Inscription around Base — "Pickwick Deluxe Whiskey"
Issued — 100 pieces

Doulton Number	Size	Variation	Height	Intro.	Discon.	Current Market Value U.K. £	U.S. $	Can. $
D —	Small	Var. 3	5"	1985	Ltd. ed.	150.00	200.00	225.00

MR. MICAWBER

STYLE TWO: CHARACTER JUG

This jug was commissioned by Pick-Kwik Wines and Spirits.

VARIATION No. 1:   Colourway — Brown hat; blue blazer; maroon cravat
Handle — Dewar's
Inscription around Base — "Dewar's"
Issued — 100 pieces

Designer: Harry Sales
Modeller: Graham Tongue
Handle: Dewar's
Colourway: Brown hat; blue blazer; maroon cravat
Inscription around Base: "Dewar's"

Backstamp: Doulton/Pick-Kwik

Doulton Number	Size	Variation	Height	Intro.	Discon.	Current Market Value U.K. £	U.S. $	Can. $
D —	Small	Var. 1	4"	1985	Ltd. ed.	150.00	250.00	275.00

VARIATION NO. 2   VARIATION NO. 3   VARIATION NO. 4

VARIATION No. 2: Colourway — White
Handle — Dewar's
Inscription around Base — "Dewar's" in red
Issued — 100 pieces

Doulton Number	Size	Variation	Height	Intro.	Discon.	Current Market Value U.K. £	U.S. $	Can. $
D —	Small	Var. 2	4"	1985	Ltd. ed.	150.00	250.00	275.00

VARIATION No. 3: Colourway — Grey hat; green blazer; light blue cravat
Handle — Pickwick Deluxe
Inscription around Base — "Pickwick Deluxe Whiskey"
Issued — 100 pieces

Doulton Number	Size	Variation	Height	Intro.	Discon.	Current Market Value U.K. £	U.S. $	Can. $
D —	Small	Var. 3	4"	1985	Ltd. ed.	150.00	250.00	275.00

VARIATION No. 4: Colourway — White
Handle — Pickwick Deluxe
Inscription around Base — "Pickwick Deluxe Whiskey"
Issued — 100 pieces

Doulton Number	Size	Variation	Height	Intro.	Discon.	Current Market Value U.K. £	U.S. $	Can. $
D —	Small	Var. 4	4"	1985	Ltd. ed.	150.00	250.00	275.00

MR. PICKWICK

CHARACTER JUG

Pick-Kwik Wines and Spirits commissioned the Mr. Pickwick jug.

VARIATION No. 1: Colourway — Green hat; black coat
Handle — No label / "Whisky"
Inscription around Base — "Pick-Kwik Derby Whiskies Wines Ales"
Issued — 2,000 pieces

MR PICKWICK
(FOUNDER & GENERAL CHAIRMAN
OF THE PICKWICK CLUB)
THE MOST FAMOUS OF
CHARLES DICKENS' CHARACTERS FROM
"PICKWICK PAPERS"
FIRST PUBLISHED IN 1846

Designer: Harry Sales
Modeller: Graham Tongue
Handle: Pick-Kwik
Colourway: Green hat; black coat
Inscription around Base: "Pick-Kwik Derby Whiskies Wines Ales"

Backstamp: Doulton/Pick-Kwik

Doulton Number	Size	Variation	Height	Intro.	Discon.	Current Market Value U.K. £	U.S. $	Can. $
D —	Small	Var. 1	4"	1982	Ltd. ed.	75.00	175.00	190.00

VARIATION NO. 4   VARIATION NO. 6   VARIATION NO. 2

VARIATION No. 2: Colourway — Brown hat; dark brown coat
Handle — Jim Beam
Inscription around Base — "Pick-Kwik Derby Sells Jim Beam Whiskey"
Issued — 2,000 pieces

Doulton Number	Size	Variation	Height	Intro.	Discon.	Current Market Value		
						U.K. £	U.S. $	Can. $
D —	Small	Var. 2	4"	1984	Ltd. ed.	75.00	175.00	190.00

VARIATION No. 3: Colourway — Beige hat; brown coat
Handle — Jim Beam
Inscription around Base — "Beam Whiskey"
Issued — 1,000 pieces

Doulton Number	Size	Variation	Height	Intro.	Discon.	Current Market Value		
						U.K. £	U.S. $	Can. $
D —	Small	Var. 3	5 1/4"	1984	Ltd. ed.	75.00	175.00	190.00

VARIATION No. 4: Colourway — Beige hat; brown coat
Handle — Beam's Black Label
Inscription around Base — "Beam Whiskey"
Issued — 1,000 pieces

Doulton Number	Size	Variation	Height	Intro.	Discon.	Current Market Value		
						U.K. £	U.S. $	Can. $
D —	Small	Var. 4	5 1/4"	1984	Ltd. ed.	75.00	175.00	190.00

VARIATION No. 5:   Colourway — White
Handle — No label / "Whiskey"
Inscription around Base — "Pick Kwik Derby"
Issued — 100 pieces

| Doulton | | | | | | Current Market Value | | |
Number	Size	Variation	Height	Intro.	Discon.	U.K. £	U.S. $	Can. $
D —	Small	Var. 5	5 1/4"	1985	Ltd. ed.	150.00	225.00	250.00

VARIATION No. 6:   Colourway — White with red transfers
Handle — Jim Beam
Inscription around Base — "Pick Kwik Derby Sells Jim Beam Whiskey"
Issued — 100 pieces

| Doulton | | | | | | Current Market Value | | |
Number	Size	Variation	Height	Intro.	Discon.	U.K. £	U.S. $	Can. $
D —	Small	Var. 6	5 1/4"	1985	Ltd. ed.	150.00	225.00	250.00

THE PICKWICK COLLECTION

MR. PICKWICK AND SAM WELLER

THE PICKWICK COLLECTION

LIQUOR CONTAINER

This two-faced liquor container was commissioned by Pick-Kwik Wines and Spirits in a limited edition of 2,000 pieces.

Designer: Harry Sales
Modeller: Graham Tongue
Handle: Jim Beam, plain bottle
Colourway: Black coat; pink bow tie; grey coat;
yellow cravat

Backstamp: Doulton/Pick-Kwik

Inscription on Base: "Beam Whiskey" and "The World's Finest Bourbon"

Doulton Number	Size	Backstamp	Height	Intro.	Discon.	Current Market Value U.K. £	U.S. $	Can. $
D —	Small	Doulton	5"	1985	Ltd. ed.	75.00	175.00	195.00

OLD MR. TURVERYDROP

LIQUOR CONTAINER

Commissioned by Pick-Kwik Wines and Spirits, Old Mr. Turverydrop was produced in a limited edition of 2,000 pieces.

THE PICKWICK COLLECTION
Specially Commissioned
from
Royal Doulton®

200ml.   JIM BEAM BOURBON WHISKEY   40%Vol.
PICK-KWIK WINES & SPIRITS
MICKLEOVER, DERBY, ENGLAND
with special permission from
JAMES B. BEAM DISTILLING INTERNATIONAL CO.

Designer: Harry Sales
Modeller: Graham Tongue
Handle: Jim Beam
Colourway: Yellow hat; black coat
Inscription on Base: "Beam Whiskey"

Backstamp: Doulton/Pick-Kwik

Doulton Number	Size	Backstamp	Height	Intro.	Discon.	Current Market Value		
						U.K. £	U.S. $	Can. $
D —	Small	Doulton	5"	1985	1985	75.00	175.00	195.00

THE POACHER

LIQUEUR CONTAINER

The Falstaff, Poacher and Rip Van Winkle character jugs were adapted by Doulton to liqueur containers for Bols liqueurs for the bottling firm W. Walklate Ltd. The small-size jugs were commissioned about 1960 by W. Walklate Ltd.

Designer: Max Henk
Handle: A salmon
Colourway: Green coat; red scarf; light brown hat

Backstamp: Doulton

Doulton Number	Size	Backstamp	Height	Intro.	Discon.	Current Market Value U.K. £	U.S. $	Can. $
D6464	Small	Doulton	4"	c. 1960	c. 1960	60.00	175.00	195.00

RIP VAN WINKLE

LIQUEUR CONTAINER

The Falstaff, Poacher and Rip Van Winkle character jugs were adapted by Doulton to liqueur containers for Bols liqueurs for the bottling firm W. Walklate Ltd. The small-size jugs were commissioned about 1960 by W. Walklate Ltd.

Designer: Geoff Blower
Handle: A man resting against a tree
Colourway: Grey-blue cap; brown robes; figure resting against tree dressed in blue

Backstamp: Doulton

Doulton Number	Size	Backstamp	Height	Intro.	Discon.	Current Market Value U.K. £	U.S. $	Can. $
D6463	Small	Doulton	4"	c. 1960	c. 1960	60.00	175.00	195.00

SAMURAI WARRIOR

THE INTERNATIONAL COLLECTION
ONE OF FOUR

LIQUOR CONTAINER

Commissioned by Pick-Kwik Wines and Spirits, the Samurai Warrior was produced in a limited edition of 2,000 pieces.

FOURTH OF A SERIES
THE INTERNATIONAL COLLECTION
Specially Commissioned
from
Royal Doulton®

200ml.　JIM BEAM BOURBON WHISKEY　40% Vol.
PICK-KWIK WINES & SPIRITS
MICKLEOVER, DERBY, ENGLAND
with special permission from
JAMES B. BEAM DISTILLING INTERNATIONAL CO.

Designer: Harry Sales
Modeller: Graham Tongue
Handle: Sword
Colourway: Black hair; white face
Inscription on Base: "Samurai Warrior"

Backstamp: Doulton/Pick-Kwik

Doulton Number	Size	Backstamp	Height	Intro.	Discon.	Current Market Value U.K. £	U.S. $	Can. $
D —	Small	Doulton	5"	1986	1986	70.00	140.00	160.00

SCOTSMAN

WHISKY DECANTERS

Two whisky flasks, one depicting a Scotsman and the other an Irishman (page 485), were made in the 1920s for Asprey and Co., New Bond Street, London, England. Each was set within a wooden tantalus, and the head of the flask was detachable. The Scotsman contained Scottish whisky, and the Irishman, Irish whiskey. These two flasks are usually traded as a set.

ASPREY & Cº LTD
LONDON
Rᵈ Nº 675852

Designer: Harry Fenton
Colourway: Red tam; black coat

Backstamp: Doulton

Doulton Number	Size	Backstamp	Height	Intro.	Discon.	Current Market Value		
						U.K. £	**U.S. $**	**Can. $**
D6873	Large	Doulton	9 1/2"	1920	1930	800.00	2,000.00	2,000.00

SGT. BUZ FUZ

CHARACTER JUG

This character jug was commissioned by Pick-Kwik Wines and Spirits.

VARIATION No. 1:   Colourway — White hair; black coat
Handle — Dewar's
Inscription around Base — "Pick-Kwik Derby Sells Dewar's Whisky"
Issued — 2,000 pieces

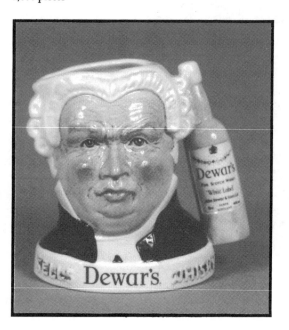

Designer: Harry Sales
Modeller: Graham Tongue
Handle: Dewar's
Colourway: White hair; black coat
Inscription around Base: "Pick-Kwik Derby Sells Dewar's Whisky"

Backstamp: Doulton/Pick-Kwik

Doulton Number	Size	Variation	Height	Intro.	Discon.	Current Market Value U.K. £	U.S. $	Can. $
D —	Small	Var. 1	4"	1982	Ltd. ed.	75.00	225.00	240.00

VARIATION No. 2:   Colourway — White with red transfers
Handle — Dewar's
Inscription around Base — "Pick-Kwik Derby Sells Dewar's Whisky"
Issued — 100 pieces

Doulton Number	Size	Variation	Height	Intro.	Discon.	Current Market Value U.K. £	U.S. $	Can. $
D —	Small	Var. 2	4"	1985	Ltd. ed.	150.00	250.00	275.00

VARIATION No. 3:   Colourway — White
Handle — Plain bottle
Inscription around Base — "Pick-Kwik Derby Sells Whisky"
Issued — 100 pieces

Doulton Number	Size	Variation	Height	Intro.	Discon.	Current Market Value U.K. £	U.S. $	Can. $
D —	Small	Var. 3	4"	1985	Ltd. ed.	150.00	250.00	275.00

THE INTERNATIONAL COLLECTION

TOWN CRIER OF EATANSWILL

LIQUOR CONTAINER

This Town Crier was commissioned by Pick-Kwik Wines and Spirits and was issued in a limited edition of 2,000 pieces.

Designer: Harry Sales
Modeller: Graham Tongue
Handle: Jim Beam
Colourway: Black hat; maroon coat with yellow trim
Inscription around Base: "Beam Whiskey"

Backstamp: Doulton/Pick-Kwik

Doulton Number	Size	Backstamp	Height	Intro.	Discon.	Current Market Value		
						U.K. £	U.S. $	Can. $
D —	Small	Doulton	5"	1986	Ltd. ed.	75.00	150.00	165.00

UNCLE SAM

THE INTERNATIONAL COLLECTION
ONE OF FOUR

STYLE ONE: HANDLE — JIM BEAM BOTTLE

Commissioned by Pick-Kwik Wines and Spirits, Uncle Sam was issued in a limited edition of 2,000 pieces.

VARIATION No. 1: Inscription around Base — "Uncle Sam"

Specially Commissioned
from
Royal Doulton
200ml. JIM BEAM BOURBON WHISKEY 40% Vol.
PICK-KWIK WINES & SPIRITS
MICKLEOVER, DERBY, ENGLAND
with special permission from
JAMES B. BEAM DISTILLING INTERNATIONAL CO.

Backstamp: Doulton/Pick-Kwik

Designer: Harry Sales
Modeller: Graham Tongue
Handle: Jim Beam bottle
Colourway: Red, white and blue

Doulton Number	Size	Variation	Height	Intro.	Discon.	Current Market Value U.K. £	Current Market Value U.S. $	Current Market Value Can. $
D —	Small	Var. 1	5"	1984	Ltd. ed.	75.00	175.00	195.00

VARIATION No. 2: Inscription around base — "Beam Whiskey"

Doulton Number	Size	Variation	Height	Intro.	Discon.	Current Market Value U.K. £	Current Market Value U.S. $	Current Market Value Can. $
D —	Small	Var. 2	5"	1984	Ltd. ed.	75.00	175.00	195.00

UNCLE SAM

STYLE TWO: HANDLE: EAGLE

Commissioned by Pick-Kwik Wines and Spirits, Uncle Sam was issued as promotional item in a limited edition of 500 pieces.

VARIATION No. 1: Inscription around base — "In God We Trust"

Designer: Harry Sales
Modeller: Graham Tongue
Handle: Eagle
Colourway: Red, white and blue

Backstamp: Doulton/Pick-Kwik

Doulton Number	Size	Variation	Height	Intro.	Discon.	Current Market Value U.K. £	U.S. $	Can. $
D —	Small	Var. 1	5"	1986	Ltd. ed.	135.00	275.00	295.00

VARIATION No. 2: Inscription around base —"Jim Beam"

Doulton Number	Size	Variation	Height	Intro.	Discon.	Current Market Value U.K. £	U.S. $	Can. $
D —	Small	Var. 2	5"	1986	Ltd. ed.	135.00	275.00	295.00

WILLIAM GRANT

LIQUOR CONTAINER

STYLE ONE: HANDLE — FOUR OAK CASKS

Issued to commemorate the centenary of the founding of the Glenfiddich Distillery, this jug contains 750 ml of 25-year-old Grants Whisky. The uniform is that of a major of the 6th Volunteer Battalion of the Gordon Highlanders. The Glengarry cap features the symbol of a stag's head, which also appears on all of the company's bottles of whisky.

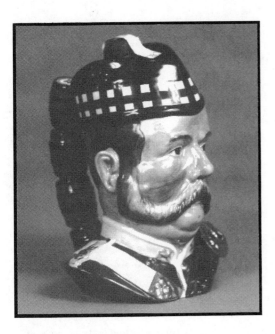

William Grant
Founder of William Grant & Sons Ltd
An independent family company for five generations
Specially Commissioned from
Royal Doulton ®
Hand Modelled and Hand Painted
Designed and Modelled by *Graham Tongue*
Grant's 25 Year Old Very Rare Scotch Whisky
One of 500, specially filled in 1986, celebrating the 100 years
since William Grant laid the foundation stone of his
Highland Distillery.

Blended and Bottled by
William Grant & Sons Ltd
The Glenfiddich Distillery, Banffshire, Scotland
Product of Scotland

750ml 43% vol.

BACKSTAMP A

William Grant
Founder of William Grant & Sons Ltd
An independent family company for five generations
Specially Commissioned from
Royal Doulton ®
Hand Modelled and Hand Painted
Designed and Modelled by *Graham Tongue*
Grant's 25 Year Old Very Rare Scotch Whisky
Specially filled in 1987, celebrating the 100 years since
the first whisky flowed from the stills of William Grant's
Highland Distillery.

Blended and Bottled by
William Grant & Sons Ltd
The Glenfiddich Distillery, Banffshire, Scotland
Product of Scotland

750ml 43% vol.

BACKSTAMP B

Designer: Graham Tongue
Handle: Four oak casks
Colourway: Scarlet

Backstamps: A. Doulton/William Grant 100th Anniversary
Issued in 1986 in a limited edition of 500 pieces to commemorate
the 100th anniversary of the laying of the foundation stone.
B. Doulton / William Grant 100 Years
Issued in 1987 in a limited edition of 2,500 pieces to celebrate the
100 years since whisky first flowed from the stills.

Doulton Number	Size	Backstamp	Height	Intro.	Discon.	Current Market Value		
						U.K. £	**U.S. $**	**Can. $**
D —	Large	Doul/100th Ann.	7"	1986	Ltd. ed.	300.00	500.00	550.00
D —	Large	Doulton/100 yrs.	7"	1987	Ltd. ed.	200.00	350.00	375.00

WILLIAM GRANT

LIQUOR CONTAINER

STYLE TWO: HANDLE — FIELD OFFICERS' SWORD

Commissioned by Grants Glenfiddich Distillery, this liquor container was issued in 1988 in a limited edition of 5,000 pieces.

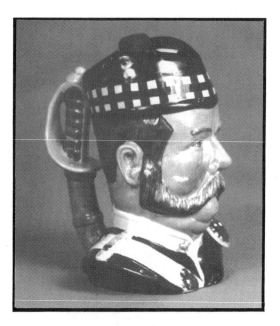

William Grant
Founder of William Grant & Sons Ltd
An independent family company for five generations
Specially Commissioned from
Royal Doulton®
Hand Modelled and Hand Painted
Designed and Modelled by *G.G. Tongue*
William Grant's 25 Year Old
Very Rare Blended Scotch Whisky
One of a limited edition of 5000
William Grant Character Jugs specially styled
with a Field Officer's sword handle
Blended and Bottled by
William Grant & Sons Ltd
The Glenfiddich Distillery, Banffshire Scotland
Product of Scotland
750ml 43% vol.

Designer: Graham Tongue
Handle: Field officers' sword
Colourway: Scarlet

Backstamp: Doulton/William Grant

Doulton Number	Size	Backstamp	Height	Intro.	Discon.	Current Market Value U.K. £	U.S. $	Can. $
D —	Large	Doulton/Grant	7"	1988	Ltd. ed.	200.00	450.00	475.00

LOVING CUPS AND JUGS

ADMIRAL LORD NELSON

This cup was issued in a limited edition of 600 pieces.

Designer: Charles Noke / Harry Fenton

Handles: Block and tackles

Main Colours: Brown, blue, yellow and green

Inscription around base: "England Expects" and "It was in Trafalgar Bay"

Backstamp: Doulton

Doulton Number	Type	Backstamp	Height	Intro.	Discon.	Current Market Value		
						U.K.£	**U.S.$**	**Can.$**
—	Cup	Doulton	10 1/2"	1935	Ltd. ed.	750.00	2,400.00	2,400.00

THE APOTHECARY

The Apothecary was issued in a limited edition of 600.

Designer: Charles Noke/Harry Fenton
Handles: Distorted faces
Main Colours: Green, red, yellow

Backstamp: Doulton

Doulton Number	Type	Backstamp	Height	Intro.	Discon.	Current Market Value		
						U.K.£	U.S.$	Can.$
—	Cup	Doulton	6"	1934	Ltd. ed.	650.00	1,300.00	1,300.00

CAPTAIN COOK

The Captain Cook loving cup was issued in a limited edition of 350 pieces.

Designer: Charles Noke/Harry Fenton
Handles: Coconut palms with flag the of
St. George and the Union Jack
Main Colours: Green, blue, yellow and red

Backstamp: Doulton

Doulton Number	Type	Backstamp	Height	Intro.	Discon.	Current Market Value		
						U.K.£	U.S.$	Can.$
—	Cup	Doulton	9 1/2"	1933	Ltd. ed.	1,500.00	6,500.00	3,500.00

CAPTAIN PHILLIP

This jug was issued in a limited edition of 350 pieces.

Designer: Charles Noke/Harry Fenton
Handle: Eucalyptus tree trunk
Main Colours: Yellow, blue, red and green
Spout: Face of Captain Phillip
Inscription around base: "Colony New South Wales founded January 1788 Sydney"

Backstamp: Doulton

Doulton Number	Type	Backstamp	Height	Intro.	Discon.	Current Market Value U.K.£	U.S.$	Can.$
—	Jug	Doulton	9 1/4"	1938	Ltd. ed.	2,000.00	6,500.00	4,500.00

CHARLES DICKENS

This jug was issued in a limited edition of 1,000.

Designer: Charles Noke/Harry Fenton
Handle: Open book
Spout: Face of Charles Dickens
Main Colours: Brown, green and red

Backstamp: Doulton

Doulton Number	Type	Backstamp	Height	Intro.	Discon.	Current Market Value U.K.£	U.S.$	Can.$
—	Jug	Doulton	10 1/2"	1936	Ltd. ed.	750.00	2,000.00	2,000.00

DICKENS DREAM

Although Dickens Dream was issued in a unlimited edition, probably only 1,000 pieces were produced.

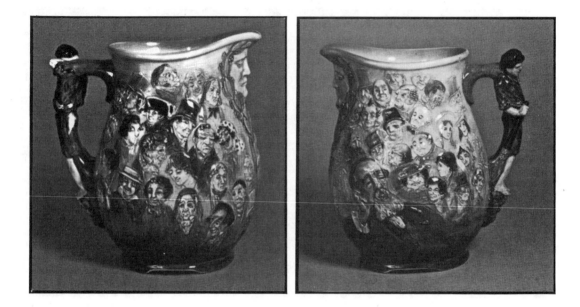

Designer: Charles Noke
Handle: Poor Jo
Main Colours: Brown, green and red

Backstamp: Doulton

Doulton Number	Type	Backstamp	Height	Intro.	Discon.	Current Market Value		
						U.K.£	U.S.$	Can.$
—	Jug	Doulton	10 1/2"	1933	Unknown	750.00	2,500.00	2,000.00

GEORGE WASHINGTON

PROTOTYPE

The handle of this prototype differs from the production model in that the stars are moulded in relief and set atop a striped background.

*Photograph
Not Available
At Press Time*

Designer: Charles Noke/Harry Fenton
Handle: Stars and Stripes
Main Colours: Brown, blue, red and cream
Spout: Face of George Washington
Inscription around base: "Declaration of Independence"

Backstamp: Doulton

Doulton Number	Type	Backstamp	Height	Intro.	Discon.	Current Market Value U.K.£	Current Market Value U.S.$	Current Market Value Can.$
—	Jug	Doulton	10 1/4"	1932	1932		Extremely rare	

GEORGE WASHINGTON

This jug was issued in a limited edition of 1,000 pieces.

STYLE ONE

Designer: Charles Noke/Harry Fenton
Handle: The Stars and Stripes
Main Colours: Brown, blue, red and cream
Spout: Face of George Washington
Inscription around base: "Declaration of Independence"

Backstamp: Doulton

Doulton Number	Type	Backstamp	Height	Intro.	Discon.	Current Market Value		
						U.K.£	U.S.$	Can.$
—	Jug	Doulton	10 1/4"	1932	Ltd. ed.	3,500.00	12,000.00	8,000.00

GEORGE WASHINGTON

This George Washington loving cup was issued to commemorate the 200th anniversary of his birth.

STYLE TWO

Designer: C. J. Noke	
Handle: Laurel leaves	**Backstamp:** Doulton
Main Colours: Browns, green and red	

Doulton Number	Type	Backstamp	Height	Intro.	Discon.	Current Market Value		
						U.K. £	U.S. $	Can. $
—	Cup	Doulton	8 1/4"	1932	Unknown	Extremely rare. Only three known.		

Note: A pitcher, 9" high, with the same design as the George Washington, style two, loving cup is known.

GUY FAWKES

The Guy Fawkes jug was issued in a limited edition of 600 pieces.

Designer: Harry Fenton

Handle: Flaming torch

Main Colours: Green, brown and red

Backstamp: Doulton

Doulton Number	Type	Backstamp	Height	Intro.	Discon.	Current Market Value U.K.£	U.S.$	Can.$
—	Jug	Doulton	7 1/2"	1934	Ltd. ed.	650.00	1,500.00	1,500.00

I.T. WIGG, BROOM-MAN

This is believed to have been a trial piece only. There are no production pieces known to exist.

Designer: Unknown

Handle: Unknown

Main Colours: Unknown

Backstamp: Unknown

Doulton Number	Type	Backstamp	Height	Intro.	Discon.	Current Market Value U.K.£	U.S.$	Can.$
—	Jug	Doulton	Unknnown	Unknown			Unique	

Note: We have no information or photographs for this jug. We would appreciate anyone with further particulars contacting the Charlton Press.

JACKDAW OF RHEIMS

This jug is believed to have been a trial piece only. No evidence exists that this jug actually went into production.

Designer: Unknown
Handle: Candle, candlestick and candle-snuffer
Main Colours: Brown, red and green

Backstamp: Doulton

Doulton Number	Type	Backstamp	Height	Intro.	Discon.	Current Market Value U.K.£	U.S.$	Can.$
—	Jug	Doulton	11"		c. 1934	Extremely rare. Only one known.		

JAN VAN RIEBEECK

This cup was issued in limited edition of 300 pieces.

Designer: Charles Noke / Harry Fenton
Handles: Van Riebeeck figures
Main Colours: Yellow, green, blue and red

Backstamp: Doulton

Doulton Number	Type	Backstamp	Height	Intro.	Discon.	Current Market Value		
						U.K.£	U.S.$	Can.$
—	Cup	Doulton	10 1/4"	1935	Ltd. ed.	1,750.00	5,000.00	3,750.00

JOHN PEEL

The John Peel cup was issued in a limited edition of 500 pieces.

Designer: Unknown
Handles: Fox heads on riding whips
Main Colours: Green, red and brown

Backstamp: Doulton

Doulton Number	Type	Backstamp	Height	Intro.	Discon.	Current Market Value		
						U.K.£	U.S.$	Can.$
—	Cup	Doulton	9"	1933	Ltd. ed.	750.00	2,400.00	2,000.00

KING EDWARD VIII CORONATION

STYLE ONE: ENGLISH EDITION, LARGE SIZE

This coronation cup was issued in a limited edition of 2,000 pieces, of which 1,080 were sold.

Designer: Charles Noke/Harry Fenton
Handle: Names of Commonwealth countries
Main Colours: Green, yellow and red

Backstamps: Doulton

Doulton Number	Type	Backstamp	Height	Intro.	Discon.	Current Market Value U.K.£	U.S.$	Can.$
—	Cup	Doulton	10"	1937	Ltd. ed.	450.00	1,400.00	1,200.00

KING EDWARD VIII CORONATION

STYLE TWO: ENGLISH EDITION, SMALL SIZE

This small cup was issued in a limited edition of 1,000 pieces, of which only 454 were sold because the coronation never took place.

Designer: Charles Noke
Handle: Names of Commonwealth countries
Main Colours: Green, red and yellow

Backstamp: Doulton

Doulton Number	Type	Backstamp	Height	Intro.	Discon.	Current Market Value		
						U.K.£	U.S.$	Can.$
—	Cup	Doulton	6 1/2"	1937	Ltd. ed.	400.00	2,000.00	1,000.00

KING EDWARD VIII CORONATION

STYLE THREE: WELSH EDITION, SMALL SIZE

Style three was issued in limited edition of 2,000 pieces and made especially for the Welsh market. The portrait of Edward, Prince of Wales, differs from that on the previous cup. The words "I am still the same man" appear on the jug, taken from a speech Edward made while on his first visit to Wales as sovereign.

Designer: Charles Noke

Handle: Names of Commonwealth countries

Main Colours: Green, red and brown

Backstamps: Doulton

Doulton Number	Type	Backstamp	Height	Intro.	Discon.	Current Market Value U.K.£	U.S.$	Can.$
—	Cup	Doulton	6 1/2"	1937	Ltd. ed.	700.00	2,000.00	1,500.00

KING GEORGE V AND
QUEEN MARY SILVER JUBILEE

This jubilee cup was issued in a limited edition of 1,000 pieces.

Designer: Charles Noke/Harry Fenton
Handles: Names of Commonwealth countries and provinces
Main Colours: Green and brown

Backstamp: Doulton

Doulton Number	Type	Backstamp	Height	Intro.	Discon.	Current Market Value U.K.£	U.S.$	Can.$
—	Cup	Doulton	10"	1935	Ltd ed.	550.00	1,400.00	1,200.00

KING GEORGE VI AND
QUEEN ELIZABETH CORONATION

STYLE ONE: LARGE DESIGN — UNCROWNED CONJOINED PORTRAITS
WITHOUT FLEUR-DE-LIS

Designer: Charles Noke/Harry Fenton
Handles: Plain
Main Colours: Yellow, red and green

Backstamp: Doulton

Doulton Number	Type	Backstamp	Height	Intro.	Discon.	Current Market Value		
						U.K.£	U.S.$	Can.$
—	Cup	Doulton	10 1/2"	1937	Unknown	650.00	1,400.00	1,400.00

KING GEORGE VI AND
QUEEN ELIZABETH CORONATION

STYLE TWO: LARGE DESIGN — CROWNED CONJOINED PORTRAITS
WITH FLEUR-DE-LIS

Style two was issued in limited edition of 2,000 pieces.

Designer: Charles Noke / Harry Fenton
Handles: Plain
Main Colours: Yellow, red and green

Backstamp: Doulton

Doulton Number	Type	Backstamp	Height	Intro.	Discon.	Current Market Value U.K.£	U.S.$	Can.$
—	Cup	Doulton	10 1/2"	1937	Ltd. ed.	500.00	1,300.00	1,200.00

KING GEORGE VI AND
QUEEN ELIZABETH CORONATION

STYLE THREE: SMALL DESIGN

Style three was issued in a limited edition of 2,000 pieces.

		Designer:	Charles Noke/Harry Fenton							
Handles:	Plain					
Main Colours:	Yellow, green, blue and red					

Backstamp: Doulton

| Doulton | | | | | | Current Market Value | | |
Number	Type	Backstamp	Height	Intro.	Discon.	U.K.£	U.S.$	Can.$
—	Cup	Doulton	6 1/2"	1937	Ltd. ed.	350.00	800.00	800.00

MASTER OF FOXHOUNDS

This presentation jug was issued in a limited edition of 500 pieces.

Designer: Charles Noke
Handle: Whip
Main Colours: Green, red and brown
Spout: Rooster's head

Backstamp: Doulton

Doulton Number	Type	Backstamp	Height	Intro.	Discon.	Current Market Value U.K.£	U.S.$	Can.$
—	Presentation jug	Doulton	13"	1930	Ltd. ed.	650.00	2,300.00	1,500.00

PIED PIPER

The Pied Piper jug was issued in limited edition of 600 pieces.

Designer: Charles Noke/Harry Fenton
Handle: Tree
Main Colours: Yellow, brown and green
Spout: Window

Backstamp: Doulton

Doulton Number	Type	Backstamp	Height	Intro.	Discon.	Current Market Value		
						U.K.£	U.S.$	Can.$
—	Jug	Doulton	10"	1934	Ltd. ed.	750.00	2,100.00	1,750.00

POTTERY IN THE PAST

The Pottery in the Past cup was issued exclusively for the members of the Royal Doulton International Collectors Club.

Designer: Graham Tongue
Handles: Plain
Main Colours: Brown and green

Backstamp: Doulton / RDICC

Doulton Number	Type	Backstamp	Height	Intro.	Discon.	Current Market Value U.K.£	U.S.$	Can.$
D6696	Cup	Doulton	6"	1983	1983	150.00	300.00	325.00

QUEEN ELIZABETH II CORONATION

Elizabeth became Queen of England on February 6, 1952. This commemorative cup features depictions of both Queen Elizabeth II and Elizabeth I. The handles are plain. It was issued in a limited edition of 1,000 pieces.

LOVING CUP

Designer: Cecil J. Noke / Harry Fenton
Handles: Plain
Main Colour: Brown

Backstamp: Doulton

Doulton Number	Type	Backstamp	Height	Intro.	Discon.	Current Market Value U.K.£	U.S.$	Can.$
—	Cup	Doulton	10 1/2"	1953	Ltd. ed.	425.00	1,100.00	1,000.00

QUEEN ELIZABETH II CORONATION

This small jug features a portrait of Queen Elizabeth II flanked by the Union Jack and the royal standard, with "Elizabeth R" underneath. A scene of Windsor Castle is on the other side. This piece was not issued in a limited edition.

JUG

Designer: Unknown
Handles: Plain
Main Colour: Brown

Backstamp: Doulton

Doulton Number	Type	Backstamp	Height	Intro.	Discon.	Current Market Value U.K.£	U.S.$	Can.$
—	Jug	Doulton	6 1/4"	1953	1953	125.00	275.00	295.00

QUEEN ELIZABETH II SILVER JUBILEE

This Queen Elizabeth II Silver Jubilee cup was issued in limited edition of 250 pieces.

Designer:	Reg Johnson
Handles:	Lion heads
Main Colours:	Red, brown and green

Backstamp: Doulton

Doulton Number	Type	Backstamp	Height	Intro.	Discon.	Current Market Value U.K.£	U.S.$	Can.$
—	Cup	Doulton	10 1/2"	1977	Ltd. ed.	850.00	2,750.00	2,500.00

REGENCY COACH

The Regency Coach jug was issued in a limited edition of 500 pieces.

Designer:	Charles Noke
Handle:	Tree branch
Main Colours:	Green and brown
Spout:	A parchment and inn sign

Backstamp: Doulton

Doulton Number	Type	Backstamp	Height	Intro.	Discon.	Current Market Value		
						U.K.£	**U.S.$**	**Can.$**
—	Jug	Doulton	10"	1931	Ltd. ed.	750.00	1,850.00	1,750.00

ROBIN HOOD

This cup was issued in a limited edition of 600 pieces.

Designer: Charles Noke / Harry Fenton
Handles: Plain, incised names of "The Merry Men"
Main Colours: Green, red and brown

Backstamp: Doulton

Doulton Number	Type	Backstamp	Height	Intro.	Discon.	Current Market Value U.K.£	U.S.$	Can.$
—	Cup	Doulton	8 1/2"	1938	Ltd. ed.	750.00	1,500.00	1,500.00

ROGER SOLEMEL, COBBLER

TRIAL PIECE

This is believed to have been a trial piece only. There are no production pieces known to exist.

Designer: Geoff Blower
Handle: Unknown
Main Colours: Unknown

Backstamp: Doulton

Doulton Number	Type	Backstamp	Height	Intro.	Discon.	Current Market Value U.K.£	U.S.$	Can.$
—	Jug	Doulton	10 1/2"		Unknown		Unique	

SIR FRANCIS DRAKE

The Sir Francis Drake jug was issued in limited edition of 500 pieces.

Designer: Charles Noke/Harry Fenton
Handle: Rope and lantern
Main Colours: Brown, red, green and blue

Backstamp: Doulton

Doulton Number	Type	Backstamp	Height	Intro.	Discon.	Current Market Value U.K.£	U.S.$	Can.$
—	Jug	Doulton	10 1/4"	1933	Ltd. ed.	750.00	1,850.00	1,750.00

THE THREE MUSKETEERS

This cup was issued in a limited edition of 600 pieces.

Designer: Charles Noke / Harry Fenton
Handles: Trophies of war and the accoutrements of pleasure
Main Colours: Yellow, green brown and red

Backstamp: Doulton

Doulton Number	Type	Backstamp	Height	Intro.	Discon.	Current Market Value		
						U.K.£	U.S.$	Can.$
—	Cup	Doulton	10"	1936	Ltd. ed.	750.00	1,900.00	1,750.00

TOWER OF LONDON

This jug was issued in a limited edition of 500 pieces.

Designer: Charles Noke / Harry Fenton
Handle: Axes, pikes, chains and armour
Spout: Shield bearing the lions of England
Main Colours: Red, green, grey and brown

Backstamp: Doulton

Doulton Number	Type	Backstamp	Height	Intro.	Discon.	Current Market Value U.K.£	U.S.$	Can.$
—	Jug	Doulton	10"	1933	Ltd. ed.	750.00	2,000.00	1,750.00

TREASURE ISLAND

The Treasure Island jug was issued in a limited edition of 600 pieces.

Designer: Charles Noke / Harry Fenton

Handle: Palm tree

Spout: Palm leaves

Main Colours: Yellow, green and brown

Backstamp: Doulton

Doulton Number	Type	Backstamp	Height	Intro.	Discon.	Current Market Value U.K.£	U.S.$	Can.$
—	Jug	Doulton	7 1/2"	1934	Ltd. ed.	650.00	1,300.00	1,300.00

THE VILLAGE BLACKSMITH

This jug was issued in a limited edition of 600 pieces.

Designer: Charles Noke
Handle: Branch with milestone at base of handle;
milestone incised "Longfellow" on one side
and "Long-fellow 1842" on the other
Spout: Leaves
Main Colours: Brown, green and red

Backstamp: Doulton

Doulton Number	Type	Backstamp	Height	Intro.	Discon.	Current Market Value		
						U.K.£	U.S.$	Can.$
—	Jug	Doulton	7 3/4"	1936	Ltd. ed.	650.00	1,500.00	1,500.00

THE WANDERING MINSTREL

The Wandering Minstrel cup was issued in limited edition of 600 pieces.

Designer: Charles Noke/Harry Fenton   **Backstamp:** Doulton
Handles: Trees
Main Colours: Green, brown and yellow

Doulton Number	Type	Backstamp	Height	Intro.	Discon.	Current Market Value U.K.£	U.S.$	Can.$
—	Cup	Doulton	5 1/2"	1934	Ltd. ed.	650.00	1,500.00	1,500.00

WILLIAM SHAKESPEARE

Thw William Shakespeare jug was issued in a limited edition of 1,000 pieces.

Designer: Charles Noke
Handle: Masks of tragedy and comedy; swords
Spout: Face of Shakespeare
Main Colours: Green, brown and red

Backstamp: Doulton

Doulton Number	Type	Backstamp	Height	Intro.	Discon.	Current Market Value U.K.£	U.S.$	Can.$
—	Jug	Doulton	10 1/2"	1933	Ltd. ed.	650.00	1,800.00	1,800.00

WILLIAM WORDSWORTH

This cup was issued in an unlimited edition, but few are known to exist.

Designer: Charles Noke
Handles: Tied vines
Main Colours: Green, yellow and red

Backstamp: Doulton

Doulton Number	Type	Backstamp	Height	Intro.	Discon.	Current Market Value		
						U.K. £	U.S.$	Can.$
—	Cup	Doulton	6 1/2"	1933	Unknown	950.00	2,500.00	2,250.00

BESWICK
TOBY JUGS

MARTHA GUNN

Photograph not available
at press time

Designer: Arthur Gredington
Handle: Plain
Colourway: Unknown

Backstamp: Impressed —
Beswick England
1113

Beswick Number	Size	Backstamp	Height	Intro.	Discon.	Current Market Value U.K. £	U.S. $	Can. $
1113	Small	Beswick	3 1/2"	1948	1966	125.00	250.00	265.00

MIDSHIPMAN TOBY

Designer: Arthur Gredington
Handle: Plain
Colourway: Purple coat; red trousers; blue shirt and socks;
dark blue hat; green and yellow waistcoat

Backstamp: Impressed —
Midshipman
Beswick England 1,112
Black ink stamp — Old Castle

Beswick Number	Size	Backstamp	Height	Intro.	Discon.	Current Market Value U.K. £	U.S. $	Can. $
1112	Medium	Beswick	5 1/4"	1948	1973	150.00	300.00	325.00

TOBY PHILLPOT

STYLE ONE: WITH JUG

Designer: Arthur Gredington	**Backstamp:** Impressed —
Handle: Plain	Beswick England
Colourway: Green coat with maroon cuffs; yellow	(model no.)
waistcoat; brown brown trousers and	
hat; blue cravat and socks; brown jug	

Beswick Number	Size	Backstamp	Height	Intro.	Discon.	Current Market Value U.K. £	U.S. $	Can. $
1110	Large	Beswick	8"	1948	1973	165.00	350.00	375.00
1114	Small	Beswick	3 1/2"	1948	1966	125.00	250.00	275.00

TOBY PHILLPOT

STYLE TWO: WITH GLASS AND JUG

Designer: Arthur Gredington
Handle: Plain
Colourway: Red coat with yellow cuffs; green waistcoat; purple trousers and hat; blue cravat and socks; brown jug and glass

Backstamp: Impressed —
Toby Phillpot Beswick
England (model no.)
Black ink stamp —
Beswick England

Beswick Number	Size	Backstamp	Height	Intro.	Discon.	Current Market Value		
						U.K. £	U.S. $	Can. $
1111	Medium	Beswick	6 1/2"	1948	1973	110.00	225.00	250.00

WINSTON CHURCHILL

STYLE ONE: WITHOUT HAT

Photograph not available
at press time

Designer: Mr. Watkin
Handle: Unknown
Colourway: Black, white, red and blue

Backstamp: Impressed

Beswick Number	Size	Backstamp	Height	Intro.	Discon.	Current Market Value U.K. £	U.S. $	Can. $
931	Large	Beswick	7"	1941	1954	250.00	500.00	550.00

WINSTON CHURCHILL

STYLE TWO: WITH HAT

Photograph not available
at press time

Designer: Mr. Watkin
Handle: Unknown
Colourway: Black, white, red and blue

Backstamp: Impressed

Beswick Number	Size	Backstamp	Height	Intro.	Discon.	Current Market Value U.K. £	U.S. $	Can. $
931	Large	Beswick	7"	1941	1954	350.00	700.00	750.00

BESWICK
CHARACTER JUGS

AIR FORCE

ARMED FORCES,
ONE OF THREE

This Air Force jug is one of a set of three. The others are the Army jug and the Navy jug.

Designer: Mr. Watkin
Handle: Flying bird
Colourway: Dark brown hair; blue hat and bird

Backstamp: Impressed —
Made in England
Beswick
737

Beswick Number	Size	Backstamp	Height	Intro.	Discon.	Current Market Value		
						U.K. £	U.S. $	Can. $
737	Medium	Beswick	5"	1939	1954	225.00	450.00	500.00

ARMY — OLD BILL

ARMED FORCES,
ONE OF THREE

Photograph not available at press time

Designer: Mr. Watkin
Handle: Unknown

Backstamp: Impressed
Colourway: Unknown

Beswick Number	Size	Backstamp	Height	Intro.	Discon.	Current Market Value		
						U.K. £	U.S. $	Can. $
735	Medium	Beswick	5"	1939	1954	225.00	450.00	500.00

BARNABY RUDGE

Designer: Arthur Gredington
Handle: Black crow
Colourway: Light brown hair; reddish brown coat;
blue shirt; grey hat; black bird with yellow beak

Backstamp: Impressed —
Barnaby Rudge
Beswick England
1,121
Black ink stamp —
Beswick England

Beswick Number	Size	Backstamp	Height	Intro.	Discon.	Current Market Value		
						U.K. £	U.S. $	Can. $
1121	Small	Beswick	4 1/2"	1948	1969	45.00	90.00	100.00

BETSY TROTWOOD

Designer: Albert Hallam
Handle: Knitting needles and wool
Colourway: Dark green dress with mauve collar and cuffs; light blue mobcap with pink ribbon; dark brown hair; light brown needles; yellow wool

Backstamp: Impressed —
Beswick England
2075
Betsy Trotwood

Beswick Number	Size	Backstamp	Height	Intro.	Discon.	Current Market Value U.K. £	U.S. $	Can. $
2075	Medium	Beswick	5"	1966	1973	110.00	225.00	250.00

CAPTAIN CUTTLE

Designer: Arthur Gredington
Handle: Hook
Colourway: Black hat and coat; white collar; light blue cravat; brown hair

Backstamp: Impressed —
Captain Cuttle
Beswick England
1120
Black ink stamp —
Beswick England Circle

Beswick Number	Size	Backstamp	Height	Intro.	Discon.	Current Market Value		
						U.K. £	U.S. $	Can. $
1120	Small	Beswick	4 1/2"	1948	1973	45.00	90.00	100.00

FALSTAFF

Designer: Albert Hallam
Handle: Feather from cap
Colourway: Red cap; green coat with gold trim

Backstamp: Impressed —
Beswick England
2095
Falstaff

Beswick Number	Size	Backstamp	Height	Intro.	Discon.	Current Market Value		
						U.K. £	U.S. $	Can. $
2095	Medium	Beswick	6 3/4"	1965	1973	75.00	150.00	165.00

HENRY VIII

Designer: Albert Hallam
Handle: Garter
Colourway: Brown coat; light brown shirt;
black hat with white trim and feather

Backstamp: Impressed —
Beswick England
2099
Henry VIII

Beswick Number	Size	Backstamp	Height	Intro.	Discon.	Current Market Value		
						U.K. £	U.S. $	Can. $
2099	Large	Beswick	7"	1967	1973	125.00	250.00	275.00

LITTLE NELL'S GRANDFATHER

Designer: Albert Hallam
Handle: Candle snuffer
Colourway: Grey-green hat and coat; red shirt;
light brown hair; yellow handle

Backstamp: Impressed —
Made In England
2031
Little Nell's Grandfather
Black ink stamp —
Beswick England Circle

Beswick Number	Size	Backstamp	Height	Intro.	Discon.	Current Market Value U.K. £	U.S. $	Can. $
2031	Medium	Beswick	5 1/2"	1965	1973	95.00	200.00	225.00

MARTIN CHUZZLEWIT

Designer: Albert Hallam
Handle: "Last will and testamony Martin Chuzzlewit"
Colourway: Brown hat and hair; green coat; white shirt

Backstamp: Impressed — Made in England 2030

Beswick Number	Size	Backstamp	Height	Intro.	Discon.	Current Market Value		
						U.K. £	U.S. $	Can. $
2030	Small	Beswick	4 3/4"	1965	1973	75.00	150.00	165.00

MICAWBER

STYLE ONE: MAROON CRAVAT WITH CREAM DOTS, EYES LOOK DOWN

VARIATION No. 1:   Colourway — Green hat and coat

Designer:	Mr. Watkin
Handle:	Scroll reading "Title Deeds" (painted black)
Colourway:	Green hat and coat; white collar; maroon cravat with cream dots

Backstamp: Impressed —
Beswick England
310
Micawber
Beswick ink stamp:
Beswick Ware
Made in England

Beswick Number	Variation	Backstamp	Height	Intro.	Discon.	Current Market Value		
						U.K. £	**U.S. $**	**Can. $**
310	Var. 1	Beswick	9"	1935	1970	75.00	150.00	165.00

VARIATION No. 2:   Colourway — Black hat and coat

Designer: Mr. Watkin
Handle: Scroll reading "Title Deeds"(not painted)
Colourway: Black hat and coat; white collar;
white cravat

Backstamp: Impressed —
310
Made in England
Micawber
Beswick ink stamp —
Beswick Ware

Beswick Number	Variation	Backstamp	Height	Intro.	Discon.	Current Market Value		
						U.K. £	U.S. $	Can. $
310	Var. 2	Beswick	9"	1935	1970	100.00	200.00	225.00

Micawber Derivatives

Photograph not available
at press time

Designer: Mr. Watkin
Handle: Walking cane (on cream jug)
Colourway: Brown coat; green hat;
brown and yellow walking
cane on cream jug

Backstamp: Impressed —
Beswick * England
674
Micawber

Beswick Number	Item	Backstamp	Height	Intro.	Discon.	Current Market Value		
						U.K. £	U.S. $	Can. $
674	Cream	Beswick	3 1/4"	1939	1973	35.00	70.00	75.00
690	Salt	Beswick	3 1/2"	1939	1973	30.00	60.00	65.00

MICAWBER

STYLE TWO: MAROON CRAVAT, EYES LOOK TO THE RIGHT

Designer: Unknown
Handle: Scroll reading "Title Deeds"
Colourway: Green hat and coat; white collar;
maroon cravat

Backstamp: Impressed —
Beswick England
310
Micawber
Black ink stamp —
Beswick Ware
Made in England

Beswick Number	Size	Backstamp	Height	Intro.	Discon.	Current Market Value		
						U.K. £	U.S. $	Can. $
310	Large	Beswick	9"	1970	1973	110.00	225.00	250.00

MR. BUMBLE THE BEADLE

Designer:	Albert Hallam
Handle:	Walking cane
Colourway:	Black hat with yellow trim; light brown hair; light green cravat

Backstamp: Impressed —
Beswick England
2032
Mr Bumble Parish Beadle

Beswick Number	Size	Backstamp	Height	Intro.	Discon.	Current Market Value U.K. £	U.S. $	Can. $
2032	Medium	Beswick	5"	1965	1973	50.00	100.00	110.00

NAVY HMS WINK

ARMED FORCES,
ONE OF THREE

The Navy jug is one of a set of three, the Army and Air Force jugs being the other two.

Designer: Mr. Watkin
Handle: Rope
Colourway: Brown hair; blue and white hat with *"H.M.S. Wink"* printed in black; light brown rope

Backstamp: Impressed —
Made in England
Beswick
736

Beswick Number	Size	Backstamp	Height	Intro.	Discon.	Current Market Value		
						U.K. £	U.S. $	Can. $
736	Medium	Beswick	5"	1939	1954	225.00	450.00	500.00

PECKSNIFF

Derivatives

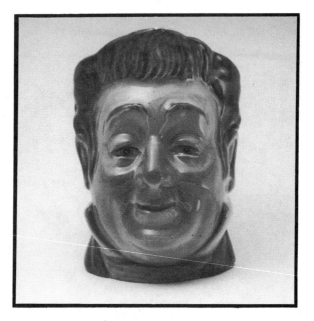

Designer: Arthur Gredington
Handle: Plain (cream jug)
Colourway: Reddish brown coat with black trim;
blue shirt; brown hair; light brown
handle on cream jug

Backstamp: Impressed —
Pecksniff
Beswick England
(model no.)
Black ink stamp —
Beswick England

Beswick Number	Item	Backstamp	Height	Intro.	Discon.	Current Market Value		
						U.K. £	U.S. $	Can. $
1117	Cream	Beswick	3 1/2"	1948	1973	35.00	70.00	75.00
1129	Sugar	Beswick	3 1/2"	1948	1973	35.00	70.00	75.00

P. G. W. COLONEL

This jug was produced by Beswick in 1967 for the 35th anniversary of Peter, Griffin, Woodward, Inc.

Designer: Unknown
Handle: Plain, Peters, Griffin, Woodward, Inc.
Colourway: Black, white and red

Backstamp: Black ink stamp —
Beswick

Beswick Number	Size	Backstamp	Height	Intro.	Discon.	Current Market Value U.K. £	U.S. $	Can. $
—	Medium	Beswick	5 1/8"	1967	1967	95.00	200.00	225.00

PICKWICK

Derivatives

Designer: Arthur Gredington
Handle: Plain (on cream jug)
Colourway: Reddish brown coat; green shirt;
blue bow tie; brown hair;
grey hat; yellow glasses

Backstamp: Impressed —
Pickwick
Beswick England
(model no.)
Black ink stamp —
Beswick England

Beswick Number	Item	Backstamp	Height	Intro.	Discon.	Current Market Value		
						U.K. £	U.S. $	Can. $
1118	Sugar	Beswick	3"	1948	1973	35.00	70.00	75.00
1119	Cream	Beswick	3 1/4"	1948	1973	35.00	70.00	75.00

SAIREY GAMP

Designer: Mr. Watkin
Handle: Umbrella
Colourway: Green hat with cream polka dots; maroon coat; maroon umbrella with brown handle

Backstamp: Impressed —
Made in England
371
Sairey Gamp
Black ink stamp

Beswick Number	Size	Backstamp	Height	Intro.	Discon.	Current Market Value U.K. £	U.S. $	Can. $
371	Large	Beswick	7"	1936	1973	65.00	125.00	140.00

Derivatives

Beswick Number	Item	Backstamp	Height	Intro.	Discon.	Current Market Value U.K. £	U.S. $	Can. $
689	Pepper	Beswick	2 1/2"	1939	1973	40.00	80.00	90.00
691	Teapot	Beswick	5 3/4"	1939	1973	95.00	200.00	225.00
1206	Preserve and lid	Beswick	3"	1950	1973	40.00	80.00	90.00

SCROOGE

Designer: Mr. Watkin
Handle: Part of hat and tassle
Colourway: Green hat with white dots; maroon coat and scarf; light brown hair

Backstamp: Impressed —
Made in England
372
Black or green ink stamp —
Beswick Ware
Made in England

Beswick Number	Size	Backstamp	Height	Intro.	Discon.	Current Market Value		
						U.K. £	U.S. $	Can. $
372	Large	Beswick	7"	1936	1973	75.00	150.00	175.00

TONY WELLER

STYLE ONE: HANDLE TOUCHES HAT, GREEN CRAVAT

Designer: Mr. Watkin
Handle: Whip
Colourway: Green hat; red-brown coat;
patterned green cravat

Backstamp: Beswick

Beswick Number	Size	Backstamp	Height	Intro.	Discon.	Current Market Value		
						U.K. £	U.S. $	Can. $
281	Large	Beswick	6 34/"	Unknown		100.00	200.00	225.00

TONY WELLER

STYLE TWO: WHIP TOUCHES EAR, SMILE SHOWS TEETH

VARIATION No. 1: Colourway — Gloss

Designer: Mr. Watkin
Handle: Whip
Colourway: Green hat; maroon coat; white shirt; green polka-dot cravat with cream horseshoe-shaped pin on scarf (gloss)

Backstamp: Impressed —
Made in England
281
Tony Weller
Black ink stamp

Beswick Number	Variation	Backstamp	Height	Intro.	Discon.	Current Market Value		
						U.K. £	U.S. $	Can. $
281	Var. 1	Beswick	7 1/4"	1935	1973	75.00	150.00	165.00

Tony Weller Derivative

Designer: Unknown
Colourway: Brown coat; green hat; green and cream scarf

Backstamp: Impressed —
Beswick * England
Tony Weller
Black ink stamp —
Beswick England

Beswick Number	Item	Backstamp	Height	Intro.	Discon.	Current Market Value		
						U.K. £	U.S. $	Can. $
673	Sugar	Beswick	2 3/4"	1939	1973	35.00	75.00	85.00
1207	Preserve and lid	Beswick	3"	1950	1973	35.00	75.00	85.00

VARIATION No. 2: Colourway — Matt

Designer: Mr. Watkin	**Backstamp:** Impressed —
Handle: Whip	Made in England
Colourway: Beige hat with dark blue band; dark	281
blue coat with light green collar;	Dark blue ink stamp —
brown bow tie with gold horseshoe-	7796
shaped pin (matt)	Beswick Ware
	Made in England

Beswick Number	Variation	Backstamp	Height	Intro.	Discon.	Current Market Value		
						U.K. £	U.S. $	Can. $
281	Var. 2	Beswick	6 3/4"		Unknown	95.00	195.00	295.00

TONY WELLER

STYLE TWO: WHIP TOUCHES EAR

VARIATION No. 3:   Closed-mouth smile

Designer: Mr. Watkin	**Backstamp:** Impressed —
Remodeller: Mr. Tangeel	Made in England
Handle: Whip	Ink stamp —
Colourway: Green collar; black coat;	Beswick Ware
yellow hat with black band;	
yellow bow tie and horseshoe pin	

Beswick Number	Variation	Backstamp	Height	Intro.	Discon.	Current Market Value U.K. £	U.S. $	Can. $
281	Var. 3	Beswick	7"	1969	1973	95.00	195.00	295.00

BESWICK
MISCELLANEOUS

CAT TEAPOT

Photograph not available
at press time

Designer: Unknown
Handle: Unknown
Colourway: Variation No. 1 — White
Variation No. 2 — Black and white

Backstamp: Beswick

Beswick Number	Item	Variation	Height	Intro.	Discon.	Current Market Value U.K. £	U.S. $	Can. $
3138	Teapot	Var. 1	6"	1989	1990	65.00	125.00	140.00
3138	Teapot	Var. 2	6"	1989	1990	65.00	125.00	140.00

DOLLY VARDEN TEAPOT

Designer: Arthur Gredington
Handle: Feather
Colourway: Yellow hat; blue bow and ribbons with dark
blue polka dots; bow tie with blue and dark
blue dots

Backstamp: Impressed —
Beswick England
1203
Dolly Varden

Beswick Number	Item	Backstamp	Height	Intro.	Discon.	Current Market Value U.K. £	U.S. $	Can. $
1203	Teapot	Beswick	6 1/4"	1950	1973	165.00	325.00	350.00

FALSTAFF

Designer: Unknown
Handle: Plain
Main Colours: Browns, green and maroon
Inscription Around Jug Base: "'Falstaff' Myself & skirted page"
Inscription Around Mug Base: "Ritol-with Wit or Steel"

Backstamp: Impressed —
Beswick England
2095
Falstaff

Beswick Number	Item	Backstamp	Height	Intro.	Discon.	Current Market Value		
						U.K. £	U.S. $	Can. $
1126	Jug	Beswick	8"	1948	1973	100.00	200.00	225.00
1127	Mug	Beswick	4"	1948	1973	45.00	90.00	100.00

HAMLET

Designer: Unknown

Handle: Plain

Main Colours: Browns, greens, black and yellow

Inscription Around Jug Base: "Hamlet-Be Thou A Spirit of Health"

Inscription Around Mug Base: "To Be or Not To Be"

Backstamp: Beswick

Beswick Number	Item	Backstamp	Height	Intro.	Discon.	Current Market Value		
						U.K. £	U.S. $	Can. $
1146	Jug	Beswick	8 1/4"	1949	1973	100.00	200.00	225.00
1147	Mug	Beswick	4 1/4"	1949	1973	45.00	90.00	100.00

JULIET

Designer: Unknown
'Handle: Plain
Main Colours: Browns, greens, maroon and blue
Inscription Around Jug Base: "Romeo and Juliet"
Inscription Around Mug Base: "Sweet Sorrow"

Backstamp: Beswick

Beswick Number	Item	Backstamp	Height	Intro.	Discon.	Current Market Value U.K. £	U.S. $	Can. $
1214	Jug	Beswick	8 1/4"	1951	1973	100.00	200.00	225.00
1215	Mug	Beswick	4"	1951	1973	45.00	90.00	100.00

LAUREL AND HARDY CRUET SET

Photograph not available
at press time

Designer: Mr. Watkin
Colourway: Black and fleshtone

Backstamp: Beswick

Beswick Number	Item	Backstamp	Height	Intro.	Discon.	Current Market Value U.K. £	U.S. $	Can. $
575	Cruet set	Beswick	4 1/2"	1938	1969	75.00	150.00	175.00

MIDSUMMER NIGHTS DREAM

Designer: Unknown
Handle: Plain
Main Colours: Greens, browns, blue and maroon
Inscription Around Jug Base: "A Midsummer Nights Dream"
Inscription Around Mug Base: "A Midsummer Nights Dream"

Backstamp: Beswick

Beswick Number	Item	Backstamp	Height	Intro.	Discon.	Current Market Value U.K. £	U.S. $	Can. $
1366	Jug	Beswick	8"	1955	1973	125.00	250.00	275.00
1368	Mug	Beswick	4 1/4"	1955	1973	75.00	150.00	175.00

MOUSE TEAPOT

Photograph not available
at press time

Designer: Unknown
Handle: Unknown
Colourway: Unknown

Backstamp: Beswick

Beswick Number	Item	Backstamp	Height	Intro.	Discon.	Current Market Value U.K. £	U.S. $	Can. $
3139	Teapot	Beswick	7"	1989	1990	65.00	125.00	140.00

MR VARDEN CREAMER

Designer: Arthur Gredington
Handle: Key
Colourway: Purple coat; dark brown hair; blue ribbon; green hat; yellow key

Backstamp: Impressed —
Beswick * England
1204
Mr Varden
Black ink stamp —
Beswick England

Beswick Number	Item	Backstamp	Height	Intro.	Discon.	Current Market Value		
						U.K. £	U.S. $	Can. $
1204	Creamer	Beswick	3 1/2"	1950	1973	35.00	70.00	75.00

MRS VARDEN SUGAR BOWL

Photograph not available
at this time

Designer: Arthur Gredington
Colourway: Unknown

Backstamp: Beswick

Beswick Number	Item	Backstamp	Height	Intro.	Discon.	Current Market Value		
						U.K. £	U.S. $	Can. $
1205	Sugar bowl	Beswick	3"	1950	1973	35.00	70.00	75.00

PEGGOTY TEAPOT

Designer: Arthur Gredington
Handle: Rope
Colourway: Light brown hair and rope; black coat and hat; light blue shirt; grey spout

Backstamp: Impressed —
Peggotty
Beswick England
1,116
Green ink stamp —
Beswick Ware
Made in England

Beswick Number	Item	Backstamp	Height	Intro.	Discon.	Current Market Value U.K. £	U.S. $	Can. $
1116	Teapot	Impressed	6"	1948	1973	120.00	250.00	275.00

ROBERT BURNS

Photograph not available
at press time

Designer: Unknwon
Handle: Plain
Colourway: Unknown
Inscription Around Base: Unknown

Backstamp: Beswick

Beswick Number	Item	Backstamp	Height	Intro.	Discon.	Current Market Value U.K. £	U.S. $	Can. $
1045	Jug	Beswick	8"	1946	1967	120.00	250.00	275.00
1596	Mug	Beswick	4 1/2"	1959	1967	95.00	200.00	225.00

SAM WELLER TEAPOT

Designer: Arthur Gredington
Handle: Umbrella handle
Colourway: Green, brown, maroon and yellow

Backstamp: Beswick

Beswick Number	Item	Backstamp	Height	Intro.	Discon.	Current Market Value U.K. £	U.S. $	Can. $
1369	Teapot	Beswick	6 1/4"	1955	1973	165.00	325.00	350.00

SQUIRREL TEAPOT

Photograph not available
at press time

Designer: Unknown
Handle: Unknown
Colourway: Unknown

Backstamp: Beswick

Beswick Number	Item	Backstamp	Height	Intro.	Discon.	Current Market Value U.K. £	U.S. $	Can. $
3142	Teapot	Beswick	7"	1989	1990	65.00	125.00	140.00

INDEX

INDEX BY ROYAL DOULTON MODEL NUMBER

D6873	The Yeoman of the Guard (large)	480
D6873	Irishman (whiskey decanter)	485
D6873	Scotsman (whiskey decanter)	499
D6874	The Fortune Teller (style two - large)	226
D6875	The Sailor (style one)	402
D6876	The Soldier (style one)	440
D6877	The Jockey (style two - small)	276
D6878	Baseball Player (style two - small)	132
D6879	The Snooker Player	438
D6880	John Shorter	287
D6881	Terry Fox	445
D6882	The Yeoman of the Guard (large)	480
D6883	The Yeoman of the Guard (large)	480
D6884	The Yeoman of the Guard (large)	480
D6885	The Yeoman of the Guard (large)	480
D6886	Home Guard	268
D6887	Auxiliary Fireman	128
D6888	King Henry VIII	293
D6891	Christopher Columbus (style one - large)	178
D6892	Genie	234
D6893	The Witch	474
D6895	Town Crier (style two - large)	453
D6896	Bowls Player	148
D6898	The Master/Equestrian	324
D6899	Leprechaun (small)	300
D6900	Santa Claus (style five - miniature)	415
D6901	Charles Dickens (style two - small)	171
D6903	The Airman	101
	(Royal Canadian Air Force - style one)	
D6904	The Sailor (style two)	403
D6905	The Soldier (style two)	441
D6906	The Collector (small)	187
D6907	Winston Churchill (style one - large)	472
D6908	Field Marshall Montgomery	222
D6909	The Wizard (small)	475
D6910	Jester	62
D6911	Christopher Columbus (style two - small)	179
D6912	Bahamas Policeman	130
D6912	The Snake Charmer	437
D6913	Queen Victoria (variation 1 - small)	383
D6914	Liverpool Centenary Jug (Bill Shankly)	304
D6916	The Graduate (male)	248
D6917	King Charles I	291
D6918	The Piper	373
D6920	Town Crier (medium)	94
D6921	Sir Henry Doulton/Michael Doulton	430
D6922	Mrs. Claus (miniature)	340
D6923	King Edward VII	292
D6924	Manchester United (Football Club)	318
D6925	Celtic (Football Club)	168
D6926	Everton (Football Club)	212
D6927	Arsenal (Football Club)	120
D6928	Leeds United (Football Club)	298
D6929	Rangers (Football Club)	385
D6930	Liverpool (Football Club)	303
D6931	Aston Villa (Football Club)	122
D6932	Vice-Admiral Lord Nelson	461
D6933	William Shakespeare (style two - large)	471
D6934	Winston Churchill (style two - small)	473
D6935	The Clown	47
D6936	Abraham Lincoln	99
D6937	General Eisenhower	232
D6938	Shakespeare	424
D6939	Charles Dickens (125th Anniversary)	172
D6940	Father Christmas	51
D6941	Napoleon	341
D6942	Elf	209
D6943	Thomas Jefferson	446
D6944	Earl Mountbatten of Burma (style two - large)	207
D6945	Len Hutton	299
D6946	Punch and Judy	380

D6947	Captain Hook (style two - large)	160
D6948	Leprechaun	69
D6949	Charlie Chaplin (large)	173
D6950	Santa Claus (style four - tiny)	414
D6951	Dick Turpin (tiny)	196
D6952	John Barleycorn (tiny)	278
D6953	Jester (tiny)	273
D6954	Granny (tiny)	251
D6955	Parson Brown (tiny)	360
D6956	Simon the Cellarer (tiny)	426
D6957	Baseball Player (Philadelphia)	134
D6958	Sheffield Wednesday (Football Club)	425
D6959	Mr. Pickwick (style two - large)	337
D6961	Francis Rossi (small)	227
D6962	Rick Parfitt	388
D6965	George Washington (style two - large)	239
D6967	Captain Bligh	156
D6968	Oliver Cromwell (large)	355
D6969	King and Queen of Diamonds	67
D6970	Glenn Miller	242
D6971	Aladdin's Cave	103
D6972	Snowman	439
D6973	Baseball Player (Toronto Blue Jays)	133
D6974	Honest Measure (tiny)	57
D6975	Toby XX (tiny)	93
D6976	Jolly Toby (tiny)	64
D6977	The Best is not too Good (tiny)	35
D6978	Old Charlie (tiny)	83
D6979	Happy John (tiny)	56
D6980	Santa Claus (style six, var. 1 - tiny)	416
D6981	Bill Sykes (style two - large)	141
D6982	The Airman (style two)	102
D6983	The Soldier (style three)	442
D6984	The Sailor (style three)	404
D6985	Charles I (small)	169
D6986	Oliver Cromwell (small)	356
D6987	Alfred Hitchcock	104
D6988	The Judge and The Thief	65
D6990	Henry VIII (style two - tiny)	295
D6991	Victoria (tiny)	295
D6992	Elizabeth I (tiny)	295
D6993	Edward VII (tiny)	295
D6994	Henry V (tiny)	295
D6995	Charles I (tiny)	295
D6997	Charles Dickens (small)	40
D6998	Robin Hood (large)	396
D6999	King and Queen of Clubs	66
D7000	George Tinworth	237
D7001	Napoleon (small)	342
D7002	Caroler (miniature)	161
D7003	Confucius (large)	188
D7004	Cyrano De Bergerac (large)	190
D7005	Dennis The Menace (large)	194
D7006	Desperate Dan (large)	195
D7008	Laurel (small)	296
D7009	Hardy (small)	264
D7010	Cabinet Maker (large)	154
D7020	Santa Claus (tiny)	418
D8074	Charrington & Co. Ltd.	43
HN1615	Mr. Micawber (bookend)	335
HN1616	Tony Weller (bookend)	450
HN1623	Mr. Pickwick (bookend)	336
HN1625	Sairey Gamp (bookend)	406
M57	Mr. Pickwick (napkin ring)	336
M58	Mr. Micawber (napkin ring)	335
M59	Fat Boy (napkin ring)	221
M60	Tony Weller (napkin ring)	450
M61	Sam Weller (napkin ring)	408
M62	Sairey Gamp (napkin ring)	406

INDEX BY BESWICK MODEL NUMBER

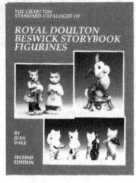